RETURN
TO THE FOUNTAINHEAD
OF THE FAITH

Explore World Ideologies
Church History
and
Christianity's Jewish Origins

Revised Edition

RETURN
TO THE FOUNTAINHEAD
OF THE FAITH

Explore World Ideologies
Church History
and
Christianity's Jewish Origins

Shelley Wood Gauld

Revised Edition

Return to the Fountainhead of the Faith: Revised Edition
Written and illustrated by Shelley Wood Gauld

Reviewed by Rev. Frank Lenihan

Published by means of Lulu Enterprises, Inc
860 Aviation Parkway
Suite 300 Morrisville, NC 27560
Phone: (919) 459-5858
Fax: (919) 459-5867

First Edition published through Pleasantword Publishing: A division of Winepress Publishing
Nominated for the 2004 Koret Foundation Jewish Book Awards
Copyright © 2003 by Shelley Gauld

Scriptures quoted with permission from:
The *Holy Bible, New International Version* (NIV)
Copyright © 1973, 1978, 1984 International Bible Society
Zondervan Bible Publishers

The Jewish New Testament (JNT)
Copyright © 1979, 1989, 1990 David H. Stern
Jewish New Testament Publications
PO Box 615, Clarksville, MD 21029. (410) 764-6144

Paperback and hardcover editions available from bookstores including Amazon.com and Barnes and Noble
E-book, paperback and hardcover editions available online from lulu.com
Visit http://www.lulu.com/grownupsbook

ISBN: 978-1-4303-0865-2

Contents

The Holy Place:
Fellowship and the Table of Showbread
Prayer and the Altar of Incense
Revelation and the *Menorah*

The Most Holy Place:
God's Providence and the Ark of the Covenant
Eternal Life and the Mercy Seat

Return to the Fountainhead of the Faith

This book explores valuable subject matter that is seldom taught from the pulpit: fourteen major world ideologies, the convoluted history of the Church, and the New Testament's inherent "Jewishness."

Preface

In February of 1994, in a small RV park in the USA, I was commissioned to complete a painting on a flat river stone. It was about 7 x 5 inches in diameter. That stone would be the first of many such art works that Geraldine Nusbaum would request over a three-and-a-half-year period. Each of her pieces—drawings, thirty paintings on stone, and designs for sixteen banners—had a distinctive Hebrew ambiance. She was a Messianic Jew—a "Christian Jew."

I had been a believer for almost twenty years before meeting Geri. In South Africa, after being introduced to the Zionist Movement by a fellow Art student who was a sabra Israeli, I'd traveled to Israel. For over a decade I'd taught Religious Education and Fine Art and had also held two major one-woman art exhibitions entitled "Maranatha" and "Alpha and Omega" respectively. Yet, in my fortieth year, Geri made me realize just how little I understood of the Bible's inherent "Jewishness." It was this unique mentor who opened doors into the world of Messianic literature, music, and art.

While working on her commissions, I began to keep a record of what I was discovering about the Messianic perspective. Geri was always deeply engrossed in the Word itself. She documented her findings by selecting biblical quotes and then rearranging them in such a way as to express her ideas. We would produce a series of studies: the "*Stonewood Hebrew Studies.*" They were another important step in an exhilarating learning process; further evidence of an extraordinarily creative phase in our lives. It was these experiences became the springboard for *Return to the Fountainhead of the Faith.*

After Geri left the park, I worked alone. For the next five-and-a-half years, pertinent imagery and data were methodically documented. At that time, the Messianic Movement was still in its infancy—it only emerged in the late 1960s. Information reflecting the Jewish origins of the Faith was therefore relatively scarce. Messianic ministries tended to publish newsletters and "booklets" rather than books—and these were not always available to the general public. In addition, cultural differences between Jews and Gentiles often made their writings somewhat unintelligible to curious Gentiles. I hoped that by writing from a gentile perspective, my book would help bridge that gap.

In the publishing of the first edition of *Return to the Fountainhead of the Faith,* I chose Pleasantword; a division of Winepress Publishing. I have since published a second illustrated work entitled *Much Bigger than Grownups: Chronicles of a Native South African.* It tells the Wood Gauld story. While editing this second book with Cynthia Miller, an editor par excellence, I became increasingly aware of the need to create an updated revised edition of *Return to the Fountainhead of the Faith.*

In this book important general knowledge, seldom taught from the pulpit, is intended to educate, reinforce cultural foundations, strengthen confidence, and broaden perspectives. Because many key New Testament teachings are reassessed in the light of the history, worship, customs, calendar, and language of the Jews, readers are equipped to distinguish between elements that are indigenous to the early Judeo-Christian heritage and the deadwood that has accumulated over time. The word *Return*, as opposed to *The Return,* in the title, is an invitation to side-step the manmade discrepancies that alienate various denominations and to unite on common ground. In the subtitle "Jewish origins," as opposed to "Hebrew origins," was chosen, because it relates more closely to the Messianic term "Jewish roots." "Yeshua," the Messiah's Hebrew name, has been used in place of the more familiar "Jesus" in the main body of the text. Likewise, the term "Messiah" replaces "Christ." This is intended to accentuate the New Testament's Jewishness.

Because *Return to the Fountainhead of the Faith* has been created for both Gentile *and* Jewish readers, the universally recognized symbol of the cross has not been used. Its association with anti-Semitism makes it offensive to many Jews.

In this revised edition, the illustrations have been trimmed to include only the strongest images. A total of seventy-five line drawings now parallel the text in instructional value. Sequential cameos within the illustrations are often arranged, in Hebrew fashion, from right to left. In addition, four of the part titles of the book help to paint a picture of a nomadic Middle Eastern community: The Olive Tree; Stones, Tents and Clay; The Dwelling Place; Stars and Seasons.

Scriptures have been quoted, with permission, from both the *New International Version* of the Bible (NIV) and David Stern's *Jewish New Testament* (JNT). The latter translation is unique in that it clearly expresses the Bible's true origins. *Webster's New World Hebrew Dictionary* by Hayim Baltsan also proved to be an invaluable resource and is recommended for all who are interested in pursuing the study of this language. For gentile readers, it is more user-friendly than other Hebrew dictionaries. Words are arranged in the familiar Latin alphabet order, as opposed to the order of the Hebrew *alef bet*. The transliteration spelling used in the book and glossary is not Baltsan's, however. I have used a more traditional Hebrew transliteration spelling.

The section on the Hebrew language at the end of the book features a glossary of over 300 Hebrew words and several well-known Jewish blessings and proclamations. As a Gentile, I was aware of the difficulty of adjusting to reading from right to left, so I designed a reverse transliteration method that facilitates the deciphering of Hebrew words for the uninitiated.

All Hebrew terms within the main body of the text and in biblical quotes have been highlighted by means of *italics*—except for the name "Yeshua." Most of these, and others relating to dominant themes, reappear in the glossary at the end of the book.

Many Messianic writers, musicians, and artists, with their distinctly Hebrew perspectives, are gratefully acknowledged as being important sources of inspiration and information in the compilation of this book. The writings of several rabbis and gentile theologians have also been helpful, and the Institute of Talmudic Research in Denver graciously answered questions relating to the Hebrew language.

I would also like to thank Mary Krueger, for her gentle perceptiveness and sustained confidence in the value of this undertaking; Cathy Keene, for being such a careful custodian of the original stones, banners and drawings (Geri's daughters); Darlene Nelson, the first to read the entire manuscript, for her enthusiastic response; Rev. James Knapp for his encouragement; my mother, Ethne Harrison, for her insightful appraisal of the original text; Ruth Kersell for her consistent prayerful support; Kathleen Martinez, a former Christian missionary to Japan, for her perspective on Shinto; Gail Keyser (a "kindred spirit"), one of the founding members of the Christian publishing company, NavPress, and a teacher of

Jewish history, for his endorsement of the first edition; my husband, Roderick, for providing the shade under which the "firstfruit" grew to maturity, for prompting me to include the section on world religions and ideologies, and for help in designing the book's cover; my daughters, Zoë and Quanta, for being such stalwart little backstops ("Sure Mom, that definitely looks like a lion"); Bob Rice for his sensitive guidance in technical matters; the Johnson family for providing a safe haven in which to work; and close friends and family members for their continued interest in this endeavor.

Geraldine Nusbaum (Underwood) passed away on March 7, 2000. She is now, undoubtedly, at one with "the lover of her soul"—Yeshua Messiah. During her lifetime she experienced more than her share of heartache, and yet so often stated, in the words of the Psalmist, "The boundary lines have fallen for me in pleasant places. . . ." (Ps. 16:6) This dedicated student of the Word will be remembered with deep affection for her strength of character, creative energy, infectious enthusiasm, and "tough-mindedness." *Shalom aleikhem* Geri.

As we now return to the fountainhead of the Faith, let us seek the face of the God of Israel and glorify him alone. May his *shalom*—peace—rest upon all who journey through the pages of this book. It is my hope that *Return to the Fountainhead of the Faith* will become a useful resource for many who are scholars at heart.

Deo volente: God willing.

Abbreviations

Although most of the non-Christian world uses the abbreviations C.E. ("of the Common Era") and B.C.E. ("before the Common Era"), only the Christian A.D. (Anno Domini, "in the year of our Lord") and B.C. ("before Christ") appear in this work. More recent dates, such as the year 1948, do not feature the A.D. abbreviation.

Other abbreviations:

AV: Authorized (King James) Version
CJB: Complete Jewish Bible
JNT: Jewish New Testament
NAS: New American Standard
NIV: New International Version
OT: Old Testament
NT: New Testament

Many nations will come and say,

"Come, let us go up to the mountain of the Lord,
   to the house of the God of Jacob.
He will teach us his ways,
   so that we may walk in his paths."

The law will go out from Zion,
   the word of the Lord from Jerusalem.

Micah 4:2

Micah 4:2 (overleaf) illustrated by means of familiar symbols of the Hebrew heritage: fruits of Israel, *menorah*, tablets of the Law, *Torah* scroll, Star of David, and the greeting "*Shalom*," meaning "Peace."

Part 1

A Matter of Choice

The Quest for Meaning

Where Do We Come From? Who Are We? Where Are We Going? In this nineteenth century painting by the French artist, Paul Gauguin, Eden is depicted under yellow skies as a tropical Tahitian Island paradise. A Polynesian Eve reaches up to pluck the fruit from the tree under the watchful gaze of a stone goddess. Other female figures portray the cycle of life, from infancy to old age. A melancholy introspection pervades the work. Gauguin's subjects are solitary, preoccupied, contemplative.

Figure 1: Line drawing illustrating the use of imagery in Paul Gauguin's painting: *"Where Do We Come From? Who Are We? Where Are We Going?"* (1897)

The questions in the title lead to two possible interpretations of the painting. The influence of French colonists was causing the islanders to query their traditional South Pacific worldview. Or, despite the exquisite beauty and apparent harmony of their utopic surroundings, these women were troubled by the uncertainties of life, the ceaseless potential for violence and suffering, and, perhaps, the ultimate enigma—the unavoidable grand finale of death.

The latter interpretation reflects a *universal* dilemma; one that reverberates down the centuries. Mankind's inherent will to survive is at odds with the fragility and transience of life. Each generation therefore grapples with abstract quintessentials, delves for bedrock principles that govern humanity's existence, and reaches beyond the material world for assistance—seeking empowerment from unseen forces.

15

The majority of wisdom traditions therefore reject the idea that there is no afterlife—that we are born, grow, wither, and die like wild flowers. They also manifest humankind's natural inclination to actively worship omnipotent supernatural beings. A myriad of religions and ideologies have been spawned as a means of easing the soul, of establishing a sense of equilibrium and control.

For many, a belief system is as inherited as social norms. Others weigh up the evidence and make choices based on knowledge. Then there are those who amalgamate various world ideologies into esoteric eclectic belief systems—in part, because religious differences have often been the cause of social conflict. Unfortunately, however, as the following pages will reveal, Earth's major religions are inherently incompatible. Contradictory doctrinal fundamentals will forever separate them. It therefore remains a matter of choice—and, having made that choice, a matter of genuine mutual tolerance. Individuals belong first and foremost to the brotherhood of humankind—regardless of religious persuasion.

Pertinent material relating to fourteen major ideologies is the first body of information to be presented in this book. This is intended to serve simply as an introduction to prevalent worldviews; enabling readers to identify distinguishing principles, assess underlying differences, and more accurately pinpoint the origins of the various ideological tendencies that now permeate Western civilizations.

World Religions and Ideologies

The order of the following corresponds with their arrangement on the time charts.

Judaism

Judaism is the faith of the Jews or *Yehudim*; meaning "Those who praise." It is directly linked to the oldest of the world's monotheistic religions.

In the twentieth century B.C., in response to the call of his god, a Mesopotamian Semite by the name of *Avram* (Abram), later renamed *Avraham* (Abraham), set out from Ur and traveled to Haran (see Figure 2). There an exclusive divine contract, or covenant, was established; making him the founder of a "holy nation" and heir to the land of Canaan. Abraham was also promised that his god, *Y-H-V-H*, would reveal himself to the nations of the earth through the offspring of his wife, *Sarai* (later renamed Sarah) —starting with *Yitzkhak* (Isaac), "the son of promise."

In the seventeenth century B.C., Isaac's twelve grandsons—the sons of *Ya'akov* (Jacob), renamed *Yisra'el* (Israel) —migrated from Canaan to the land of Egypt. There, within a period of 430 years, they grew into a nation consisting of twelve large tribes known as the Hebrews or Israelites. They initially prospered in this country, but were eventually forced into slavery. In the thirteenth century B.C., *Moshe* (Moses), a Hebrew who had been raised in the Egyptian court, led them to freedom. Their departure from Egypt is known as the Exodus. During the ensuing forty years in the Sinai desert, Moses united the tribes in the worship of *Y-H-V-H*, before their return to Canaan.

The Hebrew monarchies of *Sha'ul* (Saul), *David*, and *Shlomoh* (Solomon) flourished in Canaan between 1025 and 928 B.C. After Solomon's death, the tribes split into two independent kingdoms. The Kingdom of Israel, or Ephraim, was situated in the north; the

Kingdom of Judah, in the south. The Northern Kingdom was conquered by the Assyrians in the eighth century B.C. and the southern tribes of Judah were taken captive by the Babylonians for seventy years in the sixth century B.C.

After the return of the southern tribes, Judah was ruled as a Persian province until 332 B.C., when it was conquered by Alexander the Great. Foreign occupation of the land then alternated between Syria and Egypt. In 165 B.C., the Jews, under the leadership of a family known as the Maccabees, successfully staged a revolt against the Syrian, Antiochus IV (called Epiphanes), when he attempted to outlaw Judaism. This led to a period of Jewish independence, but it was later lost when Jerusalem was captured by the Romans in 63 B.C.

During the Roman occupation, Jewish zealots favored aggressive political action to regain independence. By the end of the second century A.D., after two unsuccessful revolts, virtually the entire nation had been scattered among the Gentiles. "Diaspora," (*HaGolah*) a Greek term meaning "scattering" or "dispersion," came to be applied to Jews living outside their homeland.

The Jewish nation had gradually lost political and economic control as a succession of major powers occupied the region. They realized that this state of affairs contradicted the promises that had been made to their forefathers. The original God-given covenants had not been fully accomplished, they were no longer a great nation, and they had not restored knowledge of the one true God to humanity. Many Jews came to believe, in accordance with the writings of the Hebrew prophets, that in the last days God would gather the tribes and restore them to their homeland; and that an "Anointed One," or *Mashiach* (Messiah), from the royal line of David, would be sent to rule the nations. They expected that he would usher in an age of peace and social justice on the earth.

From the time of Moses, the Israelites were commanded to separate themselves from their polytheistic neighbors, so as to avoid adopting their religious practices. Initially, a portable worship center, the *Mishkan* (Tabernacle), served their religious needs. This later provided the prototype for two majestic stone temples that were built in Jerusalem: the first during the golden age of King Solomon's reign; the second initiated by King Herod the Great, in about 9 B.C. Animal sacrifices were repeatedly offered as a means of paying the price for the transgressions of the people. In 70 A.D., during the first Jewish revolt, the destruction of Herod's Temple by the Romans brought this early system of worship to an abrupt end.

Directives from *Y-H-V-H* through the Hebrew prophets had abated during the period following the Babylonian exile. This is considered to mark the starting point of Judaism. It was only after 70 A.D., however, that rabbinic Judaism completely replaced the sacrificial rituals of temple worship. The role of the priesthood was then assumed by teachers, or rabbis. Since that time, worship has centered on the study of the *Torah* (Five Books of Moses) in Jewish synagogues.

Two groups of Jews, still recognized today, emerged during the Middle Ages in Europe. *Sephardic* Jews, in more southerly regions, originally had strong ties with Babylon. *Ashkenazic* Jews, in central and northern Europe, were linked to Rome and Palestine. Toward the end of the nineteenth century, the development of the Zionist Movement—a movement that encouraged Jews to return to their ancestral homeland—was kindled in response to anti-Semitic sentiment. This led to the establishment of the State of Israel in 1948 and to the return of millions of Jews.

The majority of Jews still live outside of Israel today; but wherever they live, religious

Jews, as opposed to non-religious or secular Jews, remain distinctive as a people. They have retained many of their ancient customs and are firmly bound to the observance of the Law of Moses, or Mosaic Law. Their sacred year is regulated by the Hebrew lunar calendar. Ancient feast days are faithfully celebrated. Unique rites of passage, from the circumcision of a newborn to the burial of the dead, also distinguish them from other cultural groups. Every Saturday morning, Jews across the globe congregate in synagogues in traditional attire and, under the guidance of rabbis, participate in *Shabbat* (Sabbath) services. The language of worship is often, at least in part, Hebrew.

Because Judaism stresses the importance of family and community, most special synagogue services, such as *Pesakh* (Passover), have their counterpart in a family gathering in the home. Meticulous meals are prepared in compliance with the *kasher* (kosher) food laws that were introduced during the time of Moses.

Modern Judaism, as with all major religions, is not uniform, however. It is represented by a number of different subdivisions; ranging from the distinctly orthodox and conservative, to reformed and more mystical forms—such as *Hasidism* and the elucidation of the *Kabbala*. Furthermore, because the *Torah* assumes belief in God but does not enforce it, agnostic and atheistic elements also exist within this faith. There is no attempt to proselytize other groups.

The holy writings of Judaism consist of the *Tanakh* (Hebrew Scriptures), which includes the *Torah*; the *Midrash* (the rabbinic interpretation of biblical texts, legends, and traditions); the *Mishna* (Rabbinic Law); and the *Talmud* (a commentary on the *Mishna*).

Some understanding of Judaism is a necessary prerequisite to the appreciation of this book as a whole. For this reason, more information has been provided on this faith than will be found in other examples in this section. (Please refer to the "Transliteration Guidelines" on page 229 for the correct pronunciation of all Hebrew words.)

Christianity

Prophets of all ideologies are typically preoccupied with the concept of divine truth. Only one, however, has claimed to *be* the truth. He was *Yeshua* (Jesus) of *Natzrat* (Nazareth), Palestine.

Yeshua was born into the monotheistic Jewish tradition in approximately 4 B.C. As a member of this "chosen" race, he appeared to fulfill key messianic prophecies featured in the ancient Hebrew Scriptures. Christians claim that he was the long awaited Jewish Messiah; the pivotal figure in a new agreement made between the God of Israel and humanity. They view the *Tanakh* as being the indispensable foundation for this new agreement or "New Covenant." Christianity is therefore firmly rooted in Judaism.

The Christian belief system is cradled in the conviction that union with the Almighty God and the revelation of absolute truth can be a present reality. This is not perceived as being the product of mankind's own efforts, but as a precious gift bestowed on humanity by a compassionate god. Christianity's most holy book, the Bible's New Testament, asserts that people's sins separate them from their Creator and that the forgiveness of sin and the divine gift of the Holy Spirit result in the restoration of the soul to God. Furthermore, it gives the assurance that this process of spiritual regeneration leads to eternal life.

These unique privileges are believed to be dependent on an individual's acceptance of a powerful vicarious sacrifice. In approximately A.D. 30, Yeshua, the Messiah or "Anointed One," was executed on a crucifixion stake during the Roman occupation of Palestine. He is said to have suffered and died on behalf of humanity in order to pay off the enormous debt of human sin. He is therefore viewed as being the bridge between fallible human beings and the holy God of the universe. Christians refer to him as the "Savior," claiming that he not only rescues mankind from debilitating personal guilt and spiritual death, but from the malevolent influences of Satan, "the enemy of God." This gift of salvation is therefore also perceived to be a gift of happiness and inner peace. Yeshua's followers are encouraged to go out and disseminate this "good news," or "gospel," and live their lives in the service of others.

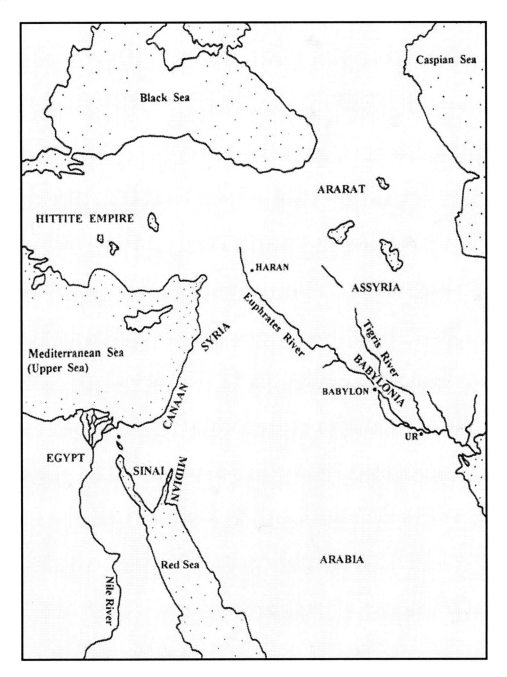

Figure 2: The ancient Middle East prior to the Exodus. Abraham traveled from Ur in southern Mesopotamia to Haran in the north, before journeying westward to Canaan

Although the vast majority of Yeshua's first followers were Jewish, gentile Christianity has dominated this faith over the past sixteen centuries. As a result, awareness of the Faith's Jewish roots has all but disappeared. Over the past two to three decades a notable spiritual awakening has been gaining momentum among the Jews, however. The name "Jesus" is still anathema to most Israeli Jews, but on the international stage increasing numbers are acknowledging Yeshua as the Messiah. These "Jewish Christians" or Messianic believers are emerging as a group of powerful witnesses. Jewish writers, rabbis, musicians, and artists, while ministering to both Jews and Gentiles, are adding an invigorating new dimension to traditional gentile Christianity.

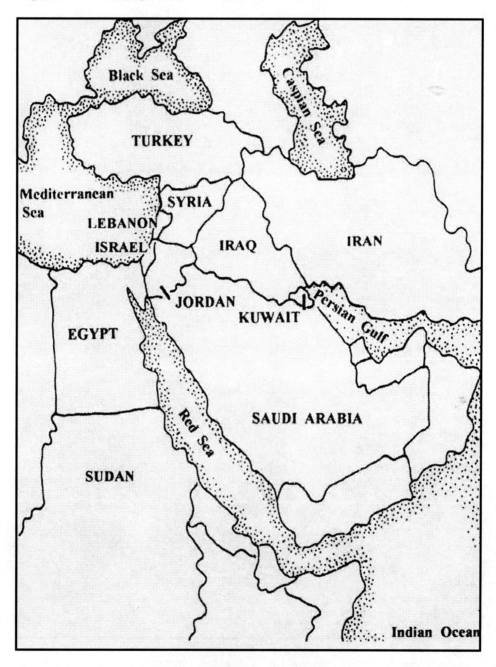

Figure 3: The Middle East today

The Catholic Church is the largest denomination in existence today, comprising about half of all Christians. Eastern Orthodox churches, a great variety of Pentecostal and mainstream Protestant churches, Messianic groups, and fringe sectarian offshoots of this faith make up the rest.

The Christian Bible consists of the Old Testament (*Tanakh*) and the New Testament (*Brit Khadashah*). They are translations of the ancient Hebrew Scriptures and the Greek New Testament respectively. It is the latter that focuses on Yeshua as the Jewish Messiah. New Messianic translations highlighting the Bible's essential "Jewishness," such as David Stern's *Jewish New Testament* (JNT) and the *Complete Jewish Bible* (CJB), have been published by Jewish New Testament Publications in recent years.

Islam

Those who practice the Islamic faith are called Muslims. They are strictly monotheistic. As in Judaism and Christianity, Islam is believed to have originated with *Ibrahim* (Avraham, or Abraham) the Hebrew. However, the emphasis lies not on the Mosaic Law (as in Judaism) or on a Messiah (as in Christianity) but on the revelation of the will of Allah (God) through the prophet Mohammed, the founder of this faith.

Mohammed was born in Mecca (Saudi Arabia) in approximately A.D. 570. He rejected the prevailing polytheism of the region and turned instead to the monotheistic models of Judaism and Christianity. When he was about forty years old, he secluded himself in a cave and is said to have been visited by the Angel Gabriel, who recited the Word of God to him. It was the written form of this "recitation" that became the holy book of Islam; the *Koran*.

Muslims accept the Old and New Testaments and honor Abraham, Ishmael, Isaac, Jacob, and Moses. They reject the divinity of *Yeshua*, however. Mohammed is viewed as being the last and greatest of the messengers of the Bible. Therefore, although these monotheistic faiths have common roots, there are differences in perception with regard to pivotal figures. For example, Muslims view Mohammed as being "the prophet like Moses," mentioned in Deuteronomy 18:15 and 18; whereas Christians regard Yeshua as being this prophet.

Isma'il (Ishmael), the firstborn son of Abraham, is traditionally regarded as being the forefather of the Arab race. Based on this premise, Mohammed, as an Arab, was his descendant. Today, although 95 percent of Arabs are Muslims, they constitute only 20 percent of Islam. This faith is practiced around the globe by about 1.3 billion people.

As in the Judeo-Christian tradition, Muslims believe in one supreme God who is both the creator of the world and judge of humankind. They accept that the dead will be resurrected on the last day and will be rewarded in heaven or punished in hell. Pride is viewed as being an individual's primary weakness, making believers prone to disbelief in Allah and disobedient to his will. Humanity, they believe, has been deluded by Satan, but Allah pardons repentant individuals and restores them to the state of purity in which they were born.

When Abraham was called to leave Haran in Mesopotamia (Gen. 12:1), he separated himself from all that was familiar and adopted an attitude of child-like trust in his relationship with his God. It is this example of absolute trust and submission that constitutes the very core of the Islamic faith. The term "Islam" means "surrender" or "submission" to the will of Allah, and its essential tenets, or "Five Pillars of Islam," are as follows:

- Its creed: "There is no God but Allah, and Mohammed is the Prophet of Allah."
- Prayer, five times a day.
- If at all feasible, at least one pilgrimage to Mecca during a believer's lifetime (hajj).
- Dawn to dusk fasting once a year for the entire Islamic month of Ramadan.
- Charitable contributions (zakat).

Muezzins, chanting from raised platforms or minaret towers, call the faithful to prayer with the Arabic words, "Allah u akba," meaning "God is great!" Muslims emulate Abraham's obedience and submission to the will of Allah, as they stop to pray or gather for worship in mosques. Each year thousands make the annual pilgrimage to the holy city of Mecca, where they visit the holiest of Islamic shrines; the Kaaba in the Great Mosque.

This mosque was originally used in the worship of pagan gods. Mohammed and his followers were ridiculed and persecuted when they proclaimed belief in one God and, after ten years, were forced to flee to the city of Medina. There Mohammed found a more accepting audience for his message. Several years later, he returned to Mecca with a small armed force and, after capturing the city, destroyed the idols of the Kaaba before rededicating it to Allah. The Islamic term "hegira" refers to Mohammed's flight from Mecca to Medina in A.D. 622. Their lunar calendar, indeed the religion itself, dates from this point in time. Islam spread rapidly throughout the Middle East, North Africa, and central Asia during the ensuing century.

Islam is split into two main groups by a controversy regarding the Imams; Mohammed's immediate successors. They are the orthodox Sunni and the more fundamentalist Shiites. The Sunni tend to be predestinarian, believing in the overpowering influence of Allah in their lives. Shiites emphasize humanity's free will and the ability to make choices based on reason. Sufism, the mystical branch of Islam, stressing a personal relationship with Allah, is common among both Sunni and Shiite believers. In the Islamic faith, there is no supreme authority to discipline radical elements. For Muslims, the Koran itself is the highest authority.

Islam is the fastest growing religion in the world today. Muslims are taught to spread their faith, but not to use coercive tactics in doing so. This is prohibited by the Koran. When deemed necessary, however, extremists use force—jihad, or holy war—to achieve their goals. (The word jihad is *normally* used with reference to a believer's personal inner battle between good and evil.) Some Islamic countries, such as Iran and Saudi Arabia, base their governments on Sharia; that is, Islamic religious law.

The holy books of Islam are the Koran (*al-Qur'an*), meaning "recitation," and the Sunna, a record of Mohammed's actions and words.

Nowhere in the Koran is the name of Ishmael's mother mentioned. The Hebrew *Torah* records, however, that because Sarah was infertile, she asked Abraham to father a child through Hagar, her Egyptian servant. The child born from this union was called Ishmael.

In 1844, a Persian by the name of Mirza 'Ali Mohammed, claiming to be a divine spokesman (or *Bab*), predicted that a new prophet, or messenger of Allah, would soon appear. This met with strong resistance from the ruling Islamic party, resulting in the death of this man and the intense persecution of his followers. It gave rise to an offshoot of the Islamic faith known as Bahaism.

Humanism and Rationalism

In the fifth century B.C. a Greek by the name of Protagoras declared: "Man is the measure of all things." The ancient Greeks perceived human intelligence, honed by the faculty of reason, to be the crowning glory of the natural order; placing humankind far above all other creatures. They believed that a life lived in harmony with the orderly perfection of nature, which could be unveiled by human reason, led to the achievement of happiness. Experimentation and innovation became the hallmarks of ancient Greek culture; evident in their mathematics, science, logic, philosophy, art, and architecture. Democracy, rationalism, and the scientific method—which form the basis of modern Western societies— all have their roots in the culture of the ancient Greeks.

Although the ancient Greeks held rational human beings in high esteem, they were well aware of the human anguish that arises when irrational passions and desires conflict with an individual's faculty of reason. They therefore acknowledged the existence of a supernatural realm; a reality that was entirely beyond the control of humanity.

Unlike the ancient Egyptians, the Greeks did not worship animals, or gods in the form of animals. Their gods and goddesses, although immortal, assumed human forms and exhibited the foibles and passions common to all men and women. They also displayed qualities of wisdom, nobility, beauty, and strength—but on a much grander scale. Twelve major gods and several lesser gods, under the authority of Zeus, ruled and harassed humankind from the pleasantness of their Mt. Olympian utopia. These divinities were simply personifications of the forces of nature or the abstract attributes of humanity. Poseidon, for example, was the god of the sea; Apollo rode the chariot of the sun across the skies every day; Artemis was the goddess of the moon; Hephaestus, the god of fire; Aphrodite, the goddess of love; and Athena, the goddess of wisdom.

The ancient Romans later adopted this Greek polytheism, but changed the names of the mythological deities; and then added a few of their own. This form of classical humanism and worship was outlawed once Christianity was adopted as the official religion of the Roman Empire in the late fourth century A.D. Eleven centuries later classical humanism reemerged during the Italian Renaissance. The French word "Renaissance" means "rebirth"; alluding to the renewed interest in the cultures of ancient Greece and Rome.

During the fifteenth century, the anonymity of medieval existence—whole societies subjugated by feudal lords and submissive to the church—slowly gave way to an acknowledgment of the worth of the individual again. This, in turn, gave rise to an increased spirit of exploration and experimentation. The humanism of the Renaissance period was generally tempered by a deep-seated faith in the God of the Bible. The multi-faceted genius of Renaissance "universal men," such as Leonardo Da Vinci, was regarded as being a gift from God; not just extra-ordinary human versatility, talent, and skill.

The eighteenth century Age of Enlightenment laid foundations for the modern era. It was a philosophic movement characterized by a rejection of religious, social, and political norms. Reason, as opposed to tradition and faith, were emphasized. The sublime age-old question "What is *true*?" was gradually superceded by the more pragmatic "What is *real*?"

During the past two centuries, humanism and rationalism have gradually become substitutes for religious belief in the West. The most notable example of this phenomenon has been the adoption of mid-nineteenth century Darwinian theories as a basis for contemporary scientific research. Darwin's hypotheses have increasingly been accepted as fact. This has drastically altered our perception of the origins of life and the governing principles of nature. It is interesting to note that the physicist Albert Einstein, most well known for his "theories of relativity," never disputed the existence of God. In fact, one of the chief motivations behind his mathematical delving into the composition of the universe was to demonstrate that its underlying harmony and order disclosed the very mind of God.

Communism

Communism, as opposed to capitalism or private enterprise, is a socialist system that has its roots in the French Revolution of 1789—preceding the Russian Revolution of 1917 by well over a century. Although the principle of communal reliance—evident in the early Christian communities and in the Israeli *kibbutz* system—has been indispensable at various stages in history, as a political doctrine, Communism's origins were radical and revolutionary. They were spawned by the rebellion of a poor working class majority against a wealthy ruling class minority.

The Russian, Karl Marx, is the most well known theorist of Communist doctrine. However, it was a Frenchman, Francois-Noel Babeuf, who, in 1795, first proposed the abolition of all private property in industry and agriculture and the transference of its ownership to the workers. He saw this as a means of redistributing land and wealth; ensuring an equal share of all economic benefits in a society. Although noble in concept, when this proposal was put to the test in Communist Russia after the Revolution of 1917, individuals soon lost their freedom and became subjugated to the demands of the State—the grand orchestrators of Communist ideology.

The government dictated wages and the supply and prices of goods; regardless of supply and demand in the market place. Consequently, healthy competition, in terms of the quality of products and the expertise of the workers, lost all relevance; resulting in a lowering of standards and a general attitude of apathy in the workplace.

Communist systems have, unquestionably, had a leveling effect; but this has seldom been advantageous. In these countries, governmental control has often resulted in the repression and persecution of individuals. This has impacted freedom of worship, independent academic experimentation, and advancement in the arts, humanities, sciences, and industry. The attempt to devise an impartial socio-economic system that would produce happy, self-motivated citizens backfired on the very people it was designed to assist.

In 1989, the Berlin wall, symbolizing the political and psychological barrier between capitalism and communism, was torn down. In 1991, the Communist Party in Russia collapsed, leaving the country in economic chaos.

Animism

The term "animism" has its root in the Latin "*anima*," meaning "breath of life" or "soul." Animists believe that the natural world is vested with a powerful life force and that all objects or elements have "spirits" that should be treated with deep respect. They therefore attempt to live in harmony with nature; demonstrating an attitude of reverence toward such things as rivers, rocks, trees, mountains, and animals. Animists often seek permission from the spirit of the object before it is used, or "sacrificed." They also make sure, out of respect for the spirit, that nothing is wasted. For this reason, North American Indians, to this day, use every part of a slain buffalo.

Rituals, prayers, and gifts are important aspects of animist worship; particularly with regard to good crops and fertility. In their rituals, "*shaman*," or "medicine men (or women)," often don masks and other distinctive clothing and then dance and chant until a hallucinatory trance-like state is achieved. They believe that by this means the spirits enter their bodies and speak directly to the community.

This very ancient form of worship with its complex mythology, rituals, and symbolism is still practiced in various tribal cultures today. Beginning in the 1960s, animism aroused interest on a more global level; particularly among first world Neo-Pagans who are dedicated to the preservation of the earth's ecology.

Spiritism or Spiritualism

Necromancy—communication with the spirits of the dead—and ancestor worship, fertility cults and the deification of nature, are mankind's most primal religious systems. Although in the West the practice of necromancy died out centuries ago, probably due to the influence of Christianity, in 1848 it reemerged in the United States in upstate New York.

In its modern form, Spiritualism—a term used by Spiritualists in preference to "Spiritism"—combines Eastern and Christian doctrines. Its adherents embrace the concepts of reincarnation and karma, and accept Yeshua as a "master"—merely one of many great teachers. They rely instead on personal "spirit guides."

During special meetings known as "séances," Spiritualists attempt to make contact with the spirits of the dead. Certain believers claim to have extraordinary powers such as mediumship, allowing the spirits to assume control of their bodies and speak through them; clairvoyance, the ability to see the spirits of the dead; "audio-voyance," hearing the spirits; and healing, the supernatural ability to heal the sick. The ultimate aim at each sitting is to witness the misty "materialization" of a spirit. This practice has strong appeal for those who have recently lost loved ones.

Although many assert that there is inadequate scientific evidence to support Spiritualist claims and discredit the supernatural phenomena as hoaxes, the curious are often warned, by those who have managed to extricate themselves from this alluring realm of the spirits, to be wary of the powers at work in this movement.

We should also note that seeking out mediums and spiritists was strictly forbidden among the ancient Israelites (Deut. 18:9–12) —reliance on their visions and "utterances" all too easily becoming substitutes for faith in the God of Israel. The account of King Saul defying Mosaic Law by consulting the witch of Endor, in order to gain advice from the spirit of Samuel, is the exception that proves the rule.

Eastern Perspectives

One of the overriding principles that separates the following major Eastern perspectives from Western religions is the perception that it is the duty of each person to refine the soul by means of a process of gradual self-improvement—that there is no *personal* God to rescue individuals from the "self" or assist individuals through the trials of life.

Hinduism

"Hindu" means "Dwellers of the Indus River." Hinduism is thought to have arisen from the combination of the Vedic religion of migrating Aryans with the ancient beliefs of the indigenous peoples of India. It is regarded as being the world's oldest religion and it is unlike any other belief system. Hinduism has no known founder, no single body of doctrine, a great diversity of religious practices, and several holy books.

Hindus worship many gods, but hold to the view that all are aspects of one supreme unknowable power in the universe—*Brahman*. Three principal forms of Brahman are demonstrated in the gods *Vishnu* and *Shiva* and the goddess *Shakti*. These gods, in turn, are seen to be incarnated or manifested in various more minor gods.

They believe that all living things are of the same essence and that every soul revisits the earth many times in human, animal, or even vegetable form. This cycle of birth and rebirth, known as *samsura*, is determined by the quality of past deeds (*karma*). Because it is believed that what one does in the present life has its consequences or rewards in the next, pure acts, thoughts, and devotions are viewed as being a means of improving one's karma and escaping samsura. The ultimate goal of every Hindu is to escape this continuum in order to become part of the "absolute soul," or Brahman.

The role of the Hindu priestly caste, the *Brahmins*, is to orchestrate or assist in the performance of rituals, to assess the ritual purity of believers, and to preside over Hindu temples and organizations. Private ceremonies focus on rites of passage (birth, initiation, marriage, and death) and daily devotions, but a variety of more public ceremonies are performed within temples. The most common of these being the *paja*; a dinner prepared for a Hindu god.

The most important holy writings of the Hindus are the *Veda*, but a great variety of other sacred literature exists. The Veda feature the *Upanishads*, *Bhagavad-Gita*, *Mahabharata*, and *Ramayana*.

Jainism

Jainism was founded by Vardhamana Mahavira and is one of four major Eastern religions that originated in India. The aim of this belief system is reflected in its name. The root word "*jina*" means "conqueror," or "victor." As in other Eastern belief systems, Jainism is characterized by the attempt to attain union with supreme beings by means of a process of gradual self-improvement. Jainists believe that individuals evolve spiritually through a series of planes or stages of spiritual perfection, until they are freed from the contamination of "self" and the material world. Their primary means of liberating the soul is through meditation and the discipline of Yoga. The overriding principle in Jainism is nonviolence toward all living things.

All souls are seen to be equal, but *Tirthankaras*, or "Liberated Souls," who have escaped the cycle of cause and effect, are worshipped; as are numerous lesser divinities. An extensive body of literature exists within Jainism.

Buddhism

Buddhism originated in India in approximately 525 B.C. with the vision of Siddhartha Gautama. It was this man who came to be known as the *Buddha*, meaning "The Awakened One" or "The Enlightened One."

Gautama taught that individuals are born to a life of pain and suffering, and that there is no underlying purpose or reality to our physical existence. Humanity, he believed, is caught up in a recurring cycle of birth, decay, death, and rebirth—reincarnation—because of an unwillingness to relinquish the attachment to the "unreal self." He maintained that in order to escape this misery, individuals must renounce "self" by means of an "Eightfold Path" of enlightenment. The ultimate goal of Buddhists is to attain a state of "nothingness," or Nirvana—The Void. As in many other Eastern religions, the journey along the path of life is more important to Buddhists than the realization of its sublime destination.

Gautama did not leave written records and, by the time the Buddhist oral tradition was written down, various schools of thought had evolved with different interpretations of his teachings. This generated some dissension within the world of Buddhism during ensuing centuries.

The three main Buddhist groups are the *Theravada*, who emphasize good deeds and purity of thought; the *Mahayana*, who stress the discipline of meditation, the redemptive powers of higher beings, and ritual practices; and the *Tantrism*, who exercise a combination of philosophic belief and ritual magic. Buddhist practices often include austere meditation, magical incantations, and complex temple rites.

The Buddhist holy writings consist of the *Tripitaka*, the teachings of Buddha; commentaries on these teachings and rulings regarding Buddhist monastic life; and the *Sutra*, general Buddhist teachings and commentaries.

Shinto

Shinto, Japan's oldest known religion, means "way of the gods." It is comprised of a complex system of rituals and philosophic ideas that lack firm historical foundations or a clear system of theology.

There is little emphasis on the after-life and no congregational worship. Individuals pay homage to their deities in small domestic or roadside shrines, and in larger public shrines. Distinctive wooden entrance gates, the *torii*, lead into structures that are quite bare; with the exception of a mirror—symbolic of the sun goddess—offering dishes, and straw and paper hangings.

In the past, the emperor of Japan was believed to be a direct descendant of the sun goddess and was venerated as "the son of god." In the late nineteenth century, State Shinto was introduced, which reemphasized emperor worship and patriotism. It was abolished in 1945 after Japan's defeat in World War II. Although still revered, Japan's emperor no longer has a god-like status.

One unifying aspect of Shinto is its veneration of the "*kami*"; impersonal positive or negative life forces or spirits, believed to be in evidence in awe-inspiring objects or phenomena in the physical world. Up until 1945, the emperor was viewed as being "manifest-kami"—or kami incarnate. In general, kami are believed to be present in majestic scenery and the forces of nature; in such creatures as birds, foxes, and wolves; in creativity, disease, sexual intercourse, growth, and healing; in the ancestral spirits of brave warriors and noblemen; and in such "mystical" objects as paper, hair, and mirrors.

According to Shinto mythological writings, kami created the world and established its laws and customs. Individuals therefore recite prayers and offer gifts of flowers, money, and cakes to these deities. Shinto priests conduct "*matsuri*"—ceremonies that focus on themes such as successful harvests, repentance, peace, health, and longevity.

In modern day Japan, Shinto is generally associated with joyful occasions, whereas Buddhism is associated with more somber events. The basic tenets of Confucianism have also been absorbed, forming a code of ethics. The Japanese draw from all three traditions.

Written records of their ancient mythology were only established in the eighth century A.D., after the introduction of the art of writing from the Chinese mainland. Holy books include the *Nihongi*, or Chronicles of Japan; and the *Kojiki*, or Record of Ancient Matters.

Sikhism

In Sikhism we find a combination of Islamic and Hindu beliefs and practices. The Sikh religion was founded in the fifteenth century by *Guru* ("Teacher") Nanak. It is dominant in the Punjab region of northern India, where Sikhs have attempted to establish a homeland. The word *Sikh*, meaning "disciple," refers to the devotees of Nanak and his nine successors.

This religion has its roots in the Hindu devotion to Vishnu and in the practices of Muslim Sufis, or mystics. The teachings of Nanak reflect much of the Eastern worldview. He taught that there is one unknowable god and creator who can only be perceived in nature by those who have relinquished all forms of worldliness. Nanak believed that the goal of humanity's existence is to escape the cycle of reincarnation and to become one with this god by means of the discipline of meditation. Sikh scriptures—known as *Adi Granth*, or "First Book"—festivals, pilgrimages, and places of worship were developed over time by Nanak's followers.

Persecution by the Muslims in the seventeenth century prompted the Sikhs to form a special combative group called the *Khalsas*, or "Pure." This militant brotherhood remains active today.

Confucianism

Confucianism is more a system of conduct than a religion. Its founder was a Chinese philosopher by the name of Confucius, or *K'ung-fu-tzu*, meaning Master K'ung. Although he never claimed to be a prophet, on his death he was immediately elevated to a god-like status. Temples were built to honor him and his grave became a site of pilgrimage.

Confucius (551–479 B.C.) is known for his wise sayings, or "analects." He spoke not so much of God, however, but of goodness; not so much of religion, but of moral conduct. He encouraged people to live in a virtuous manner. Based on his teachings, Confucianism advocates social justice, loyalty and devotion to family members and friends, self-control, and the cultivation of the intellect. Despite the impact of the Communist ideology in the twentieth century, this philosopher of ancient times is still venerated by the people of China.

Taoism

The primary influence in the formation of the Taoist philosophy in the sixth century B.C. was the teaching of a Chinese man by the name of Lao-tzu. The word *Tao* means "the way" and alludes to a manner of thinking, an attitude toward life. Initially, Taoism was a complex abstract philosophy understood by a privileged few. With the development of its religious counterpart, Taoist influence spread and, like Confucianism, eventually came to permeate the Chinese culture.

Taoist philosophy differs from the Taoist religion that emerged from it. The philosophy focuses on the existence of a "permanent Tao," which is believed to be an essential underlying reality or life force that unifies everything in existence. Apparent discrepancies are viewed as being merely different aspects of the same thing. Conflict is said to arise when people hold fast to an independent perception of reality—thereby losing sight of "the Tao."

Followers of the Taoists religion, on the other hand, believe that the universe is governed by an assortment of gods who punish corrupt conduct by means of ill health, death, and suffering in the hereafter, and reward good conduct by means of abundant gifts and longevity. In their daily lives, adherents claim to consult and placate the numerous spirits that inhabit the objects in their surroundings. A priestly order performs complex rituals and exorcisms.

Taoists emphasize the importance of ceremony, magic, and mystical religious experience. Because their focus is on the essence of life and on the attainment of immortality, they tend not to actively pursue education, social status or wealth.

Atheism, Agnosticism, and Deism

No study of this kind would be complete without making some reference to the three philosophical attitudes that reflect a *rejection* of Earth's formal belief systems. Atheists deny the very existence of God and therefore reject all religions. Agnostics question the concept of divine revelation, claiming that there is insufficient substantive evidence, or "knowledge," to prove the actuality of God—or any ultimate reality. Deists affirm the concept of God as a powerful influential force, but see him as being above and beyond all of Earth's formal religions. The term "Deism" was first applied to eighteenth-century rationalists.

Adherents to Dominant World Religions: A Broad Approximation

Buddhism	360,000,000
Christianity	2,000,000,000 (Over 50% Catholic)
Confucianism	6,300,000
Hinduism	900,000,000
Islam	1,300,000,000
Jainism	4,200,000
Judaism	14,430,000
Shinto	2,800,000
Sikhism	23,260,000
Spiritism	12,340,000
Taoism and Chinese folk religions	382,000,000

World Religions and Ideologies

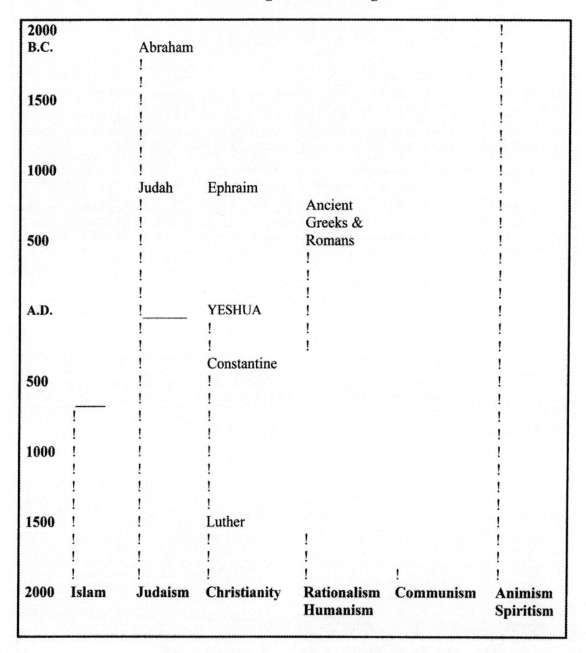

Eastern Religions and Ideologies

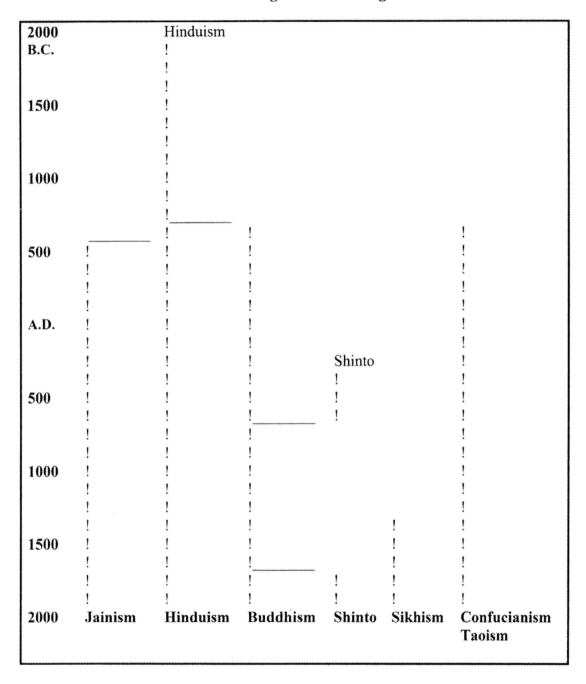

Relative and Absolute Truth

Not all members of a society can be regarded as being truly representative of its religious ideals. Sincere and nominal belief are worlds apart in any cultural group. Of those who search for meaning, some are content to accept that truth is a relative concept; that it is determined by differing cultural backgrounds or whatever each individual perceives to be the truth. Others, dissatisfied with spiritual truths that are relative or compromising, yearn for fundamental principles that are enduring and absolute; remaining constant from generation to generation, regardless of culture.

If truth is discerned on the basis of varying opinions and shifting worldviews, it is merely the product of human innovation, intellectual guesswork, and persuasion—and there *is* no all-encompassing truth. Furthermore, world ideologies are contradictory in so many respects, it must be assumed that they are either all man-made or that only *one* is divine— the expression of *actual* spiritual realities.

The latter—the concept of one absolute, divine eternal truth—by its very nature, cannot be formulated by means of humanity's fallible powers of reasoning. If spiritual absolutes exist, they must be determined by a supreme deity or governing factor—which is, in essence, beyond human comprehension.

An attempt should therefore be made to distinguish between noble human aspiration, as humanity searches for God, and divine revelation, as God discloses himself to humanity. We should also clearly distinguish between the two fundamentally different perceptions of truth: the one being nonspecific, variable, and relative; the other, permanent, unchangeable, and absolute.

A Jewish Messiah

If all religions were equally true and it was of no consequence whatsoever as to what one believed, then biblical teachings regarding the "chosen nation" of Israel and a Jewish Messiah would be nullified. In fact, the whole concept of salvation would be irrelevant. If, for instance, souls evolve slowly toward perfection by means of the cycle of reincarnation, there was no need for Yeshua's crucifixion. The Eastern concept of reincarnation renders his death absolutely meaningless. It completely negates the belief that the problem of human sin was resolved by means of an atoning sacrifice.

This book is based on the premise that the Israelites *were* the "holy people" of God, that Yeshua of Nazareth was indeed the Jewish Messiah, and that ancient Hebrew monotheism holds the key to the revelation of the living God and to absolute truth. It is precisely when viewed in the light of major world ideologies that the unique power and utter simplicity of this perspective emerges. The New Testament teaches that this message must continue to be disseminated across the globe—because there is "no other name under heaven given to mankind by whom we must be saved!" (Acts 4:12; JNT page 158).

Yeshua in First Century Roman Palestine

We will begin our study of Yeshua by painting a picture of the world in which he lived. The name of the country into which he was born has changed several times during the course of its history. It has been called Canaan. During the period of the Divided Kingdom, it was Israel and Judah. Today much of this "Promised Land" or "Holy Land" is known as the Land of Israel (*Eretz Yisra'el*). At the time of the Messiah's incarnation, the region was called Palestine; a name derived from the word *Philistia*, meaning "the land of the Philistines."

Palestine became part of the Roman Empire in 63 B.C. It had been under Roman rule for about sixty years prior to the birth of Yeshua. Of the local princes who were employed to govern the country, Herod the Great, a pro-Roman Idumaean, is the most well known. He ruled for thirty-four years. Although a superb diplomat, he was ambitious and ruthless. Herod was therefore hated by the Jews. In order to protect his position, he established a mercenary army and system of strongholds; one of which was the fortress of Masada in the Dead Sea region.

This king made an attempt to win the support of the Jews by rebuilding the Temple in Jerusalem, but his gesture was not indicative of any religious or political allegiance—he also built a temple to Augustus in Samaria and orchestrated the building of the Roman port city of Caesarea. It was Herod who ordered the wholesale slaughter of the "babes of Bethlehem"; he had all Jewish boys less than two years of age murdered when he learned of the birth of the Messiah, "the King of the Jews."

When Herod died, his kingdom was divided into three separate regions so that it could be governed by his three sons. Two of these sons warrant particular attention. Archelaus governed Judea (*Yihudah*) and Samaria (*Shomron*), but was deposed after a decade of incompetent rule. Pontius Pilate, a procurator under the authority of Rome, was sent to replace him.

Galilee (*Galil*) fell under the jurisdiction of Herod Antipas; Herod's second son. It was this man who was in control of the region during the time of Yeshua's ministry. It was this man who had John *(Yokhanan)* the Baptist beheaded and who met briefly with Yeshua during his trial. Herod Antipas inherited his father's flair for diplomacy, but was eventually exiled by the insane Emperor Caligula when he stepped out of rank by requesting a title. In A.D. 44, after the death of Herod Agrippa I—the grandson of Herod the Great—the entire country came under direct Roman rule.

Many Jews resented the Roman presence, not only because of the heavy taxes that they found themselves having to pay, but because it was contrary to their heritage as God's people to be subject to foreign rule in their own country. Sporadic acts of rebellion therefore occurred, particularly in Galilee. The term "Galilean" came to be associated with revolutionary tendencies. These acts of insurrection eventually led to two Jewish revolts against Rome. The first started in A.D. 66 and ended in A.D. 73 with the last stand of the Jews of Masada. At that time, Herod's Temple in Jerusalem was destroyed and thousands of Jews massacred. The second revolt, known as the *Bar Kokhba* Revolt, took place between 132 and 135 A.D.

The two most important religious groups in Yeshua's day were the Sadducees (*Tz'dukim*) and Pharisees (*P'rushim*). The Sadducees, although primarily concerned with temple ritual, were the more materialistic of the two and were more willing to cooperate with the Romans. The Pharisees focused on the requirements of the *Torah*, or Law. Apart from their Roman rulers, a seventy-one member Jewish judicial council, known as the Sanhedrin—in force from 100 B.C. to 425 A.D.—also governed the Jews in first century Palestine. Under the leadership of the high priest, this council—consisting of Sadducees, Pharisees, and two scribes—had the authority to judge, punish, and imprison Jews. Only the Romans had the authority to impose the death penalty.

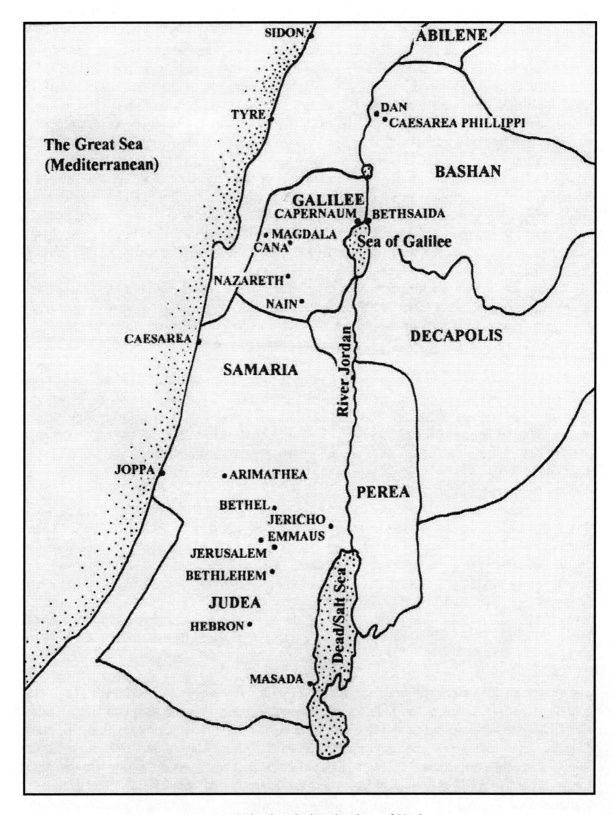

Figure 4: Palestine during the time of Yeshua

After the Temple was destroyed in A.D. 70, it was the scholastic tradition of the Pharisees that united the Jews of the Diaspora (*Galut*). Indeed, that tradition constitutes the basis of the *Talmud* and modern day Judaism.

Son of Man, Son of God

> For to us a child is born, to us a son is given, and the government will be on his shoulders. And he will be called Wonderful Counselor, Mighty God, Everlasting Father, Prince of Peace. Of the increase of his government and peace there will be no end. (Isa. 9:6–7)

In approximately 4 B.C., during the reign of Emperor Caesar Augustus and shortly before the death of Herod the Great, a virtuous young Jewess named *Miryam* (Mary) gave birth to her first son. She named him Yeshua (Jesus). *Miryam* had fallen pregnant prior to her marriage to *Yosef* (Joseph), during the period of their engagement. But *Yosef* was not the child's father. Yeshua is said to have been conceived by the Spirit of God—making him the son of the God.

The birth took place in the Judean town of *Bet-Lekhem* (Bethlehem) during a Roman census, in the most lowly circumstances imaginable—in the animal shelter of a crowded inn. He was raised in a middle class home in the Galilean town of *Natzrat* (Nazareth) and apparently had brothers and sisters (Mark 6:3; John 2:12); the most well known of which being James (*Ya'akov*) and Jude *(Y'hudah)* —the writers of New Testament letters bearing these names. After the account of Yeshua's birth and early childhood, *Yosef* is no longer mentioned in the Gospels. Yeshua is simply referred to as "*Miryam's* son." It appears that at a comparatively young age, he took over *Yosef's* carpentry business in order to support his family.

Accounts of Yeshua's birth and childhood, recorded in the Gospels of Matthew and Luke, differ in some respects, but both emphasize that this was no ordinary child. When he was twelve years old—the year in which he would have been preparing for his *bar mitzvah*—Yeshua astounded the teachers of the Temple with his profound wisdom (Luke 2:42–50). This extraordinary insight into the Hebrew Scriptures at an early age heralded his unique calling.

Baptism

> [I]n the future he will honor Galilee of the Gentiles, by the way of the sea, along the Jordan. (Isa. 9:1)

Yeshua had a relative by the name of *Yokhanan* (John). He was the son of *Z'kharyah* (Zechariah), a Levitical priest. John, an ascetic of the Judean desert, is described as being one who wore camel skins and a leather belt around his waist, who ate locusts and wild honey. Yet people flocked to the *Yarden* (Jordan) in order to hear him preach and be baptized by him.

When Yeshua was approximately thirty years of age, this prophetic messenger proclaimed him to be the promised Messiah of Israel—"the Lamb of God who takes away the sin of the world!" (John 1:29) *Yokhanan* then baptized him. Yeshua's participation in this act of Jewish ritual cleansing marked the beginning of his three-year ministry—the biblical accounts include three spring festival periods; the last one being the Passover of his death and resurrection.

Ministry

Yeshua never married and, during the time of his ministry, had no settled family life. This afforded him the freedom to preach and heal throughout Palestine. He was equally at home with the affluent and the poor, and had very little in the way of worldly belongings. He taught his followers not to fear poverty, but to live by faith as he did.

Yeshua was found talking to Samaritans, the enemies of the Jews. He ate with tax collectors, the parasites of his society. He consistently responded to those in need, regardless of their social standing; showing kindness to prostitutes and adulterers, and mingling with outcasts. He was passionate in his defense of the truth and, at times, extremely fiery in his condemnation of the false teachings and hypocrisy of the scribes and Pharisees—he single-handedly drove the moneychangers out of the Temple courtyard in Jerusalem! To the religious authorities, Yeshua's rhetoric was often audacious and unacceptable. He posed a threat to the existing status quo.

This Galilean is said to have raised the dead and instantly healed the sick, blind, deaf, dumb and demon-possessed. Pitiful lepers were cured of their dreaded disease. Even nature appeared to heed his commands. The Gospels record that he walked toward his disciples' fishing boat across the waters of the Sea of Galilee on one occasion; and on another, with a few simple words, calmed a raging storm on this lake. He also claimed equality with the God of Israel by forgiving people's sins. This was no ordinary man.

Yeshua selected twelve common middle-class men to be his *talmidim* (disciples); his constant companions, helpers, and students. They were open to new ideas; unfettered by academicism and rigid religious preconceptions. Of the twelve, his three closest companions were *Shim'on Kefa* (Simon Peter), *Ya'akov* (James) and *Yokhanan* (John). With the exception of *Yehudah* from *Kri'ot* (Judas Iscariot), all were Galileans; their accents distinguishing them from the Jews of Jerusalem (*Yerushalayim*). These men, and this Messiah's fellow countrymen, would have addressed him by his Hebrew name—"Yeshua."

Throughout the centuries, Christian painters have often rendered "Jesus" as blue-eyed, brown-haired, and gentle—at times, even effeminate. Not so. As a descendant of a Semite of the Near East (*Avram*) and as a Jew of that period, he would almost certainly have been olive-skinned, with dark hair and eyes. Furthermore, he was a carpenter; a trade requiring physical strength. He often walked great distances, slept out in the open, experienced fatigue, hunger, and thirst—and seldom enjoyed luxury of any kind. Despite his divine commission he was assuredly tough, lean, and very astute; not "meek and mild." Yeshua manifested the awesome power of the Almighty—and the strength and resilience of a full-blooded Jew.

Messiah

In retrospect it is clear that numerous messianic texts in the Hebrew *Tanakh* (OT) foreshadowed the life and mission of Yeshua of Nazareth—for instance, Yeshua's crucifixion was described by King David in Psalm 22 centuries before the actual event. Yet the Gospels indicate that his followers were baffled as to his true identity. They could not help but grasp that they were witnessing something extraordinary but, it seems, were unable to assess the historic significance of the events unfolding before their eyes. Even the enlightened proclamation of *Kefa* (Peter) in Matthew 16:16, was later negated by his betrayal of his *rabbi* (teacher).

The Jewish perception of the Messiah was based on a prophecy in the Book of Isaiah (9:6–7). They expected a triumphant, royal Messiah—a great political figure. Jewish zealots had hoped that Yeshua would satisfy their yearnings for such a deliverer; that he would be the one to free them from the yoke of Roman rule. It has therefore been suggested that Judas Iscariot, by delivering Yeshua into the hands of the Jewish Sanhedrin, attempted to place him a position that would *force* him to reveal himself as God's *royal* Messiah. Yeshua never professed to be this kind of savior, however.

Although various prophetic passages in the *Tanakh* relate to the Messiah as being both a sacrificial lamb (*korban*) and king (*melekh*), it apparently never occurred to his followers that he would come first as a sacrifice and only much later as a king. His Jewish followers had to be taught time and time again that his kingdom was "not of this world." His was not an earthly kingdom. It would be an eternal spiritual kingdom.

Trial and Crucifixion

During his ministry, religious leaders became increasingly uncomfortable with Yeshua's influence over the Jewish people. His teachings were authoritative, incisive, and uncompromising. And he did not hesitate to publicly expose their hypocrisy. Yeshua became a thorn in their side. They began to fear an uprising that would topple the status quo and were forced to accept him as the Messiah, or condemn him as a blasphemer. They chose the latter.

Two charges were brought against Yeshua. The first was a false charge of insurrection against the Roman rulers, which was dismissed by Pontius Pilate. The second was an accusation of blasphemy, brought against him by the Jewish Sanhedrin. It was this second charge that led to his death by crucifixion.

> "If you [Pilate] let this man go, you are no friend of Caesar. Anyone who claims to be a king opposes Caesar." (John 19:12)

> Yeshua remained silent. The *cohen hagadol* [high priest] said to him, "I put you under oath! By the living God, tell us if you are the *Mashiach* [Messiah], the Son of God!" Yeshua said to him, "The words are your own. [NIV: "Yes, it is as you say."] But I tell you that one day you will see the Son of Man sitting at the right hand of *Ha G'vurah* [the Power, God] and coming on the clouds of heaven." At this, the *cohen hagadol* tore his robes. "Blasphemy!" he said. "Why do we still need witnesses? You heard him blaspheme! What is your verdict?" "Guilty," they answered. "He deserves death!" (Matt. 26:63–66; JNT page 40)

In the above excerpt, Yeshua responded to the charge of blasphemy by referring to a passage in the Hebrew Scriptures (Daniel 7:13–14) that related exclusively to the Messiah.

These events led to a mock trial during which Yeshua was condemned to die. He was ridiculed and taunted as, in feigned deference, Roman soldiers pressed a crown of sharp, thorny twigs onto his head and placed a purple robe—a symbol of royalty—across his shoulders. "Hail, king of the Jews!" they jeered, as they hit him in the face. He received thirty-nine lashes, probably with a Roman "cat-o-nine-tails," before being forced to carry his heavy wooden stake to a small hill called Skull, or *Gulgolta* (Aramaic), on the outskirts of the old city of Jerusalem. His lacerated body was nailed to the stake, which was then raised to stand between the stakes of two criminals.

Death by crucifixion was a common Roman method of execution at that time. The hands and feet of criminals were tied or nailed to crosses, stakes, and even the trunks of trees. Criminals were then left to suffocate to death. Death was often hastened by the breaking of the legs of criminals; a slumped body suffocated quickly. Most men were simply tied to their upright posts. Nails, brutally driven through wrists and feet, were used only when the authorities chose to make a public example of a particular crime—as they did in the case of Yeshua. Traditional images of the crucified Messiah show him wearing a loincloth, but as he hung there, in full view of the public, he was most probably completely naked. He suffered extreme pain and degradation.

> The soldiers came and broke the legs of the first man who had been put on a stake beside Yeshua, then the legs of the other one; but when they got to Yeshua and saw that he was already dead, they didn't break his legs. However, one of the soldiers stabbed his side with a spear, and at once blood and water flowed out. (John 19:32–34; JNT page 148)

Burial

Having gained special permission from Pontius Pilate, Joseph of Arimathea, a member of the Jewish Sanhedrin who accepted the teachings of Yeshua, removed the body from the stake. Together with Nicodemus the Pharisee, he wrapped it in a shroud in accordance with Jewish custom. The body was then laid in an unused burial cave and a large stone was rolled across its entrance. This conforms to the two-stage burial procedure practiced by first century Jews—the wrapped body was laid in a cave for the first year, after which the dry bones were placed in a limestone ossuary. Yeshua's tomb was "sealed" by the authorities and guards took up positions at the entrance to ensure that his followers did not remove the body. This concern arose from the fact that Yeshua had stated that he would be rejected and killed, but would rise from death on the third day. All of this took place on the eve of the Jewish Passover in approximately A.D. 30.

> "The Son of Man must suffer many things and be rejected by the elders, chief priests and teachers of the law, and he must be killed and on the third day be raised to life." (Luke 9:22)

Resurrection

The third day—Sunday, the first day of the Jewish week—was a day of bewilderment. First century witnesses claimed that Yeshua came back to life. Reports as to the actual events vary in the Gospels, but all four describe visits to the empty tomb by Yeshua's perplexed followers. They also include reports relating to the reappearance of the Messiah on that Sunday: first to Mary *(Miryam)* of Magdala, later to two men on their way to the town of Emmaus, then to Peter, and finally to the rest of the disciples (excluding Thomas) in Jerusalem. Matthew's Gospel states that the guards were paid to spread the story that the body was stolen from the tomb.

The New Testament records that in his resurrected state, Yeshua was able to appear and disappear at will. He therefore reassured his followers that he was not a ghost by encouraging them to touch his body and by eating a piece of broiled fish in their presence. Over the next forty days, he is said to have made many more supernatural appearances, before physically ascending from the earth, to the "right hand of his heavenly Father," in full view of his disciples *(talmidim)*.

It was only *after* his resurrection, that Yeshua's true identity became self-evident. Only then did all pieces of the puzzle fall into place. It was Yeshua's *resurrection* that turned a band of grief-stricken fearful followers into a group of dynamic witnesses.

Yeshua never appeared to the Jewish Sanhedrin. Although they assuredly received the disquieting reports regarding the empty tomb and the Resurrection, they chose to maintain their positions. Accordingly the Jewish nation as a whole, under the authority of the Sanhedrin, did not accept Yeshua as the Messiah.

Spirit Baptism

There is one more incident of significance that completes this account. Fifty days after that Jewish Passover, during the Feast of Weeks (Pentecost), Yeshua's followers were filled with God's Spirit (*Ruach HaKodesh*) while in the city of Jerusalem. That day has been called "the birthday of the Church," because it was on this Jewish holiday that believers were first empowered to continue Yeshua's work. Peter preached with such authority, that about three thousand people were won over to belief in the Messiah that day.

Yeshua's *talmidim* (disciples) were finally able to grasp that the phrase "kingdom of God" pertained specifically to the rule of God in their *hearts*—not in the political arena. The Resurrection ushered in God's spiritual kingdom. From that time, he has ruled in the hearts and minds of countless individuals by transforming them, inwardly, by means of his Spirit.

The triumph of Yeshua's resurrection separated him from all other great teachers and prophets. It also demonstrated that he was the Messiah of Israel—the *Mashiach*, the "Anointed One." Paul (*Sha'ul*) later stated that if the reality of the Resurrection was unfounded, then believers in Yeshua would, of all people, be the most to be pitied. Belief in Yeshua is based not only on this event, however. There is his extraordinary life, his miracles and teachings, and the baptism of the Spirit on the Day of Pentecost. There is also the undeniable inner transformation, or spiritual rebirth, that each true convert undergoes.

Good News

The news Yeshua instructed his followers to go out and disseminate was "good news." With a living faith that manifests itself in a new equilibrium, a gladness of heart, a life full of purpose and meaning, he surely never intended his messengers to "go forth" as fiery prophets of doom, despair and disaster? Furthermore, numerous man-made modifications and traditions have been cultivated over the centuries—the Scriptures have even been *tailored* at times to make them *fit* various doctrines! A balanced faith is based on knowledge and love of God, not on fear. Yeshua's original teachings must be preserved.

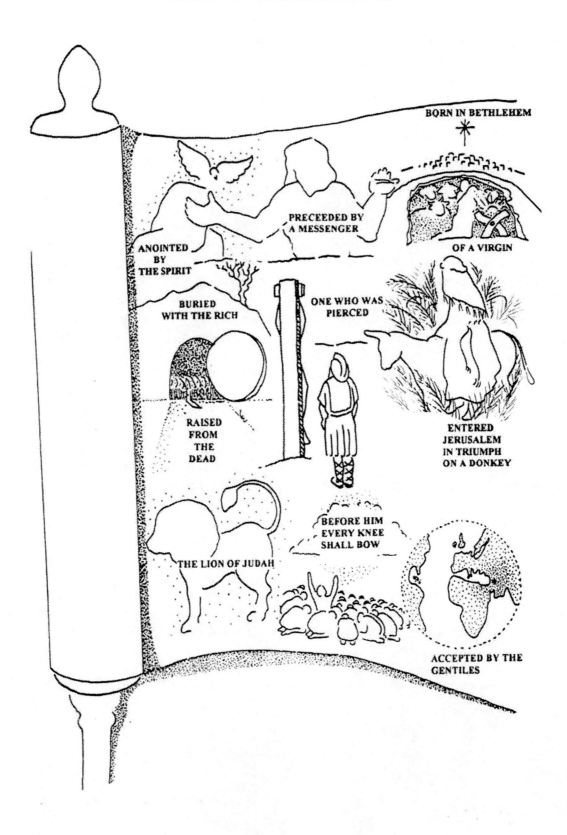

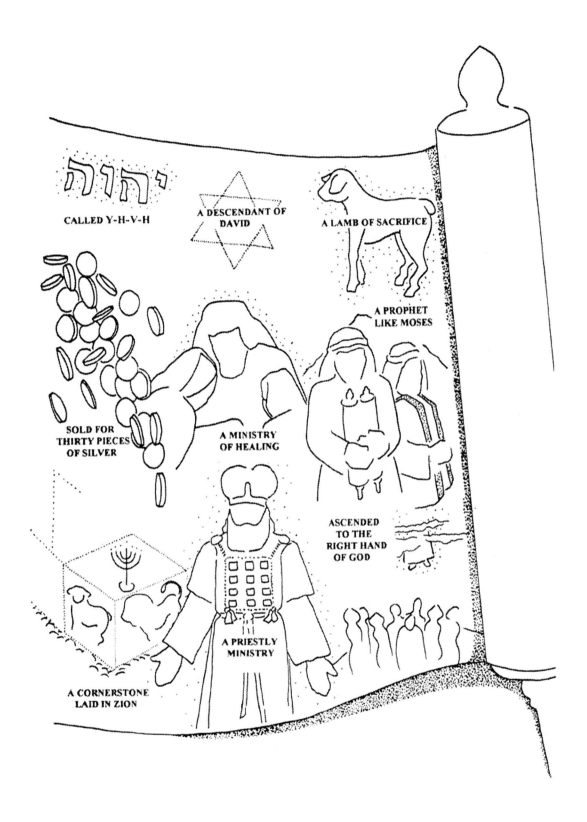

Figure 5: The fulfillment of messianic prophecies promised in advance through the prophets of the *Tanakh* [OT]. (Rom. 1:2; JNT page 199) See also page 257

Two Thousand Years of Church History

Yeshua of Nazareth has been a very real source of comfort and fortitude to millions across the globe for the past two thousand years—and the Bible has never ceased to amaze those who undertake to study it. As Jews continue to anticipate the coming of their Messiah, Christians worship and serve their Savior—while awaiting his second appearing.

The First Believers

Yeshua's first followers formed a small sect in Roman Palestine. They were essentially Messianic—"Jewish Christians." By the end of the first century, the majority of Jews were living in major cities *outside* their homeland: throughout the Mediterranean region, in Syria, and in Babylon. Wherever a community of Diaspora Jews was established, a synagogue was built. Up until the fourth century, these were used both as community centers and as places of worship. Early gentile Christians filtered into these meeting places, leading to their partial adoption of the Hebrew culture. A certain prestige accompanied this association with the Jews. After all, theirs was a very ancient and credible tradition; one that had stood the test of time.

Although belief in Yeshua was originally found within the context of Judaism, dissension soon arose in the young Church with regard to gentile circumcision and the choice and preparation of food. Such matters had to be resolved. They were at odds with the Mosaic Law.

Early Persecution

In time, Christianity would become the earth's dominant belief system and, as such, the backbone of many gentile civilizations. For sixteen centuries it would demonstrate a remarkable propensity to cleanse, refine, and revitalize itself; and would be adapted to serve the needs of numerous different cultural groups. In the Western world in particular, the supposed year of Yeshua's birth would become a giant milestone, a momentous turning point in history; dividing time into B.C. (Before Christ) and A.D. (Anno Domini; "In the Year of Our Lord"). But, before they gained religious tolerance, Christians suffered persecution for almost three hundred years.

Early Jewish and gentile believers were regarded as social outsiders and often paid a high price for their faith. Emperor Nero executed many after the fire of Rome in A.D. 64, claiming that they were responsible for the calamity. They were thrown to hungry lions in amphitheaters as a means entertaining the unemployed of Rome. Early believers therefore resorted to worshipping in secret, behind the closed doors of private homes.

Sacred images dating from this period are scarce, but some may still be seen in Rome's ancient subterranean burial grounds; the catacombs. Many of the original symbols of the Faith found there remain in use today. One such image is the fish; thought to have been a secret sign written in the sand or on the palm of the hand.

Establishing Christian Doctrines

Between about 50 and 150 A.D., the first communities of believers were established and the life and ministry of Yeshua were recorded by various witnesses. As these people started reaching old age and differing schools of doctrine emerged, it became necessary to select, from the many writings in circulation, those that most accurately conveyed the Christian message. By the end of the first century, the canon—list of books considered to be authoritative—of the Hebrew *Tanakh* had been established by the Jews. Christians adopted this Jewish canon, referring to it as the Old Testament, but changed the number and order of its twenty-four Jewish books to thirty-nine.

The four Gospels were regarded as canonical by Christians by the end of the second century, but it was only in A.D. 367 that Athanasius, the Bishop of Alexandria, drew up the complete list of New Testament books which appear in the modern Bible—with the exception of the Book of Revelation and several Catholic epistles.

When differences in perspective threatened to undermine the integrity of the Church, ecumenical councils—councils comprised of members from all churches—assembled to review and clarify doctrines. These meetings led to the formulation of such documents as the Nicene Creed (AD 325). Although the basic tenets of the Faith remained intact, those early councils determined—and to some extent engineered—the direction the Church would take. They chose, for instance, to give it more universal appeal by minimizing its deep Jewish roots. This loss is only *now* in the process of being restored to the Church by Messianic *rabbis*.

Pacifism as a State Religion

Yeshua never endorsed anger, hatred, aggressive reprisals or war. He didn't even encourage passive Ghandi-esque resistance. He promoted acts of sincere love to all, including one's enemies. According to New Testament teachings, it's not acceptable to kill, maim or injure others in any way. Nowhere in the gospels, or in the epistles, is physical warfare promoted. The cryptic apocalyptic visions of John in the Book of Revelation, mention war—including "war in heaven" (12:7) —only in the context of a great "end-time" event.

Yeshua repeatedly reminded his followers that his kingdom was "not of this world" and the epistles refer only to *spiritual* warfare—never to *physical* warfare. Messianic believers were taught that *vengeance* is always the prerogative of *Y-H-V-H*, not humankind. This is what makes the Faith unique—and counter-instinctive, without the indwelling Spirit. Christianity, an extension of Judaism, is, in its original form, superbly peaceful, comforting and compassionate. It is a non-violent, non-militant belief system.

During the first three centuries of Christianity's existence, believers, like their Messiah, were therefore pacifists. They put into practice his teachings regarding loving God, their "neighbors," and their enemies. Accordingly, early Messianic Jews refused to participate in the two major Jewish revolts staged against the Romans in Palestine in the first and second centuries—and were consequently regarded as traitors by their fellow countrymen. Furthermore, Christians living within the Roman Empire were sickened by the idolatry that permeated the Roman legions and realized that, as "soldiers of the Messiah," they were called to fight only "the good fight of Faith." New converts therefore typically resigned their military commissions. The term "Christian war" is, in essence, an oxymoron; the two words are inherently contradictory.

The Roman military was particularly anti-Christian and in the year A.D. 303, believers living within the empire suffered their most severe period of persecution. When Constantine was converted to the Faith in A.D. 313, Christianity gained religious tolerance. It was only in A.D. 392 during the reign of Theodosius I, however, that it became the official religion and paganism was outlawed. This presented Rome with a major problem. How does a massive, highly militarized empire, with a religion that is profoundly *pacifist* in doctrine, maintain control of its provinces and defend itself?

43

Early Symbols of the Faith

Alpha and Omega: Eternal God
A and Ω, the first and last letters of the Greek alphabet,
represented the eternal God

I am the Alpha [*Alef*] and the Omega [*Tav*], the First and the Last,
the Beginning and the End
(Rev. 22:13)

Dove: Peace
Relating to the account of Noah and the flood

Chi (X) and Rho (P): the Messiah
The first two letters in the Greek word "Christos," meaning Christ

Peacock: the Omnipresence of God
The numerous oculi, or "little eyes," on the male peacock's fan
represented the all-seeing eyes of God

Fish: the Messiah
The Greek word "ichthys," meaning "fish," formed an acronym for
IESOUS CHRISTOS THEOU HYIOS SOTER:
Jesus Christ, of God the Son, Savior

Stag: Baptism
As a stag travels many miles in its search for water,
so the newborn believer thirsts for the waters of baptism

Shepherd and Sheep: the Messiah and his People
"I am the good shepherd.
The good shepherd lays down his life for the sheep"
(John 10:11)

Figure 6: Early symbols of the Faith

Two men would play pivotal roles in resolving Rome's military dilemma: Constantine and a prominent bishop of the early church by the name of Augustine. The manner in which Constantine was converted appears to negate one of the core attributes of Yeshua's teachings; its compelling pacifism.

The emperor related his story to the church historian, Eusibius of Caesarea, towards the end of his life: Constantine was a dedicated worshipper of Deus Sol Invictus, "The Undefeated Sun God"; a title applied to three different Roman pagan divinities. On a certain day in A.D 313, on hearing of his enemy Maxentius' mastery of the magical arts, Constantine appealed to the "Supreme God" for assistance. As he prayed, he looked up into the midday sky at his god, the hot dazzling sun, and saw the shape of a cross above the sun with the words "*Conquer* by this." That night the Messiah appeared to him in a dream and commanded that he fight under "the sign" [Chi-Rho?] "as a safeguard in all *engagements with his enemies*." The following day Constantine's army marched on Rome and defeated Maxentius. This unverifiable story undermined the Faith's three hundred year old pacifist stance. It indicated that the Messiah *Constantine* had met, sanctioned war and bloodshed. During the rest of his life, this emperor *combined* Christian and pagan beliefs—and was only baptized in his old age.

A second very influential leader, Augustine of Hippo (A.D. 354-430), later compiled a list of principles by means of which "Christian war" could be justified. If circumstances could be made to fit his criteria, a war would be called a "Just War": 1. There had to be a just cause to go to war. 2. Every attempt had to be made to address the conflict before any blood was shed. 3. War had to be declared by a legitimate leader. 4. The damage had to be gauged likely to be less than that caused in the initial attack or injury. 5. The battle had to be waged by "moral means." 6. Success had to be virtually assured.

From A.D. 416, only "Christians" were employed by the Roman army. This would have included not only true converts, but numerous nominal Christians in the new "Christian Empire." It was these questionable events that gave credence to the concept of Christian war.

By the end of the fourth century, Christianity's influence was being felt across the known world; from Spain in the West, to Persia and India in the East. From that time forward, gentile variants of the Faith forged their own courses and a large body of traditions developed which further obscured its Hebrew origins.

Once Christianity had been sanctioned by the government of Rome, an urgent need arose to erect buildings that would exalt the new religion. The ancient Romans, always great builders, already had a suitable design. It was a large, rectangular columned hall with a side entrance and a semicircular apse, or recess, at each end. Each of the apses featured a small altar. These buildings, known as "basilicas," were constructed to accommodate large crowds and served as stock exchanges, law courts, and business or civic centers. The magistrate or judge's chair, positioned within one of the apses, was called a "*cathedra*"—the Latin word for "chair." A "cathedral" would come to be a church that is the official seat, or post, of a bishop. The term relates to a "chair of authority."

The basilican design was modified to suit the requirements of the first Christian churches. They featured only one apse (at the eastern end), the entrance was moved to the western end, and a courtyard (atrium) and entrance vestibule (narthex) were added. Later plans eliminated the courtyard; incorporated a single or double transverse section (transept), forming a cruciform or cross-shaped structure; and often featured impressive domes. The large central hall which accommodated the majority of worshippers was called the "nave"; derived from the Latin "*navis*," meaning "ship." The Church was the "ship" that carried believers through the stormy seas of life.

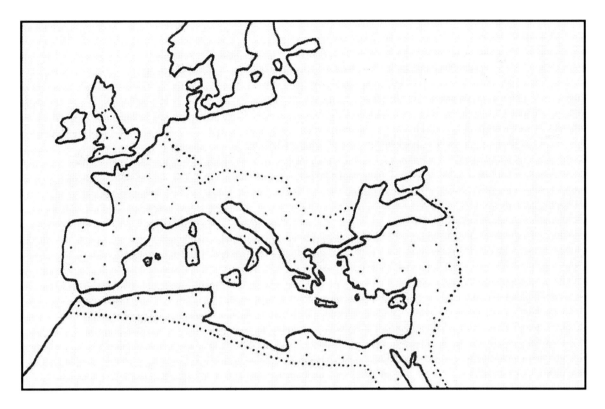

Figure 7: The Roman Empire in the fourth century A.D.

The exteriors of early Christian churches were very plain, but their interiors were lavishly decorated with shimmering iconographic mosaics. In this respect, the buildings reflected something of the qualities of the ideal believer; one who, although outwardly unadorned, possesses a rich inner life or treasure. At that time, the vast majority of Europe's population was illiterate. They had to rely on the clergy and church imagery—mosaics, stained glass, paintings, and sculpture—and for their spiritual instruction. One of the principal motivating factors in the eventual establishment of compulsory education in Western countries was that all people should be afforded the opportunity to study the Scriptures for themselves. This, of course, has become somewhat of an irony in our modern world.

The Roman basilica formed the basis of a style that epitomized ecclesiastic architecture well into the twentieth century. It is a style that is commonly regarded as having reached its zenith in the majestic Gothic cathedrals of medieval Europe.

In the hands of the godly, the Faith has had an immensely civilizing effect on nations. But in the hands of nominal believers, "Christian" governments, and state churches, it has all too often been used as a scourging whip, a means of controlling entire societies, and of justifying war and persecution. Yeshua has frequently been dishonored by deeds performed "In His Name."

After Theodosius I outlawed pagan worship, Christian doctrines came to be regarded as the basis of law and order. "Heresy" therefore became an offence against both church and state. During the twelfth and thirteenth centuries, when civil rulers were unable, or refused, to discipline dissident elements, the church assumed control. In 1231, Pope Gregory IX established a special court, known as the Inquisition. It was designed to hunt down heretics and force them to conform to church teachings.

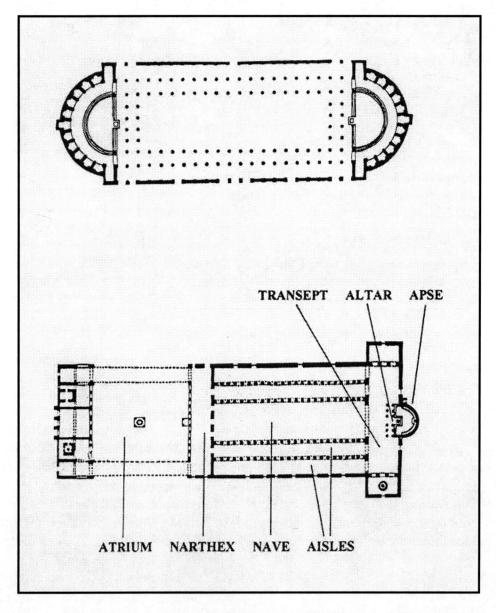

Figure 8: Roman basilica floor plan showing an apse at each end (above); and the early Christian basilican design, featuring a short transept and a small apse at the eastern end (below)

The medieval Crusades also demonstrated the dubious benefits of a marriage between church and state. Islam spread like wildfire from its inception and Christian countries found themselves having to stem the tide of its expansion in the West. The Crusades—military campaigns waged against Muslims in control of Palestine during the eleventh, twelfth, and thirteenth centuries—were products of a combination of both spiritual *and* worldly motives, however.

Ironically, with the establishment of Christianity as the dominant religion of the Western world, the marketplace of men's souls was flooded with the "pearl of great price," coercive tactics were used in selling it, and God's most priceless gift to humanity was gradually devalued.

The Time of the Gentiles

The adoption of Christianity as the official religion of the Roman Empire had both positive and negative long-term consequences. Its new status brought an end to the cruel persecutions of the early Church, resulting in a more rapid dissemination of the gospel message. But from that time citizens of the Roman Empire, and later the Western world in general, became "Christians" merely by virtue of their nationality—by birth. In addition, those of differing religious persuasions have, at times, been forced into the adoption of the Faith and conversions have not necessarily been genuine. Sincere believers in Yeshua have been swallowed up in a sea of nominal Christianity.

This change in status also led to doctrinal compromises that remain to this day. Church leaders found that it was no easy task to "convert the heathen." So, from the fourth century, various pagan concepts and practices were adapted and incorporated into worship in order to appease those resisting change. Most Christians still celebrate Yeshua's birth on 25 December; a day on which the ancient Romans celebrated the birth of the Unconquered Sun—a few days after the winter solstice and apparent "rebirth" of the sun. This Roman festival was therefore replaced by a celebration of the birth of the Son of God. There is no record regarding the birth date of Yeshua, however—and he instructed his followers to remember his death, not his birth.

The image of the jolly red-suited Father Christmas, or Santa Claus, with his sled and eight reindeer, is a more recent invention. Based on various legends relating to actual historical figures, this popular character was blown into a full scale figment of the imagination in the well-known poem entitled, "The Night before Christmas"; written in 1822 by Clement Clark Moore.

Popes and Patriarchs

After his conversion, Constantine moved his capital from Rome to the eastern city of Byzantium, and renamed it Constantinople (modern-day Istanbul, Turkey). At the end of the fourth century the massive Roman Empire split into the Western and Eastern Roman Empires. In the following century, the unwieldy Western Empire collapsed—due principally to the relentless invasions of nomadic "barbarian" tribes from central Asia. The Eastern Roman Empire, or Byzantine Empire, on the other hand, remained intact for another one thousand years under the leadership of such emperors as Justinian.

High-ranking bishops became church leaders in the major cities of Christendom. Initially, the Bishop of Rome—otherwise known as the Pope—was accepted as the supreme overseer of the Christian church. It was disputes relating to this position of preeminence that led to the first major split in the Church in A.D. 1054. The Latin Roman Catholic Church was established in the West, and the Greek Eastern Orthodox Church in the East; each under its own leadership. Constantinople became the heart of the Eastern Orthodox Church under the leadership of patriarchs, or "metropolitans." Rome remained the focus of the Western Church under the authority of Catholic popes.

Medieval Christianity

The medieval era extended from the collapse of the Western Roman Empire in the early fifth century, to the beginning of the Renaissance toward the end of the fifteenth century. Within this more volatile socio-economic period, both the Roman Catholic Church and the feudal system (from the ninth century) provided some stability. The church rapidly grew in wealth and influence, and monasteries became safe refuges in an insecure world; dependable sources of shelter, food, and medical care—and the only source of education.

Up until A.D. 1100, the majority of books were found only in monastic libraries. These were handwritten and were therefore relatively scarce. After A.D. 1200, when professional scribes and illuminators started producing books for the first European universities, they became more plentiful.

Differences that existed between Eastern and Western traditions related more to church government than to doctrine, but during the medieval period in Europe several independent groups attempted to return to more scriptural doctrinal models. It was only in the sixteenth century, during the High Renaissance—with the resurgence of the individualism of classical antiquity—that contentious doctrines were effectively challenged for the first time. This resulted in a change in attitudes that would split the Church for the second time. Traditional organized religion in the West would be torn into two entirely separate, self-governing factions—Catholicism and Protestantism; a chasm that continues to this day.

Luther and the Reformation

In 1517, Martin Luther, a German Augustinian monk and a professor of Biblical Studies at the University of Wittenberg, pinned his "Ninety-five Theses" to the door of the Castle Church in Wittenberg. This was a list of objections to the practice of selling indulgences—selling pardons for sins.

The medieval Church taught that a temporary period of punishment in hell followed the death of a believer—that the soul was, in this way, purged of all mortal sin before being admitted to heaven. This interval in hell was called purgatory. Luther did not object to this teaching in principle, but believed that the sale of indulgences, as a means of releasing sinners from penances imposed by priests, had become scandalous. As a devoted Catholic, he attempted to reform the church from within, but his observations were rejected. When he refused to recant, he was excommunicated. This marked the beginning of the Protestant Reformation—a movement of radical reform that resulted in the complete severing of ties with the mother church. The term "Protestant," as a means of describing Luther's followers, was first used in 1529.

Luther, and later reformers such as John Calvin, Ulrich Zwingli, and John Knox, held that during the medieval period, man-made church traditions had become spiritual stumbling blocks in the lives of believers. They resolved to return to the simplicity of first century New Testament teachings; insisting that salvation is attained by *grace*—the undeserved favor of God—and by faith in the Messiah.

They rejected the supremacy of the popes and emphasized the importance of preaching directly from the Scriptures, taking communion, heart-felt prayer, singing hymns, and relying on the prompting of the Spirit. They taught that all true believers are equal before God and can approach him personally, directly. This contradicted medieval Church traditions that taught that believers needed to depend on intermediaries to communicate with God; the clergymen as priests, the Virgin as a mediator, and the saints as intercessors—because the latter dwell in the presence of God.

The reformers also objected to the Church's growing materialism and the veneration of ecclesiastic icons (sacred images) and relics (artifacts such as bones, bits of wood, and cloth associated with holy personages). These were dismissed as practices that constituted serious encumbrances to the Faith, all too easily leading to a form of idolatry.

The adulation of *Miryam* (Mary), Yeshua's mother, was also rejected. They believed that the medieval Church had endowed her with attributes that were not clearly substantiated by Scripture. Protestants tended to regard this as a feminine bias which was an extension of the worship of the pagan goddesses of the ancient world.

According to Catholic tradition, *Miryam* was sinless from the time of her conception (the Immaculate Conception); remained a virgin throughout her life; and did not die, but was "assumed" into paradise (the Assumption of the Virgin) to become a heavenly queen. The Catholic Church does not accept that she had any children other than Yeshua.

Numerous Catholics profess to have seen visions of her or to have been miraculously healed by her. The veneration of *Miryam* is intricately woven into the fabric of the Catholic worldview and a new attitude of tolerance and gentle forbearance between Catholic and Protestant believers has been evident in recent years. (The ongoing conflict between Catholics and Protestants in Northern Ireland has its roots in politics. It has always been more of a political than a religious struggle.)

Protestant church architecture came to be characterized by austere simplicity, eradicating the temptation to worship realistic man-made images and ensuring reliance on the written Word. Although attempts had been made to translate the Bible into the vernacular—the everyday language of a culture—in various European countries during the Middle Ages, St. Jerome's Latin Vulgate (A.D. 400) remained the officially accepted version. Following the Reformation, an urgent need arose to translate it into the languages of Protestant countries—and to base translations on the original Hebrew and Greek, rather than on the Vulgate. Luther's contribution was to translate the New Testament into German, so that it could be studied firsthand by literate laymen. He had this advantage: Germany's Gutenburg printing press had started mass producing books in the fifteenth century. Handwritten Bibles were therefore soon replaced by printed copies; making them cheaper and more accessible to laymen.

Although Protestantism was an important catalyst in the restoration of a less embellished Faith, it has not been exempt in terms of persecuting those of other persuasions. The drawn-out, tumultuous sixteenth-century English Reformation is a case in point.

Initially, the Catholic Church in England burnt Protestant believers at the stake and attempted to halt the introduction of reformation teachings and Tyndale's English translation of the New Testament. It was a more personal motive—Henry VIII's infatuation with a vivacious and sophisticated woman of the court—that led to the irreconcilable breach between the English and the pope, however.

King Henry VIII, finding himself without a male heir to continue the royal line, and having been beguiled by the winsome Anne Boleyn, asked the pope to annul his marriage to his Spanish wife, Catherine of Aragon. He justified his request by saying that in marrying Catherine, his brother's widow, he had sinned against God by violating a law found in Leviticus 20:21 ("If a man marries his brother's wife, it is an act of impurity; he has dishonored his brother. They will be childless"). When the pope refused to grant his request, Henry resolved his quandary by seeing to it that his Parliament severed all ties that bound the English Church to the Roman papacy. Then he forced English members of the clergy to proclaim the king (himself), rather than the pope, "the only supreme head of the Church of England" (1534). This concept concerning the divine authority of kings had been suggested to him by Anne Boleyn by means of a Reformation booklet she had secretly acquired.

On dissolving his marriage with Catherine, Henry married Anne. She too failed to produce a male heir. After only a thousand days as queen, having been accused of sexual impropriety with other men, she was executed. Jane Seymour, the next royal bride, died shortly after producing the king's only male heir, Edward VI.

From early in the thirteenth century, an anti-papal reform movement had been gaining momentum in England. Many of the English did not strongly object, therefore, when, after Henry's break with the pope and subsequent excommunication, he endorsed the destruction of the Catholic monasteries of England. An added incentive in doing so was to seize Catholic land and rich treasures from their shrines. Surprisingly, this unpredictable king remained rooted in the Catholic tradition and had Protestants burnt at the stake as readily as he hanged and beheaded "traitors" who continued to support the pope.

During the reign of Henry's son, Edward VI (1547–1553), Reformation ideas started to take effect in England. Catholics were forbidden to hold Mass and the Latin Mass was replaced by readings from the *English Prayer Book*. When Edward died of tuberculosis at the age of sixteen, Mary—the daughter of Catherine and therefore a staunch Catholic—was the next royal child to succeed to the throne. During her five-year reign (1583–1588), while attempting to restore Catholicism to England, she had approximately two hundred Protestants burnt at the stake.

Following Mary's death, Lady Jane Grey ruled England for nine days. Elizabeth I, the daughter of Anne Boleyn, and therefore of questionable legitimacy, then assumed the throne and permanently established Protestantism in England during a long and difficult reign. Christianity in the political arena is certainly a far cry from the simple heartfelt faith of sincere believers!

Three major Protestant traditions developed during the period of the Reformation: the Lutheran tradition in Germany and Scandinavia; the Calvinist and Zwinglian traditions in Switzerland, France, Holland, and Scotland; and the Church of England. Since then, Protestants have continued in a cycle of protesting, dividing, and reforming; resulting in the formation of numerous denominations.

The Counter Reformation
When the seventeenth century Catholic Church found that it was rapidly losing adherents, it launched a crusade in order to win believers back into its fold. This was the Counter-Reformation or the Catholic Reformation. Although some reforms took place within the

church after the Council of Trent—a series of conferences held in Trent, Italy (1545-63) in which doctrines and traditions were reassessed—the Catholic Church would reemphasize many of the very ideas that had caused the rift. Their seventeenth-century baroque churches were opulent, awe-inspiring, and spectacular. Heaven, God, apostles, and saints were dramatically portrayed with compelling realism. Spiritual concepts were given physical form and heaven was brought down to Earth for congregations to *inspect*—in magnificent painted ceilings.

Two champions of the Catholic Reformation were Ignatius of Loyola and Teresa of Avila. Loyola founded the Society of Jesus, or Jesuit Movement; an ascetic monastic order that was sanctioned by the pope in 1540. These men put themselves at the disposal of the pope. Their primary aims were to counteract the influences of the Protestants by every means possible, to send missionaries into new regions, and to achieve and maintain standards of excellence in the area of education. They formed an elite group comprised only of handsome, healthy, highly-intelligent eloquent men. The Jesuits are still known for their outstanding achievements in the mission field and in the academic world. Many are familiar with their expression: "Give me a child until he is seven, and he will remain a Catholic the rest of his life."

A Christian mystic is one who strives for union with the very essence of God. This is often achieved in a moment of divine revelation or spiritual ecstasy. Teresa of Avila (1515–82), a Spanish nun, was one such person. Her faith was deeply personal and contemplative, yet surprisingly pragmatic. She wrote about her many ecstatic heavenly visions and, moved by the intensity of her faith, did much to revive the spiritual life of Spanish Catholics. As she traveled throughout the country, she established new places of worship and revitalized existing ones by means of her practical mysticism. She is known as the great reformer of the Carmelite order.

In 1542, in countries such as France, Germany, Spain, and Italy, the Inquisition—usually consisting of Franciscan and Dominican friars—was reinstated as an instrument of coercive conversion. Members of the Inquisition believed that it was necessary to either convert non-Catholics, or to permanently remove those with unorthodox beliefs from the "Body of Christ"—in much the same way as drastic surgery is sometimes required to save a patient with a fatal medical condition. Because these men worked in secret, they often abused their powers; their subjects were sometimes tortured, even sentenced to death, when they refused to recant. This weapon against "heretics," including Protestants, was only effective in communities that were already predominantly Catholic, however. In the light of modern standards of morality and justice, the Inquisition is universally condemned.

During the Counter-Reformation, the Catholic Church practiced extreme censorship; compiling extensive lists of books that were not to be read by parishioners. Propaganda tactics were used by both Catholics and Protestants in the battle for the souls of the European world.

Modern Apostasy
This checkered history of the gentile church has contributed to the creation of a generation that, not differentiating between genuine and nominal Christianity, is disillusioned with the Faith. There has been massive defection; particularly since World War II. The demise of nominal Christianity is healthy in certain respects, but in the present "Post-Christian Era," we are having to deal with its negative legacy.

Many see only the dead man-made Church and reject the religion of their forefathers. They renounce rigid church policies; the dry, formal stereotypes of religious ritual; hypocrisy and false piety; the racism and bigotry still found in some quarters; the wealth and power of the Catholic Church and Protestant "mega-churches"; and the factions within the Faith as a whole.

It is important to understand, however, that Yeshua himself vehemently opposed hypocritical religious attitudes in his day. Therefore, we should not reject him on this basis. The Church is not a building, an institution, or even those who attend a weekly service or mass. The true Church is invisible. It is comprised of a multitude of *unseen* relationships between individuals and their God. Belief in the Messiah has never been a contract between an empire, a country, a crusading army, or an institution and its God. Those who earnestly seek him find him; regardless of the tradition from which they come.

Despite the relatively recent decline of nominal Christianity—which will probably lead to the resurgence of religious persecution of genuine believers in the future—individuals still need to fill the spiritual vacuums within their souls. So, while some have fallen away completely, adopting the principles of modern-day rationalism as their guide, others have attempted to immerse themselves in non-Christian religions. Still others have resolved their quandary by combining traditional Christian doctrines with aspects of various Eastern ideologies; thereby forming personally tailored eclectic belief systems. Many therefore profess belief in Yeshua, but also accept the doctrines of reincarnation and karma—an illogical combination of irreconcilable ideas.

Christianity's diverse denominations, and the flaws and contradictions embedded in its history, do not negate the fact that it is a compelling belief system with a very firm historical basis. And the God of Israel has, unquestionably, been glorified through the churches of the Gentiles. Numerous men and women of great spiritual stature and integrity have provided comfort, hope, and security to millions across the globe in their efforts to spread the gospel and alleviate suffering. For over sixteen centuries, multi-cultural believers have kept the flame of faith burning. They have also provided humanity with an abundance of glorious sacred music and art works, magnificent ecclesiastic architecture, outstanding literature and pastoral work, and more acts of sacrificial love and kindness than one can imagine. These things have been borne out of the love of a gentile multitude for a Jewish Messiah.

New Directions
In 1948, the ecumenical World Council of Churches was formed in Amsterdam. It has been joined by many different denominations; including the Eastern Orthodox Church. Then, in 1962, Pope John XXIII convened an ecumenical council in St. Peters in Rome. This was known as the Second Vatican Council, or Vatican II. His aim was to reform and modernize the Catholic Church and to reconcile all Christians.

This council had far reaching consequences: The Latin Mass was translated into the vernacular. An attempt was made to be reconciled to the Eastern Orthodox Church—their mutual excommunication was lifted in 1965. All religious discrimination, particularly anti-Semitism, was condemned. The Pope was obliged to confer more regularly with his bishops and laymen were encouraged to play a more active role in church affairs. Vatican II is now viewed as being a revolutionary landmark in the history of the Catholic Church.

Pope John Paul II, the first non-Italian pope to be elected to the papacy in over 450 years, came to office in 1978. Apart from his prominent status as the "vicar of God," this man dramatically impacted the course of recent history on the international stage. In the year 2000—a year of Jubilee, marking the end of the second millennium of the Christian faith—he opened the period of Lent by publicly requesting forgiveness for the sins of the Catholic Church over the past two thousand years. This was not an attempt to discredit Catholicism, but to wipe the slate of history clean in order to face the future without the encumbrances of the past. The Pope also unequivocally condemned the use of force or violence in the name of the Christian religion. Following his lead, Catholic Church leaders throughout the world asked to be forgiven for the atrocities and injustices of such actions as the Inquisition and the Medieval Crusades, and for sins that have been committed on local levels in recent years.

Since the restoration of the Jewish homeland in 1948, another change of attitude—compounded by the emergence of the Messianic Movement in the late 1960s—has been evident among Gentiles. It is a precious thing. Because the Jews have remained steadfast in the preservation of their ancient heritage, Messianic believers, with their inherent understanding of the Hebrew tradition, have been recapturing something of the ambiance of the early Church, while redirecting gentile believers to a more exact interpretation of the Scriptures. These Jewish teachers are providing unique insights into Hebrew history and worship; the Jewish calendar and Feasts of Israel; the Hebrew language; and Jewish music, dance, and art. They present Yeshua, not as the principal character in the "old, old story" of the Christian tradition, but as a decidedly Jewish Messiah.

Although the common adage "old habits die hard" holds true, increasing numbers of Gentiles are now demonstrating a new empathy for the Jews and a lively interest in their culture. Attracted by the freshness and integrity of the Messianic vision, they are reaching beyond familiar church traditions and finding valuable treasures and a deep sense of renewal at the source of the Faith. It is now more universally acknowledged that Yeshua was a Jew, and that both Old and New Testaments were written by Jews.

This, unlike the Protestant Reformation, has been a gentle movement that has tended to edify and unify Christendom. After over sixteen centuries, the blurred Hebrew origins of the Faith are being redefined by Messianic believers. All roads no longer lead to Rome. Increasingly, they are leading back to Jerusalem. Perhaps the frustrating age-old disparities separating Protestant, Roman Catholic, and Eastern Orthodox traditions are destined to dissolve at the Hebrew fountainhead of the Faith.

The Jewish Position with Regard to Gentile Christianity

Although the earliest communities of believers were predominantly Jewish, as a nation, the Jews did not recognize Yeshua as the Messiah. From the beginning, Messianic believers faced opposition from Jewish authorities who objected to their message. This rift was compounded when Yeshua's followers refused to support the Jewish revolts against Rome in A.D. 66–73 and 132–135 (the *Bar Kokhba* Revolt). From that time, they were regarded as traitors by their fellow countrymen and few more Jews were won over to belief in Yeshua.

When Christianity later became the official religion of the Roman Empire, Messianic Jews seemingly joined ranks with the Romans; the old enemies of the Jews. The Romans had occupied Palestine, besieged Jewish cities, and massacred thousands of people during the Jewish revolts. As Christianity took root across Europe, the division between Jews and Christians deepened. For centuries this lingering animosity between Judaism and Christianity would produce an attitude of distrust on the part of the Jews, and an attitude of intolerance on the part of the Christianized world. Jews often found themselves ostracized, because it was *their* ancestors who had "crucified the Savior."

Nevertheless, there have always been Messianic Jews—Sir Benjamin Disraeli and Felix Mendelssohn are two notable examples.

Diaspora Jews have retained their distinctive heritage and maintained their guardianship of the initial God-given light—the Law. Throughout history, this adherence to a different culture has isolated them from the Gentiles among whom they lived. This, in turn, has led to periods of intense persecution. Jews have frequently been looked upon as the pariahs of their societies. They have been hounded by gentile nations—even expelled from various European countries. Christians have all too often dismissed the fact that it was through the Jews that they received the written Word, the Bible; and the Living Word, the Messiah.

Ironically, the ethnic group that provided the springboard for the Christian religion has often been shamelessly treated by Christian civilizations. The following words in the Lord's covenant with Abraham *are* "written in stone" and should serve as a permanent warning against anti-Semitism:

"I will bless those who bless you and whoever curses you will I curse." (Gen. 12:3)

Certain over-zealous groups of Crusaders, in their antipathy toward non-Christians, killed many Jews. Even Martin Luther "warned" Protestants against the Jews in his later writings. Ferdinand and Isabella of Spain used sledge hammer tactics in their zeal to "purge" their nation. First, it was the Spanish Inquisition. Then, in 1492, both Jews and Muslims were expelled from their country. Ironically, by supporting Columbus' voyages of discovery, the Spanish king and queen were instrumental in opening up a "New World" that would later become a safe haven for millions of Jews.

In Europe, Jews were forced to live in separate districts called ghettos. They were massacred in the Russian pogroms (1881–1914). During World War II, an attempt was made in Nazi Germany to exterminate them altogether in the Holocaust (*HaSho'ah*). This genocide, the obliteration of approximately six million people—a third of the world's Jewry—was Hitler's "final solution." Despite the resistance of some notable figures such as Dietrich Bonnhoeffer, the Church in Germany was ineffectual in its efforts to stem the tide of Nazi Aryanism. Approximately five million Gentiles—Poles, gypsies, homosexuals, the handicapped, Jehovah's Witnesses, and Seventh Day Adventists (who were mistaken for Jews because they worshipped on Saturdays) —were *also* Holocaust victims. They too paid the ultimate price in that most horrendous of wars.

Pope John Paul II, born in Krakow Poland in 1920 as Karol Woityla, witnessed the beginnings of the Holocaust and is said to have helped Polish Jews escape Nazi persecution. During his time in office, he demonstrated a deep sympathy for the Jewish people. By forcefully opposing anti-Semitism, he earnestly attempted to right the wrongs of the past. As a powerful world leader, this pope redirected the massive Catholic Church into a new relationship with the Jews; a relationship based on mutual respect and acceptance.

Various Protestant "missions to the Jews" started in the nineteenth century and continue to this day, but bitter memories of past persecutions remain giant stumbling blocks in many

Jewish minds. Non-Messianic Jews do not generally draw a distinction between nominal and genuine Christianity and tend to associate the Faith with cruelty and injustice. The Messianic Movement has been building strong new bridges between contemporary Christians and Jews, however. The potential exists for it to have a profoundly unifying influence in years to come.

> "And I will pour out on the house of David and the inhabitants of Jerusalem a spirit of grace and supplication. They will look on me, the one they have pierced, and they will mourn for him as one mourns for an only child, and grieve bitterly for him as one grieves for a firstborn son." (Zech. 12:10)

> Therefore God raised him to the highest place and gave him the name above every name, that in honor of the name given Yeshua, every knee will bow—in heaven, on earth, and under the earth—and every tongue will acknowledge that Yeshua the Messiah is *Adonai* [the Lord: *Y-H-V-H*], to the glory of God the Father. (Phil. 2:9–11; JNT page 265; Isa. 45:23)

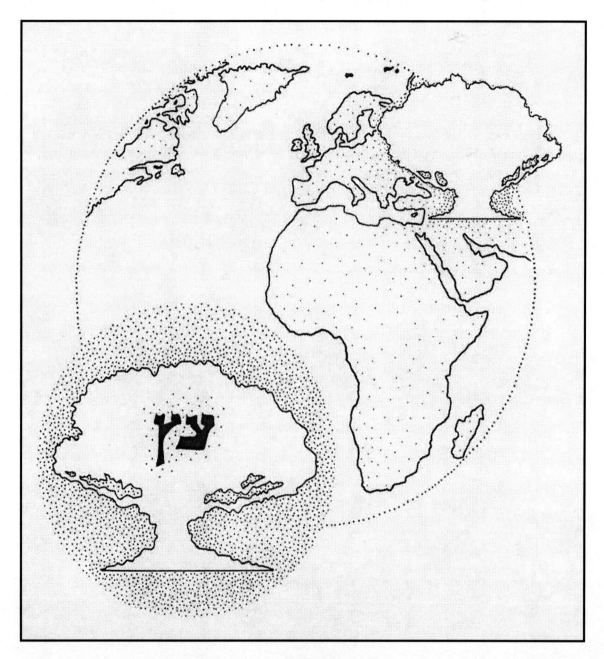

Figure 9: The cultivated olive tree of Israel and engrafted gentile nations of the earth. The Hebrew word " '*etz*," seen within the olive tree, can mean "tree," "stick" or "wood"

Part 2

The Olive Tree

After over sixteen centuries of gentile Christianity—from A.D. 392, when the Faith became the official religion of the Roman Empire, to the present time—the vast majority of Christians have lost sight of the *source* of "holy writ." The deadwood of man-made doctrines, rituals, and traditions now obscures much of the inherent "Jewishness" of the Messiah—and the original Hebrew ambiance of the Bible as a whole. Millions who have been won over by Yeshua are impoverished by a lack of awareness of the heritage into which he was born.

Those returning to the fountainhead of the Faith soon discover that, like a magnificent tapestry, the Hebrew tradition delights the senses and feeds the soul. It has a compelling ancient beauty and offers refreshing new insights. As we now return to the roots of the Faith, Hebrew images will set the stage for the correlation of New Testament principles with the language, history, worship, customs, and calendar of the Jews.

The Hebrew Heritage

When we picture the Middle East, we visualize tanned rocky landscapes—dry, dusty, and rugged. We see olive groves, fig trees, and grapevines on the stone terraces of the Judean hills; Masada-like plateaus in the sultry Dead Sea region; the giant peaks of the Sinai; nomads with their tents and flocks; and towns comprised of whitewashed boxes, shaded by towering palms. Modern cities like Tel Aviv and Haifa, with their high-rise buildings, are pushed to the backs of our minds. The land of the Hebrews is familiar to us, in part, because of what we've learned from the Scriptures.

But in the context of the ancient Hebrew heritage, there are other equally vivid images that should excite our imaginations: powerful Hebrew kings and prophets; favored firstborn sons; tribes with intriguing blessing symbols; a magnificent desert "Dwelling Place" with its priesthood and system of worship; holy feast days linked to stars, moons and harvest times; an elaborate marriage tradition with bridal canopies, Jewish bridegrooms and bejeweled brides; and a sacred language with names rich in meaning. These too are woven into the antique brocade of the Judeo-Christian legacy.

'Akedah: Typology
Those who have been raised in Christian or Jewish traditions will be familiar with many of the words and images of the *Tanakh* (OT). These take on new meaning when they parallel truths found in the New Testament (*Brit Khadashah*). This association of Old Testament historical figures or events with New Testament events or spiritual principles reinforces our understanding of the sublime truths contained within the Scriptures. It also helps to disclose the very mind of the God of Israel, whose profound wisdom forms a delicate underlying web

in the Word. The more the Bible is studied, the more luminous the silvery interconnecting strands become. In gentile theological circles, this method of comparison is called "typology." Among the Jews, it is '*akedah* or "binding."

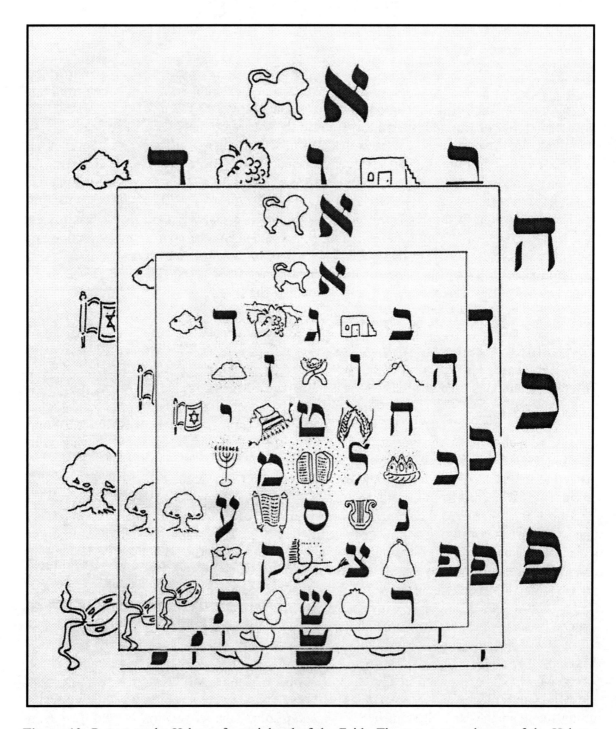

Figure 10: Return to the Hebrew fountainhead of the Faith. The twenty-two letters of the Hebrew alphabet placed alongside Jewish images that begin with those letters

A Thriving Olive Tree

Trees are linked to the fall of mankind in Genesis. In the New Testament they are linked to the redemption of humanity in the Messiah's crucifixion stake ("He hung on the tree") and the eventual restoration of each individual's privilege to eat from the Tree of Life. But there is another less exalted tree image, inseparable from our perception of the Holy Land, which warrants our attention. It is the image of the humble olive tree (*zayit*).

The olive tree is the first plant species to be mentioned by name in the Scriptures (Gen. 8:11); a reference found in the account of Noah and the flood. It was later associated specifically with the tribes of Israel and has remained an appropriate symbol for this nation to this day—the history and characteristics of the olive tree relate strongly to those of the Hebrew race.

> The Lord called you a thriving olive tree with fruit beautiful in form. But with the roar of a mighty storm he will set it on fire, and its branches will be broken. (Jer. 11:16)

Olive trees are indigenous to the Mediterranean region. They were first cultivated by Semitic peoples more than 3,500 years ago. These sturdy evergreen hardwoods can survive to an age of approximately 1,500 years; epitomizing the concept of "resolute persistence." They have gnarled trunks; smooth ash-colored bark; dark green leaves with a silvery underside; and delicate, pale cream flowers. They do not naturally produce good fruit, however. The fruit of the wild olive is small and worthless. *Good* stock has to be grafted into a wild sapling in order to improve its fruit. Olive trees are therefore *cultivated* in order to increase their yield. Although they thrive in the tropics, they do not bear fruit unless they are exposed to very cold temperatures (7°C or 44°F) for at least two to three months of the year.

The Jews, as sturdy and ancient as the olive tree, are also native to the Mediterranean region and Semitic in origin. And their race was "cultivated" to become a "holy nation." By the end of the *Bar Kokhba* Revolt in the second century A.D., the Hebrew race—the "thriving olive tree"—had been "burned" and its "branches broken." Virtually the entire nation was scattered among the "*goyim.*" (In the Scriptures, the Hebrew word *goy*—plural *goyim*—can simply mean "nation," but today it is usually used with reference to non-Jews; to gentile, pagan or heathen cultures.)

Yet the olive tree is still a fitting symbol for the Jews; the only recognizable "Israelites" among us today. They have persevered despite centuries of persecution and inhospitable conditions, and epitomize the concept of "resolute persistence." Jews are also often gifted achievers; Jewish names are frequently associated with outstanding accomplishments in the arts and sciences.

In the *Tanakh* (OT), the symbol of the olive tree pertains specifically to the Israelites. But in Paul's (*Sha'ul's*) New Testament letter to the Romans, he used this image with reference to gentile believers. He described them as *wild* olive branches that are grafted into the "cultivated tree" of Israel. Herein is a striking image of God's compassion for the Gentiles.

> After all, if you were cut out of an olive tree that is wild by nature, and contrary to nature were grafted into a cultivated olive tree, how much more readily will these, the natural branches, be grafted into their own olive tree! (Rom. 11:24)

Because Yeshua was Jewish, and therefore a product of the Hebrew tradition, like proselyte Jews, his gentile followers have always been "grafted" into this ancient tradition as "wild olive branches." *This* is the root from which Christians have "drawn their nourishing [spiritual] sap." (Rom. 11:17)

"Your people will be my people and your God my God." (Ruth 1:16)

The Sovereign Lord declares—he who gathers the exiles of Israel: "I will gather still others to them besides those already gathered." (Isa. 56:8)

First century the Jews, on the whole, did not acknowledge Yeshua as the Messiah; but Messianic Jews have always been grafted back into their "cultivated tree"—not converted into a non-Hebraic gentile tradition. And how firmly rooted Messianic believers are! How natural it is for them to be grafted in again. As Christianity was in the beginning, so it remains—an inherently Hebrew faith.

So the olive tree was used first as a symbol for the tribes of Israel (Jer. 11:16) and later by Paul with reference to engrafted Gentiles (Rom. 11). In the Book of Hosea we find one more image of the olive tree; there the *restored* nation of Israel is one splendid olive tree, one glorious holy nation.

"His splendor will be like an olive tree. . . " (Hos. 14:16)

Although the original "thriving olive tree" was "chosen" by God, the Hebrew nation would almost totally disintegrate. The Jews are the only clearly recognizable Hebrew descendants among us today. Yet the God of Israel is assuredly the God of history and all things are undoubtedly unfolding as they should. Perhaps in returning to the very beginnings of this race, and in tracing their history, systems of worship, and traditions, we will come to a greater understanding of *Y-H-V-H's* master plan. On page 16, an overview of Hebrew history was featured under the subtitle "Judaism." In the following pages the emphasis shifts to the origins and significance of Hebrew names, the composition of the twelve tribes, positions of prominence among them, periods of exile and restoration, and intriguing biblical prophecies pertaining to this nation.

The Patriarchs

"I am the God of your father, the God of Abraham, the God of Isaac and the God of Jacob." (Exod. 3:6)

The colorful early history of the Hebrew race is recorded in the Book of Genesis. At the head of the first Hebrew families were the patriarchs: Abram or *Avram* (renamed Abraham, or *Avraham*); Isaac or *Yitzkhak;* and Jacob or *Ya'akov* (renamed Israel or *Yisra'el*).

The Hebrews were called upon to separate themselves from their pagan neighbors, relinquish all vestiges of polytheism, and worship and obey the God of Israel alone. It was this monotheism that was later adopted by Christian Gentiles on their acceptance of the Jewish Messiah. The Scriptures indicate that the Israelites were *chosen* to be the means whereby God would heal the breach between himself and the nations of the earth.

As one pages through Genesis, it becomes clear that God chose ordinary men and women for this extraordinary task. Their stories—and names—reflect the frailty and fallibility of human nature. Interpersonal rivalries with far reaching consequences existed between such figures as Esau and Jacob, Leah and Rachel, Joseph and his brothers. Yet despite their failings, God cherished them and revealed his purposes through them. He did not require perfection of his people; only child-like trust.

Avraham the Hebrew

As a descendant of Noah's eldest son Shem, Abraham was a *Semite*, or "Shemite"—hence the term "anti-Semitic"; used with reference to those who are prejudiced against Abraham's descendants, the Jews.

> The sons of Noah who came out of the ark were Shem, Ham, and Japheth . . . and from them came the people who were scattered over the earth. (Gen. 9:18–19)

> One who had escaped came and reported this to Abram the Hebrew. (Gen. 14:13)

"*Hebrew*" is a term derived from the root word "*eber*" or "*ever*"; meaning "to cross over," to "pass over," or "beyond." The first use of the word is found in Genesis 14:13. It relates Abraham—the original Hebrew. He had come from *beyond* the Euphrates River in Mesopotamia, on his way westward to the promised land of Canaan. Accordingly, "Hebrews," or "*'Ivrim*," means "those who come from the other side." Although "Hebrew" was initially used as a term of derision—there is evidence to suggest they were referred to as "*Habiru*" by the ancient Egyptians—it eventually came to be regarded as an acceptable title by the Israelites.

When Abram was ninety-nine years old, God changed his Hebrew name, *Avram*, meaning "exalted father," to *Avraham*; meaning "father of many nations" or "father of a multitude." God also changed his wife's name from "*Sarai*" meaning "mockery," to "Sarah" meaning "princess." All of this astounded Abraham. Not only were he and his wife *very* old, she was barren. They were childless.

> "I am God Almighty; walk before me and be blameless. I will confirm my covenant between me and you and will greatly increase your numbers. . . . No longer will you be called Abram [*Avram*]; your name will be Abraham [*Avraham*], for I have made you a father of many nations." (Gen. 17:1, 2, 5)

Yitzkhak: The Son of Promise

Abraham was one hundred years of age when Sarah finally gave birth to Isaac; "the son of promise." The baby was given the Hebrew name *Yitzkhak*, meaning "laughter." This name reflected not only their obvious delight, but also their amazement—and evidently, slight embarrassment—at the birth of a son in their extreme old age.

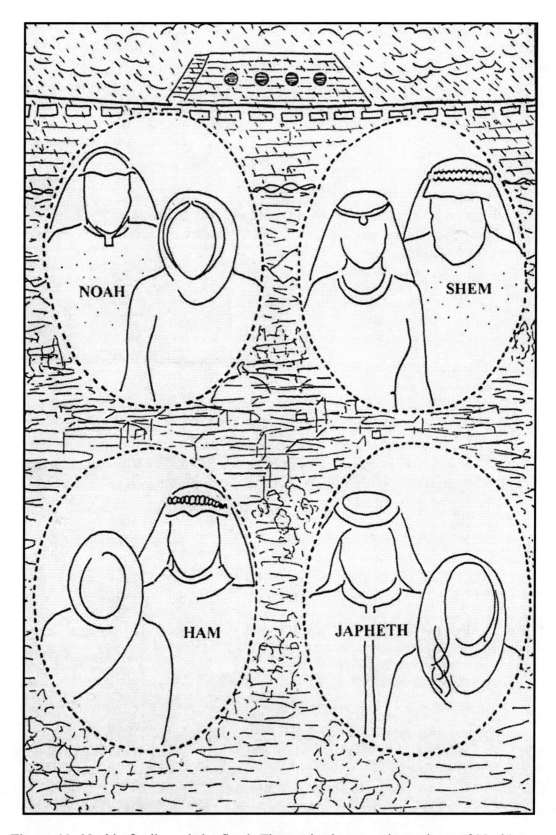

Figure 11: Noah's family and the flood. The patriarchs were descendants of Noah's son, Shem. They were Semites

Figure 12: Family cameos of Abraham and Isaac

Then God said, "Yes, but your wife Sarah will bear you a son, and you will call him Isaac [*Yitzkhak*]. I will establish my covenant with him as an everlasting covenant for his descendants after him. And as for Ishmael, I have heard you: I will surely bless him. . . . He will be the father of twelve rulers, and I will make him into a great nation. But my covenant I will establish with Isaac, whom Sarah will bear to you by this time next year." (Gen. 17:19–21)

Abraham *believed* that he would become the "father of a multitude"—despite his age and childless marriage (Gen. 15:4–6). The Scriptures state that this absolute trust made him "righteous in the sight of God." Sarah was not as trusting. She grew impatient, took matters into her own hands, and offered her Egyptian servant, Hagar, to her husband as a surrogate mother. When a child from this union was born, deep resentment developed between the two women; resulting in the eventual severing of ties. Hagar's baby was named Ishmael or *Yishma'el*; meaning "God pays attention."

Then the Lord said to Abraham, "Why did Sarah laugh and say, 'Will I really have a child, now that I am old?' Is anything too hard for the Lord?" (Gen. 18:13)

Ya'akov Becomes *Yisra'el*

When Isaac reached a marriageable age, Abraham sent a servant to his brother's family in Nahor, Mesopotamia, to find a suitable wife. By divine providence, *Rivkah* (Rebekah) was chosen. All was well with Isaac and Rebekah—until the birth of their fraternal twin sons.

As with Sarah, Rebekah had been childless for many years. When she eventually fell pregnant, twins—Esau and Jacob—jostled each other in her womb; a pattern that would characterize their relationship throughout much of their lives. During the birth, Jacob emerged holding onto the heel of his older brother, Esau. The younger son was therefore given the name *Ya'akov* ("grasp the heel"); a Hebrew expression meaning "he supplants." This name confirmed the prophetic words that had been spoken by God to Rebekah, prior to the birth of her sons: "the older will serve the younger."

Isaac prayed to the Lord on behalf of his wife, because she was barren. The Lord answered his prayer, and his wife Rebekah became pregnant. The babies jostled each other within her, and she said, "Why is this happening to me?" . . . The Lord said to her, "Two nations are in your womb, and two peoples from within you will be separated; one people will be stronger than the other, and the older will serve the younger." When the time came for her to give birth, there were twin boys in her womb. The first to come out was . . . Esau. After this, his brother came out, with his hand grasping Esau's heel; so he was named Jacob [*Ya'akov*]. (Gen. 25:21–26)

Many years later, before Isaac died, Jacob deceived his father into granting him the irrevocable "blessing of the firstborn" (Gen. 27). When Esau discovered this, he vowed to kill his younger twin. This incident forced Jacob to flee from his home in Canaan and seek refuge with his mother's family in Haran.

Jacob eventually ventured back to Canaan from Haran—with a very large family—and a conciliatory meeting took place between the brothers. Prior to this meeting, on his way home, Jacob wrestled with a heavenly being on the banks of the river Jabbok; a tributary of the Jordan. Ever the opportunist, the younger twin, realizing the magnitude of the event, asked the angel for a special blessing. The angel replied:

> "Your name will no longer be Jacob [*Ya'akov*], but Israel [*Yisra'el*], because you have struggled with God and with men and have overcome." (Gen. 32:28)

In this way, the name *"Ya'akov"* ("He supplants") was changed to *"Yisra'el"* ("He struggles with God").

The name "Israel" has become a source of controversy in recent years. It is, of course, the modern day Jewish homeland; but in the Scriptures "Israel" is used exclusively with reference to Jacob, his descendants, or to the northern tribes of the divided kingdom. In the following quote from the New Testament, Paul (*Sha'ul*) uses the term metaphorically with reference to Israelites who remain faithful to God.

> For not all who are descended from Israel are Israel. (Rom. 9:6)

Clearly, not all people have a heart for God or "hunger for the things of God." This was true in ancient times and remains true today. The name Israel means "he struggles with God." Therefore those who, like Jacob, actively seek God and "wrestle" with him as the old nature is being changed by the Spirit, might be termed "Israel"—in a figurative sense. But the title "Israel" should only be unequivocally applied to the physical descendants of Abraham, not to followers of the Jewish Messiah—despite the implication in Galatians 6:16 and Ephesians 2:13. The doctrine of Replacement Theology, claiming that the House of Israel has been *replaced* by the gentile Church, is fervently rejected by Messianic believers.

In the following name chart, each entry appears in English, as a Hebrew transliteration (Hebrew characters replaced by letters of the Latin alphabet), and as the interpretation of the Hebrew word—thereby disclosing its meaning.

The House of Jacob

By the time Jacob returned from exile in Haran, he had two wives—Leah and Rachel (*Rakhel*), who were sisters—two concubines, Bilhah and Zilpah; twelve sons and a daughter. The names of his sons form a record of the emotional struggle that took place between the sisters as they competed for Jacob's affection. In fact, these women eventually resorted to using their maids as "surrogate mothers" in order to produce more offspring and gain favor in their husband's eyes!

Jacob had originally agreed to work for Laban (*Lavan*), his father-in-law, for seven years, in order to win the hand of Rachel. However, on his wedding day Jacob was tricked into marrying Leah, Laban's heavily veiled older daughter. He was outraged! Laban pacified him by saying that he could also marry Rachel—a week later.

The Names of the Patriarchs and their Wives

English	Hebrew (Transliteration)	Meaning
Abram	*Avram*	Exalted father
changed to:		
Abraham	*Avraham*	Father of a multitude (or "Father of many nations")
Sarai	*Sarai*	Mockery
changed to:		
Sarah	*Sarah*	Princess
Isaac	*Yitzkhak*	Laughter
Rebekah	*Rivkah*	Snare
Jacob	*Ya'akov*	He grasps the heel (fig: He supplants)
changed to:		
Israel	*Yisra'el*	He struggles with God
Leah	*Leah*	Weary
Rachel	*Rakhel*	Ewe

"It is not our custom here to give the younger daughter in marriage before the older one. Finish this daughter's bridal week; then we will give you the younger one also, in return for another seven years of work." And Jacob did so . . . and he loved Rachel more than Leah. (Gen. 29:26–30)

Therefore, despite the fact that she bore Jacob only two sons, Rachel was the bride of choice, the woman he cherished. Leah remained the unhappy, disconsolate wife; a victim of unrequited love.

Before he died, Jacob conferred twelve irrevocable blessings on his twelve sons (Gen. 49). Several of these were prophetic in that they were later borne out by Hebrew history. These provided the blessing symbol imagery that features in Jewish worship to this day. As the naming of each of Jacob's sons unfolds in the following pages, the blessing symbol for the twelve tribes will be given.

Then Jacob called for his sons and said: "Gather around so that I can tell you what will happen to you in days to come." (Gen. 49: 1)

Twelve Sons

Reuben, the first child to be born into this family, was the son of Leah. She gave him the Hebrew name *Re'uven*, meaning "Behold, a son!" The blessing symbol of the tribe of Reuben was the sunrise (Gen. 49:3). This related to the idea of new life or a new beginning in the birth of a first son. The following Scripture discloses Leah's intense heartache, her longing to be loved and accepted by her husband.

When the Lord saw that Leah was not loved, he opened her womb, but Rachel was barren. Leah became pregnant and gave birth to a son. She named him Reuben [*Re'uven*], for she said, "It is because the Lord has seen my misery. Surely my husband will love me now." (Gen. 29:31–32)

The situation had not improved by the time Leah gave birth to her second son. She named him *Shim'on* (Simeon); a name that most closely approximates the Hebrew phrase "one who hears." She was referring to her God as being the one who, having heard of her plight, sent a second son as a source of comfort. The blessing symbol for this tribe was a clay jar or "vessel of wrath," in combination with a sword (Gen. 49:5–7). It sometimes appears as a fortified tower.

She conceived again, and when she gave birth to a son she said, "Because the Lord heard that I am not loved, he gave me this one too." So she named him Simeon [*Shim'on*]. (Gen. 29:33)

When Leah gave birth to her third son, she named him *L'vi* (Levi). This is thought to be a derivation of the Hebrew word for "attached." Because the tribe of Levi became the priestly tribe of Israel, its blessing symbol was the high priest's breastplate. Yet again we made aware of Leah's misery in the following words.

Again she conceived, and when she gave birth to a son she said, "Now at last my husband will become attached to me, because I have borne him three sons." So he was named Levi [*L'vi*]. (Gen. 29:34)

Figure 13: The twelve Hebrew blessing symbols. Most of these still feature in Jewish worship to this day. Read from right to left

Leah named her fourth son *Yehudah* (Judah); a name that sounds very much like the Hebrew word for "praise" *(Yadah)*. Rachel had still been unable to conceive, and Leah, realizing that she had at least enjoyed the privilege of motherhood, saw beyond her predicament and praised God. The blessing symbol of the tribe of Judah was a lion. This tribe was destined to become the royal line of the House of Israel (Gen. 49:8–10).

> She conceived again, and when she gave birth to a son she said, "This time I will praise the Lord." So she named him Judah [*Yehudah*]. Then she stopped having children. (Gen. 29:35)

When Rachel could no longer tolerate being childless, she asked Jacob to sleep with her maid Bilhah; so that this woman could act as a surrogate mother. Jacob agreed and Bilhah gave birth to a son. Rachel, believing that God had made a judgment in her favor, named him Dan. In general, the Hebrew word "*dan*" relates to the concept of judgment; but in this context it means, "He has vindicated." Dan was later appointed as judge over the House of Israel: "Dan will provide *justice* for his people" (Gen. 49:16). This tribe's blessing symbol consisted of the scales of justice and a serpent, or simply a serpent.

> Then she said, "Here is Bilhah, my maidservant. Sleep with her so that she can bear children for me and that through her I too can build a family" . . . she became pregnant and bore him a son. Then Rachel said, "God has vindicated me; he has listened to my plea and given me a son." Because of this she named him Dan. (Gen. 30:3–6)

Because this compromise had been so effective, Rachel used it a second time and Bilhah gave birth to another son. The rivalry between the two sisters was highlighted when, at the birth of this child, Rachel made a point of referring to their struggle and declaring herself the victor. She named the child *Naftali* (Naphtali), a Hebrew word meaning "my struggle." The blessing symbol of the tribe of Naphtali was a female deer (Gen. 49:21).

> Rachel's servant Bilhah conceived again and bore Jacob a second son. Then Rachel said, "I have had a great struggle with my sister, and I have won." So she named him Naphtali [*Naftali*].
> (Gen. 30:7–8)

Leah, believing that she was losing ground in the contest with Rachel, decided to try the same tactic and asked Jacob to sleep with her maid Zilpah. When yet another son was added to her family, she considered herself extremely fortunate and named him *Gad*; a Hebrew word meaning "good fortune." This name can also be interpreted as "a troop" or "a troop is coming!" Although seemingly not as logical, the latter gains credibility when one looks at the tribe's blessing symbol. It is the image of an army camp (Gen. 49:19).

> When Leah saw that she had stopped having children, she took her maidservant Zilpah and gave her to Jacob as a wife. Leah's servant Zilpah bore Jacob a son. Then Leah said, "What good fortune!" So she named him Gad. (Gen. 30:9–11)

Leah used her maid as a surrogate mother for the second time. When Zilpah gave birth to yet another son, she simply named him *Asher*; a Hebrew word meaning "happy." The tribe of Asher's blessing symbol was an olive tree (Gen. 49:20).

71

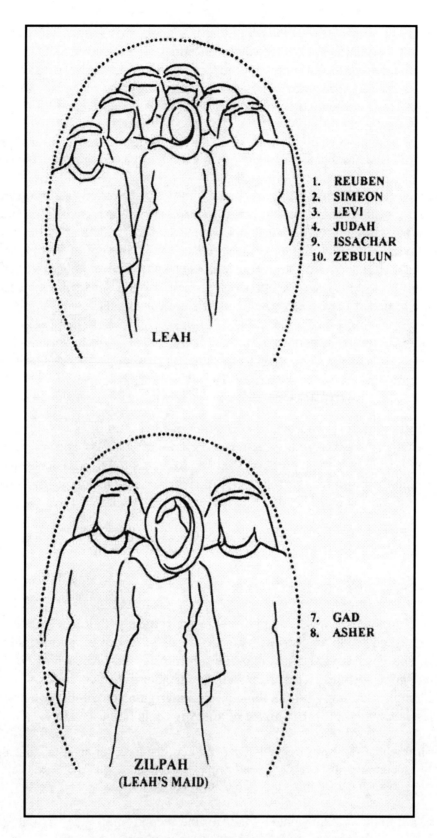

Figure 14: Family cameos of Leah and her maid Zilpah

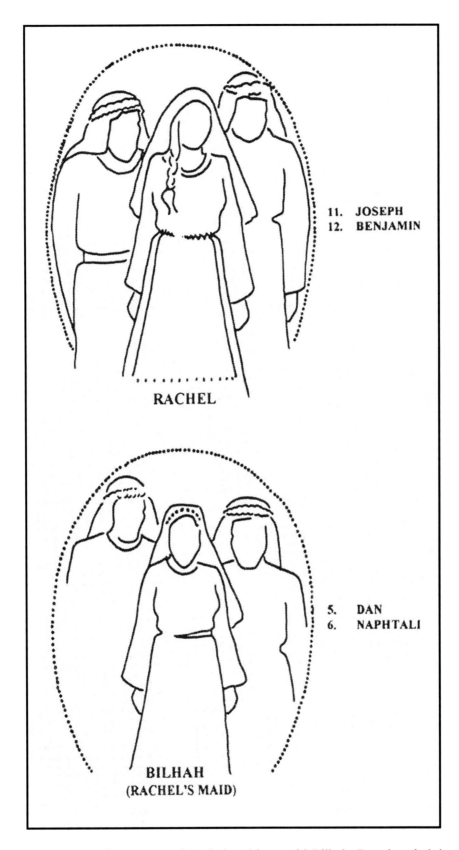

Figure 15: Family cameos of Rachel and her maid Bilhah. Bear in mind that Rachel died in childbirth. She did not survive to see her sons reach adulthood

The Sons of Jacob and Joseph

English	Hebrew	Meaning	Blessing symbols
1. Reuben	*Re'uven*	Behold, a son!	A sunrise
2. Simeon	*Shim'on*	Probably means "One who hears"	Vessel of wrath (or a fortified tower)
3. Levi	*L'vi*	Derived from root word "attached"	Breastplate
4. Judah	*Yehudah*	Sounds like Hebrew for "Praise"	Lion
5. Dan	*Dan*	He has vindicated	Serpent on scales of justice (or a serpent)
6. Naphtali	*Naftali*	My struggle	Doe
7. Gad	*Gad*	Good fortune, or a troop	Army camp
8. Asher	*Asher*	Happy	Olive tree
9. Issachar	*Yissa'khar*	Sounds like Hebrew for "Reward"	Ass
10. Zebulun	*Z'vulun*	Sounds like Hebrew for "Honor"	Ship
11. Joseph	*Yosef*	May he add	Fruitful bough
12. Benjamin	*Binyamin*	Son of the right hand, or Son of the South	Wolf
Manasseh	*M'nasheh*	Causing to forget	
Ephraim	*Efrayim*	Fruit (pl.)	

Leah's servant Zilpah bore Jacob a second son. Then Leah said, "How happy I am! The women will call me happy." So she named him Asher. (Gen. 30:12–13)

The next Scripture is rather strange. It seems that Leah gave Rachel some mandrake plants, regarded as a symbol of fertility, in exchange for the "favor" of sleeping with her husband. When she later gave birth to her fifth son, she saw this as a confirmation that she had made the correct decision in giving her maid to Jacob. She named this child *Yissa'khar* (Issachar); which sounds very much like the Hebrew word for "reward." The blessing symbol of this tribe was an ass (Gen. 49:15).

> So when Jacob came in from the fields that evening, Leah went out to meet him. "You must sleep with me," she said, "I have hired you with my son's mandrakes." So he slept with her that night. God listened to Leah, and she became pregnant and bore Jacob a fifth son. Then Leah said, "God has rewarded me for giving my maid-servant to my husband." So she named him Issachar [*Yissa'khar*]. (Gen. 30:16–18)

Leah would bear Jacob one last son and then a daughter. She named her son *Z'vulun* (Zebulun), which sounds like the Hebrew word for "honor." The following words reveal that she was still yearning for Jacob's love and respect, even if it was only on the basis of having borne him six sons. The blessing symbol of the tribe of Zebulun was a ship (Gen. 49:13; Deut. 33:19).

> Leah conceived again and bore Jacob a sixth son. Then Leah said, "God has presented me with a precious gift. This time my husband will treat me with honor because I have borne him six sons." So she named him Zebulun [*Z'vulun*]. Some time later she gave birth to a daughter and named her Dinah. (Gen. 30:19–21)

Rachel finally fell pregnant and gave birth to the eleventh son in the family. Because at that time children were considered to be gifts from God, Rachel's infertility had been a source of deep personal humiliation. She therefore named her firstborn *Yosef* (Joseph); a word meaning "may he [God] add." Joseph, born in Jacob's old age, was the precious offspring of his beloved Rachel. He soon became the apple of his father's eye and was referred to as "the prince among his brothers" (Gen. 49:26). Jacob later gave this son a special token of favor; the prestigious "richly ornamented robe." The blessing symbol of Joseph's tribe was a fruitful bough.

> Then God remembered Rachel; he listened to her and opened her womb. She became pregnant and gave birth to a son and said, "God has taken away my disgrace." She named him Joseph [*Yosef*], and said, "May the Lord add to me another son." (Gen. 30:22–24)

God did indeed "add another son," but Rachel did not live to enjoy him. She died in childbirth. It appears that this was a breach birth—the baby emerges feet first—because the mid-wife declared that it was a boy while Rachel was struggling to give birth. Rachel named him *Ben-Oni*, meaning "the son of my trouble." Jacob later renamed him *Binyamin* (Benjamin) meaning "son of the right hand" or "son of the South." The blessing symbol of the tribe of Benjamin was a wolf (Gen. 49:27; Deut. 33:12).

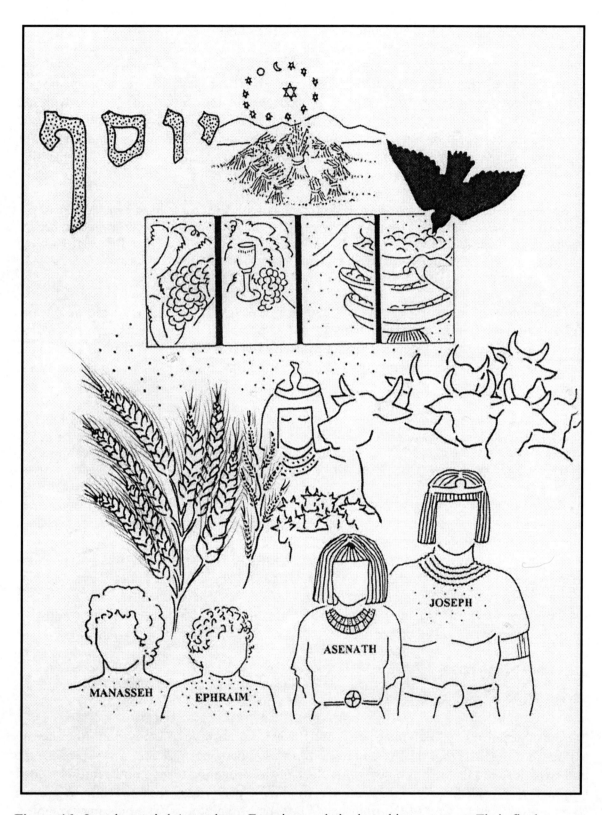

Figure 16: Joseph married Asenath, an Egyptian, and she bore him two sons. Their firstborn was Manasseh; their second, Ephraim. Other images relate to Joseph as the "interpreter of dreams"

And as she was having great difficulty in child-birth, the midwife said to her, "Don't be afraid, for you have another son." As she breathed her last . . . she named her son Ben-Oni. But his father named him Benjamin [*Binyamin*] So Rachel died and was buried on the way to Ephrath [Bethlehem]. (Gen. 35:17–19)

The Scriptures describe the battle between Leah and Rachel, but say nothing of the characters of Jacob's two concubines. Human nature dictates that they would have had their fair share of suffering. They must have bonded with their babies and then have had to take second place in their relationships with them. The contest among Jacob's women could *not* have been conducive to a happy household.

The Sons of Joseph
Manasseh and his brother Ephraim were the sons of Joseph and Asenath, their Egyptian mother. They were both born in Egypt during the period of Joseph's separation from his family, prior to the seven years of famine. Joseph named his first son *M'nasheh* (Manasseh), meaning "causing to forget"; and his second son *Efrayim* (Ephraim), meaning "fruit." (The suffix "*im*" indicates that *Efrayim* is the *plural* form of the Hebrew word for fruit.)

Before the years of famine came, two sons were born to Joseph by Asenath daughter of Potiphera, priest of On. Joseph named his firstborn Manasseh [*M'nasheh*] and said, "It is because God has made me forget all my trouble and all my father's household." (Gen. 41:50, 51)

The second son he named Ephraim [*Efrayim*] and said, "It is because God has made me fruitful in the land of my suffering." (Gen. 41:52)

Positions of Prominence

Hebrew Leadership
Various types of leadership feature in Hebrew history. The patriarchs—Abraham, Isaac, and Jacob—were the first to assume positions of prominence. Moses and Joshua were the great figures of the Exodus and the occupation of Canaan. The Levitical priesthood led the people in worship. The judges, known for their military or moral prowess, delivered Israel from subjection to other nations between the period of Joshua and the kings. The first great kings of Judah—Saul, David, and Solomon—were followed by a divided monarchy. As the nation became increasingly decadent, God sent prophets to both kingdoms. These prophets guided Israel during times of crises and, in the case of the southern Kingdom of Judah, during the period of the Babylonian exile. The ministries of these Hebrew prophets spanned a period of between 250 to 300 years.

The Birthright
Within the context of the family unit, the firstborn son enjoyed certain unique privileges. He automatically belonged to the Lord; this served to secure the priesthood within each family. The "*consecration of the firstborn*" was normally "redeemed" with the offering of an animal in the first month of a baby's life, however. Secondly, this son assumed *leadership* in the

family on the death of his father; this included the right to royal succession during the period of the monarchy. From the time of Moses, the firstborn son inherited a *double, sometimes even a triple, portion of the family estate*. He therefore enjoyed a position of prominence; a special measure of honor, authority, and wealth. These exclusive rights, "the birthright," were of great value and usually strongly defended.

The privileged status of the firstborn was sometimes forfeited and in the cases of Jacob and Ephraim, contrary to tradition, the birthright was given by God to the younger son. The stories of Jacob having to bribe his brother and trick his father in order to gain the birthright are irrelevant—Rachel had been informed by God, prior to the birth of the twins, that Jacob would have authority over Esau: "The older will serve the younger" (Gen. 25:23).

In the New Testament, the term "firstborn" is used with reference to Yeshua. He was the only begotten Son of the God, *Miryam's* (Mary's) firstborn, and the first to be resurrected to eternal life. The title alludes, above all, to his status as God's Messiah—the "Anointed One"—a position of supreme honor and authority.

Joseph and Ephraim as "Firstborn" Sons

In terms of the sons of Jacob, Reuben, the firstborn, should have inherited the birthright. We are told that he forfeited this privilege when he committed an act of incest with Bilhah, one of his father's concubines. This probably gave Jacob the excuse he needed to shift the prized birthright from Reuben, the firstborn of Leah, to Joseph, the firstborn of his beloved Rachel.

> He was the firstborn, but when he defiled his father's marriage bed, his rights as firstborn were given to the sons of Joseph, son of Israel . . . and though Judah was the strongest of his brothers and a ruler came from him, the rights of the firstborn belong to Joseph. (1 Chron. 5:1–2)

Although there was good reason for Jacob's favoritism, the gift of the robe—and Joseph's prophetic dreams regarding his dominion over his family—made his brothers uneasy (Gen. 37:3–11). They might have construed Joseph's visions as indicating that Jacob would make him his sole heir. So when the opportunity presented itself, they disposed of this "thorn in their side." They sold him to Ishmaelite slave traders, who were on their way to Egypt.

Joseph is one of the most celebrated figures in Hebrew history. His well-known life story is filled with significance and blessings, despite the hardships. The hand of God clearly guided this "highly favored one." He is therefore often regarded as being a type, or picture, of the Messiah.

When Joseph disappeared, Jacob was brokenhearted. He had been told that his favorite son was dead. Therefore, years later, when Jacob was reunited with this son and his young family in Egypt, he was overjoyed. In a gesture of loving acceptance, he declared that Joseph's sons would be awarded the same status as Reuben and Simeon; his own firstborn sons.

> "Ephraim and Manasseh will be mine, just as Reuben and Simeon are mine." (Gen. 48:5)

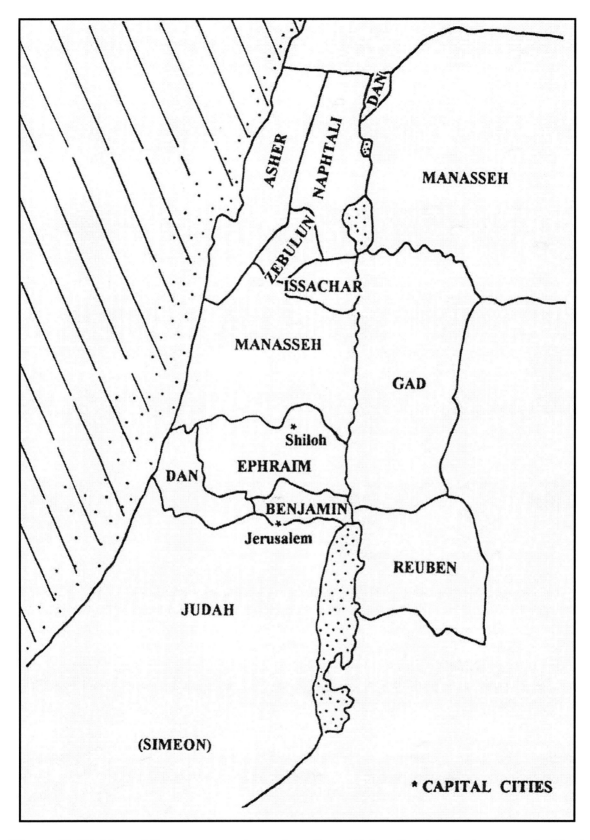

Figure 17: Division of Canaan among the twelve tribes. All the tribes inherited one parcel of land but the sons of Joseph inherited the double portion of the firstborn

The aging patriarch confirmed this statement by means of a special blessing. Joseph expected the rights of the firstborn to be passed on to his oldest son, Manasseh. But it was *Ephraim* who was touched by his grandfather's right hand, signifying that *he* was receiving "the blessing of the firstborn." Although Jacob declared that Manasseh would also "become great" (Gen. 48:19), history shows that, contrary to tradition, Ephraim's descendants assumed leadership of the Hebrew tribes. Ephraim become the greater of the two.

> "[H]is younger brother will be greater than he, and his [Ephraim's] descendants will become a group [or "multitude": NAS] of nations. (Gen. 48:19)

> "I am Israel's father, and Ephraim is my firstborn son." (Jer. 31:9)

Ephraim: A Man, Tribe, Region, and Kingdom
Unlike the name of Joseph, Ephraim's name is not associated with an outstanding personality in Hebrew history. "Ephraim" would become a prominent tribe, a portion of land in Canaan, and the name of the Northern Kingdom of Israel. By the time of the Exodus, about four centuries after the death of Ephraim, the names "Ephraim" and "Manasseh" had become synonymous with that of Joseph, their father. The wilderness camp, for example, featured the names of the two sons *instead* of that of Joseph. On entering the Promised Land under the leadership of Joshua (*Y'hoshu'a*), Joseph's share of the land—the double portion—was divided into two regions. One went to the tribe of Ephraim and the other to the tribe of Manasseh.

"Joseph's portion" was extensive compared to those of the other tribes. The land of Ephraim, in particular, was some of the richest and most fruitful hill country in Canaan. The fact that Moses' successor, Joshua, was an Ephraimite, compounded the region's status. The territory of "Ephraim" maintained a position of religious and political prominence for centuries.

> "These are the boundaries by which you are to divide the land for an inheritance among the twelve tribes of Israel, with two portions for Joseph." (Ezek. 47:13)

Shiloh, Joshua's capital city in the district of Ephraim, became home to the Tabernacle after the wilderness period. It was therefore revered as Israel's sanctuary city and used as a site for pilgrimages and religious festivals. The towns of Bethel and, at one point, Sheshem, within the district of Ephraim, also served as centers of Israelite worship.

For many centuries Ephraimites—the descendants of Joseph and Ephraim, "the firstborn"—enjoyed a position of special prestige, authority, leadership, and wealth in ancient Israel; a fact not commonly known today.

The Royal Line of Judah
It is clear from Jacob's blessings, that God chose another tribe to be the *royal* line of Israel. The Israelite monarchy commenced with the reign of Saul, a Benjamite, but it was from the line of Judah that King David and Solomon *(Shlomoh)* came. And it was into this line that the "King of Kings," the Messiah *(Mashiach)*, was born.

Figure 18: The royal line of Judah. From this line came Kings David and Solomon, and eventually the "King of Kings"—the Messiah

"The scepter will not part from Judah, nor the ruler's staff from between his feet, until he comes to whom it belongs and the obedience of the nations is his." (Gen. 49:10)

Judah was the fourth son of Jacob and Leah. Ironically, although Leah was rejected by her husband, it was from one of *her* sons that the preeminent royal line emerged. Judah's name means "praise" and his blessing symbol was a lion; a creature commonly regarded as a symbol of royalty in the ancient Near East. Yeshua, the "Holy One" of Israel, who would "inhabit the praises of his people" (Ps. 22:3), was a royal descendant of this tribe. He is often referred to as the "Lion of Judah."

"You are a lion's cub, O Judah; you return from the prey, my son. Like a lion he crouches and lies down like a lioness—who dares to rouse him?" (Gen. 49:9)

The tribe of Judah became the largest single tribe of Israel. The portion of land allotted to them was known as Judea (*Yihudah*); and the people of this region, the Jews (*Yehudim*: "Those who praise"). Both names are derived from the word Judah (*Yehudah*). This name was also later used with reference to the southern kingdom—the Kingdom of Judah.

The tribe of Simeon inhabited the extreme south-western region of Canaan (modern day Negev) and was almost totally absorbed by the more powerful tribe of Judah. All towns in the south belonged to Judah, none to Simeon.

The Priestly Tribe of Levi

From the time of Moses, the tribe of Levi also enjoyed a position of special honor. It was the priestly line of Israel. The descendants of Moses' brother, Aaron, became the priests, or c*ohanim*, who led the Israelites in worship. Other Levites acted as assistants to the *cohanim* (Deut. 33:9–10; Num. 25:13). In accordance with Jacob's blessing (Gen. 49:7), the tribe of Levi was scattered among the other tribes and did not inherit a separate portion of land. Instead, they were allocated forty-eight *cities* in the territories of Canaan.

Therefore the line of Joseph inherited the birthright of the firstborn and the *double portion* of land; the line of Levi became the priestly tribe, assuming the *right of consecration*; and the line of Judah became the royal line, assuming the privilege of *leadership*.

A Divided Kingdom

The northern tribes' attitude to an Israelite monarchy was that it contradicted the very foundations of their faith. A temporal king was considered unnecessary. The God of Israel was their king. Furthermore, after the demise of their long-standing position of prominence, they resented and resisted the establishment of the monarchy of Judah in the south. Even during the splendid golden age of King Solomon's reign, they yielded to his authority with extreme reluctance.

Indeed, a temporal monarch could not replace the leadership of a holy God. David and his son Solomon were great kings, but their lives were subject to the weaknesses common to all humanity. Their leadership was far from flawless.

82

David had a great "heart for God," but his adulterous relationship with Bathsheba led to the virtual murder of her husband, Uriah. Solomon, Bathsheba and David's second son, enjoyed special favor in God's eyes and was chosen to succeed his father. This signified that David had been pardoned for his great sin.

Solomon, for all his great wisdom, turned from God in his old age to worship the pagan gods of his pagan wives. We are told that it was this apostasy that led to the enduring division of Israel into two factions. After Solomon's reign, two lines of kings ruled two Israelite kingdoms—and neither managed to achieve the degree of unity, peace, and strength that had characterized the nation before the introduction of a monarchy. The Israelites were only truly bound together when led by God.

Joseph's richly ornamented robe is often associated with dissension and division among the sons of Israel. It is therefore appropriate that God chose a robe, the cloak of his prophet Ahijah, a priest of Shiloh, to warn his people of the impending clash that would divide the tribes into two independent kingdoms:

> . . . and Ahijah took hold of the new cloak he was wearing and tore it into twelve pieces. Then he said to Jeroboam, "Take ten pieces for yourself, for this is what the Lord, the God of Israel, says: 'See, I am going to tear the kingdom out of Solomon's hand and give you ten tribes. But for the sake of my servant David and the city of Jerusalem . . . he will have one tribe. I will do this because they have forsaken me. . . .' " (1 Kings 11:30–33).

After the death of Solomon, the Ephraimites, under the leadership of Jeroboam, assembled in Sheshem for the coronation of their new king, Rehoboam. There they implored that he lighten the heavy labor imposed on them by his father, Solomon. But Rehoboam's response was harsh and heavy-handed:

> "My father made your yoke heavy; I will make it even heavier. My father scourged you with whips; I will scourge you with scorpions." (1 Kings 12:14)

Rehoboam had finally provided the northern tribes with a legitimate excuse for a revolt against the monarchy of Judah. The result was a tragic and enduring split between the northern and southern tribes.

> So Israel has been in rebellion against the house of David to this day. (1 Kings 12:19)

The Southern Kingdom came to be known as "the House of Judah" or simply "Judah." It consisted, for the most part, of the tribes of Judah, Benjamin, and Simeon. Its capital city was Jerusalem, in the territory of Benjamin (1 Kings 11:31; 12:19–24).

The tribe of Ephraim was so prominent in the north, that its name became synonymous with the Northern Kingdom. This kingdom encompassed the rest of the tribes. It was by far the larger of the two kingdoms. In the Scriptures, the Northern Kingdom is frequently referred to as "Ephraim," "the House of Israel," or simply as "Israel." From 925 B.C. it was also referred to as the "Kingdom of Samaria"; after King Omri built a new capital city by that name.

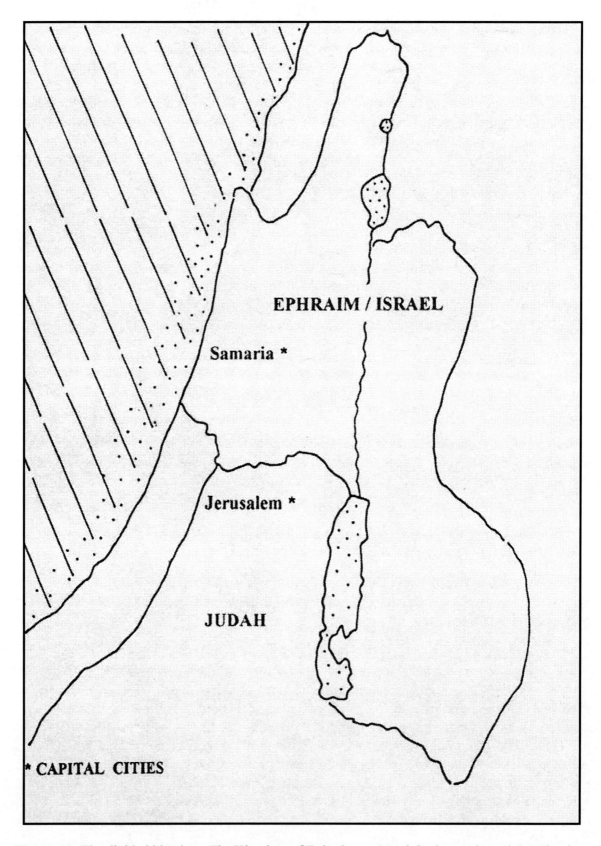

Figure 19: The divided kingdom: The Kingdom of Ephraim, or Israel, in the north; and the Kingdom of Judah in the south

Scattering and Gathering

From the beginning, the Israelites were warned that the consequence to apostasy would be the scattering of the tribes among the gentile nations of the earth:

> "If you do not carefully follow all the words of this law . . . Then the Lord will scatter you among all nations, from one end of the earth to the other." (Deut. 28:58, 64)

Despite Ephraim's initial strength and prominence, it became decadent and weak after its revolt against Judah and frequently lapsed into idolatry. Hosea was a prophet of the Kingdom of Israel for forty years during the eighth century B.C. It was during his time that the northern tribes reached an all time low in their adoption of pagan worship. Through this prophet we hear a grieving God pleading with his people and warning them of coming destruction. Yet even before the collapse of the Northern Kingdom and the exile of its tribes, we hear the same God promising to later forgive, gather and restore them to their homeland.

The tribes of Judah also proved unable to resist the religious influences of their neighbors and suffered a similar fate. In the Book of Jeremiah, we hear the Lord lamenting, "They broke my covenant, though I was a husband to them. . . ." (Jer. 31:32).

The Scattering of Ephraim and Judah

Between 734 and 722 B.C., the Northern Kingdom was taken captive by the Assyrians (2 Kings. 17:22–23). It is generally believed that the tribes were scattered across the Assyrian Empire by their captors and that foreigners were moved in to occupy Israelite territories. The Assyrians were known to have used this tactic in order to weaken and destroy the nations that they conquered. By this means, the morale and traditions of a people were quickly eroded. The following Scripture—also used in the Gospel of Matthew [2:18] in the context of the murder of the male babies of Bethlehem at the time of the Messiah's birth—relates to the exile of the northern tribes:

> A voice is heard in Ramah, mourning and great weeping, Rachel [mother of Joseph and grandmother of Ephraim] weeping for her children and refusing to be comforted, because her children are no more. (Jer. 31:15)

More than a century after the destruction of the Northern Kingdom, the Southern Kingdom of Judah was conquered by the Babylonians. Her people were taken into captivity. This period of Jewish exile lasted a mere seventy years, from 605–534 B.C.—although Jerusalem was only finally defeated in 586 B.C., their exile began in 605 B.C. The Jews were therefore able to retain their heritage. Initially, a small group returned from Babylon to rebuild Solomon's Temple in Jerusalem. More returned in stages during the ensuing decades. Others chose to remain in Mesopotamia. These Babylonian Jews, permanently separated from Jerusalem temple worship, laid the foundations of modern-day Judaism.

A second period of exile—this time a wide-spread dispersion of the Jews—occurred in A.D. 70; approximately forty years after the ascension of the Messiah. At that time, Palestine was a province of the Roman Empire. In an effort to free themselves from the yoke of Roman rule, the Jews staged a rebellion known as the Jewish Revolt. They suffered a devastating defeat. Thousands were massacred. Jerusalem and its Temple were destroyed. Survivors fled to neighboring gentile countries. To this day, travelers are able to see the spoils of that Roman victory; including the Temple's *menorah* carved in low relief on Rome's triumphal Arch of Titus—dated A.D. 81.

Another Jewish revolt, known as the *Bar Kokhba* Revolt, took place in the following century (132–135 A.D.) It was equally unsuccessful. Once again, surviving Jews fled to neighboring countries. Therefore, by the end of the second century, virtually the entire nation had been scattered among the Gentiles—a dispersion that would last for the next eighteen centuries. Until 1948, Palestine would come under the dominion of one foreign power after another.

In Search of Ephraim

Conjecture concerning the ultimate fate of the ten northern tribes has spanned the centuries. With the restoration of the Promised Land to the Jews in 1948, and the Messianic Movement gaining momentum in recent years, interest in the subject has been rekindled. Traditionally, gentile historians have maintained that the northern tribes never returned from the Assyrian exile. This has been contested by Jews who assert that they returned and merged with the tribes of Judah, both before and after the Babylonian exile. It has also been contended that only about twenty percent of the northern tribes were actually taken captive, because most had moved south and amalgamated with the Jews during the reign of Jeroboam.

The latter is based on archeological guesswork with regard to population density in Judah during that period and on a scriptural reference in 2 Chronicles 11 (vs. 13–17) which states that the Levites, and those from every tribe who had "set their hearts on seeking the Lord," went to Jerusalem, strengthened the kingdom of Judah, and supported Rehoboam for three years. This implies, however, that they returned to the north after this three-year period.

Approximately one hundred and eighty years separate the initial division of the tribes during the time of Rehoboam, from the Assyrian exile. It is therefore reasonable to assume that a certain degree of mingling between the tribes would have been inevitable during that period, and that some northern Israelites would have settled among the southern tribes.

The Scriptures support this view. In the New Testament (Luke 2:36), a reference is made to Anna, the prophetess in the Temple, who was "of the tribe of *Asher*." And Yeshua stated that his twelve Jewish followers, as representatives of the *twelve* tribes, were destined to judge the tribes of Israel. Furthermore, the letter of James starts with a reference to "the twelve tribes scattered among the nations." He could only have been addressing Jews of the Diaspora—that is, Israelites who could be traced.

> To the twelve tribes scattered amongst the nations: Greetings. (James 1:1)

We should also note that although Judah and Ephraim (or Israel) are at times referred to independently in the Scriptures, their names often appear in combination so as to emphasize the fact that reference is being made to *all* Israelites. Biblical ideas are often reinforced by means of a form of poetic repetition; such as "Let Jacob rejoice and Israel be glad!" (Ps. 14:7). Furthermore, New Testament writings use the words *Judah* and *Israel* interchangeably with reference to the Jews. So we cannot afford to be too literal in our interpretations of these terms.

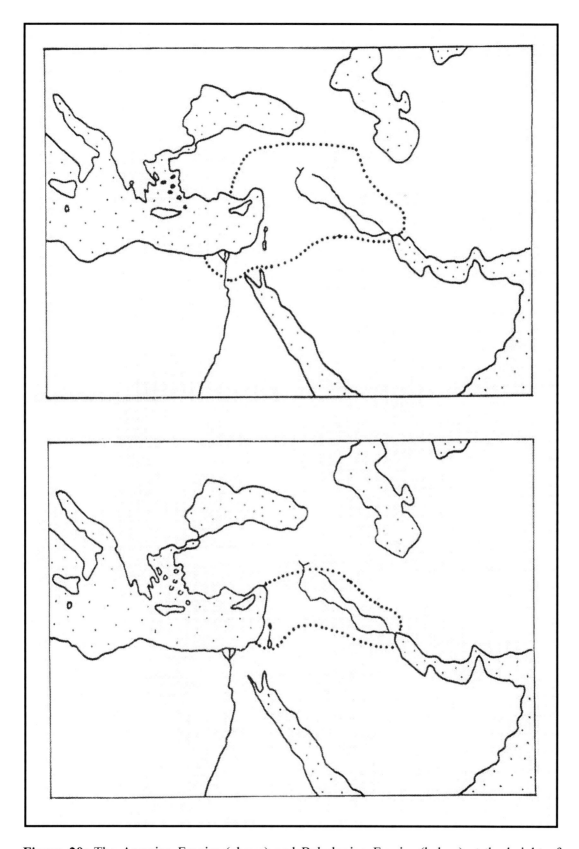

Figure 20: The Assyrian Empire (above) and Babylonian Empire (below) at the height of their powers

From a purely practical standpoint, it is also essential to look at population figures. A census of the tribes during the time of Moses is recorded in the *Tanakh* (OT). According to those figures, the Israelites numbered approximately two million during the wilderness period; a sizable increase from the seventy-member family that moved down to Egypt during the time of Joseph. This dramatic growth in population occurred over a 430 year period.

The first census number of 603,550, recorded in Numbers (1:46), included only non-Levite men over the age of twenty who were "able to serve in Israel's army." The second number given, 22,273 (Numbers 3:42), included only male Levites. The total census therefore amounted to 625,823 men. When one takes into account the women, children, and the aged, the estimate of two million is probably conservative.

The number of Jews living today has been calculated to be in the region of between thirteen and seventeen million; approximately five million in Israel, and over eight million among the Gentiles. Bearing in mind that about six million Jews died in the Holocaust, this is still far too few people to represent the descendants of all twelve tribes after a period of nearly four thousand years—from the time of Jacob in the seventeenth century B.C. to the present. These figures attest to the fact that numerous Israelites must have lost or forfeited their heritage at some point in their history.

In 1999, Simcha Jacobovici and Elliot Halpern published a video entitled, "Quest for the Lost Tribes." Based on a prophecy that appears in Isaiah 11:11, in which God promised to reclaim the remnant of his people a *second* time from "Ashur, Egypt, Patros, Ethiopia, 'Eilam, Shinar, Hamat, and the islands of the sea," they went in search of the "lost" northern tribes in the modern day equivalents of these regions. And they did, indeed, discover pockets of people who were practicing some form of Judaism, or who demonstrated a connection with the Hebrew culture. Distinguishing rituals, diet, clothing, writings, and symbols—such as the Jewish prayer shawl and Star of David—were found. The Parthans of Afghanistan, the Chiang-Min of China, and the Beta Israel, or "Falashas," of Ethiopia, who practice an ancient form of Judaism, are three of the most noteworthy examples. (The ties of many Ethiopians to an ancient form of Judaism are so strong, that many were airlifted to Israel during the economic and political crises in their country during the 1970s and 1980s.)

Therefore, fifty years after the establishment of the State of Israel and the return of the Jews, Simcha Jacobovici and Elliot Halpern claimed that the ten northern tribes had been located. This seemed to fulfill Isaiah's prophecy that the Lord will reach out his hand "a second time" to reclaim the remnant of his people—first the Jews and then these northern tribes. Notice, however, that in Isaiah 11:11 the Lord promised to reclaim only "a remnant" from these regions. That is to say, during the past twenty-seven centuries, from 722 B.C. to the present, the majority of Jacob's descendants did not remain in their tribal units, but were assimilated into gentile nations as they spread "from one end of the earth to the other." In this way Jacob's prophecy concerning Ephraim would have been fulfilled.

"[H]is descendants will become a group [or multitude: NAS] of nations. . . ." (Gen. 48:19)

Additional evidence of a Hebrew or Jewish connection has been found in other gentile countries. In Mexico and the south-western states of the USA, many are discovering a Sephardic Jew connection. In 1492, the very month Columbus set sail for the Americas, thousands of Jews were expelled from Spain. Many therefore migrated to the New World.

As a permanent reminder that they were people of the Promised Land—*Eretz Yisra'el*—"ez," the first and last letters of the word *eretz,* meaning "the land," were added to the ends of Jewish names. To this day the "ez" suffix in names such as Sanchez and Martinez is suggestive of Sephardic Jewish ancestry.

Within a group in Southern Africa, known as the Lemba Tribe, DNA testing has confirmed their claims to ancestral ties with the Jews; particularly with the Jewish *cohanim,* or priesthood. Furthermore, the Japanese language appears to be linked to the Hebrew linguistic tradition. Numerous Japanese words and place names closely approximate Hebrew terms. Faint traces of this heritage have even been linked to *pre-*Columbian America.

The Gathering of Judah

Owing to the Holy Land's strategic location as a buffer zone between the countries of Africa and Southwest Asia, it has been fought over and occupied by many different cultures at various stages in its history. These include the ancient Assyrians, Babylonians, Persians, Greeks, Romans, crusading Christians, and Muslim Arabs and Turks. A small Jewish presence has always remained in the land, however.

Christians constituted the greater part of the population of Palestine before the seventh century Arab invasions. From the seventh to early twentieth centuries—apart from a one hundred year period when Crusaders gained control of Palestine (A.D. 1099) —the region was controlled by Arabs and Turks.

During World War I, the Turks were German allies and Palestine was captured by the British. Leading the campaign was a general by the name of Allenby. As a Christian, he understood the significance of Jerusalem and prayed that it would be captured without damage being caused to its holy sites. The following day he ordered biplanes on a reconnaissance flight over the city and unwittingly terrified the Turks by means of this unfamiliar sight. And when they learned that they were up against a man by the name of Allenby—in their language, "man sent from God" or "prophet from God"—they refused to fight. Allenby took Jerusalem without Arab resistance.

The British Balfour Declaration
(Written by Arthur James Balfour in November 1917)

"His Majesty's Government view with favour the establishment in Palestine of a national home for the Jewish people, and will use their best endeavours to facilitate the achievement of this object, it being clearly understood that nothing shall be done which may prejudice the civil and religious rights of existing non-Jewish communities in Palestine. . . . "

Britain was given a mandate by the League of Nations to govern the country and to prepare it for self-rule. However, in 1917, a statement known as the Balfour Declaration indicated that the British were in favor of the establishment of a Jewish state in Palestine. This position was supported by other major world powers and even had some Arab support.

The gathering of Israel in the modern era had already begun, however. Late in the nineteenth century, Jews, inspired by the Zionist philosophy of Theodore Herzl, started filtering back to their traditional homeland of Palestine. The region was sparsely populated at that time. Under the Turks, the land had been neglected and was too undeveloped to sustain a large population. It was considered to be quite worthless. There was little demand for it. These early Jewish immigrants called themselves "Palestinians" and they lived in harmony with their Arab neighbors.

The Balfour Declaration provided a window of opportunity for Jews to "go home." It led to the first large surge of Jewish immigration. This flood of Jewish immigrants was the expression of an ancient irrepressible cultural yearning to return to the land of the *Torah*. By 1922, more than 84,000 Jews had returned. By 1939, the immigrant figure had escalated to over 445,000. After the Holocaust of World War II, there was yet another wave of Jewish immigrants. This alarmed many Palestinian Arabs; while others, attracted by growing employment opportunities, moved in from neighboring Arab countries.

By 1947 Arab nations in the Middle East were strongly contesting the Jewish presence and claim to the land. Britain therefore handed the matter over to the United Nations. The UN proposed a partitioning of Palestine into Arab and Jewish regions. On 14 May 1948, the State of Israel declared its independence.

The tiny Jewish homeland was surrounded by huge unsympathetic Arab nations from its very inception. As soon as it declared its independence, it was immediately attacked; the intention being to annihilate Israel and restore the region to Arab control. The Jews held their ground and expanded their territories in each of the subsequent Arab-Israeli Wars: 1948–1949, the War of Independence; 1956, the Sinai Campaign; 1967, the Six-Day War; and in 1973, starting on the holiest day of the year, the *Yom Kippur* War. More recently, in mid-2006, during a brief struggle against Hezbollah in southern Lebanon, Israel attempted to reestablish a corridor of security. She was unable to route this Arab resistance group who had entrenched themselves among southern Lebanese civilians, however. Israel has never been the aggressor. In each case she responded to attacks, or threats of attack.

Political instability has not been a deterrent to Jewish immigration. The establishment of the State of Israel after World War II provided the catalyst for the Jewish people to rebuild their nation and cultivate a sense of direction and purpose. Out of the ashes of the Holocaust, came the restoration of their ancient homeland. After an exile of over 1,800 years, the proclamation, "Next year in Jerusalem!" was finally a reality.

Profound irreconcilable differences between Jews and Palestinians continue to plague the land, creating a volatile political climate. Arab Palestinians now view themselves as an oppressed and disenfranchised people. Many of the present generation of Israelis are tired of warfare and disillusioned by the many thwarted attempts to establish a secure and peaceful homeland. Furthermore, many Palestinians still view Jewish claims to the land as being fundamentally illegitimate. They will not let up their resistance until they've regained full control of the region. Offering parcels of land "in exchange for peace" has proved futile. This ongoing Arab-Israeli conflict has been referred to by radical Muslim leaders as a holy war, or "jihad."

Today Jerusalem is claimed as a capital city by both Jews and Palestinians. The Temple Mount at its heart is regarded as holy by both cultures. The Muslim "Dome of the Rock" stands on the traditional Jewish temple site—the site on which the Temples of Solomon and Herod once stood. This hexagonal mosque is built around a large rock that is believed by Jews to be Mt. Moriah, the site chosen by Abraham for the sacrifice of Isaac; and by Muslims, the place where Mohammed tethered his white horse on the night of his ascent into heaven. To Jews, Jerusalem is undoubtedly the most sacred city on Earth. To Muslims, it is one of three holy cities: Jerusalem, and Mecca and Medina in Saudi Arabia.

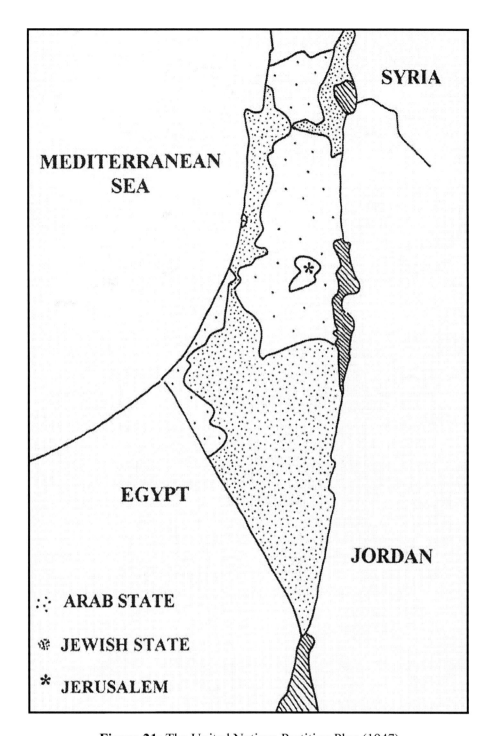

Figure 21: The United Nations Partition Plan (1947)

How ironical it is that it was the monotheism of Judaism and Christianity that attracted Mohammed in the seventh century A.D.—and that both Arabs and Jews claim Abraham as their forefather and worship his God.

Peace in the Middle East remains as elusive as ever.

Restoration

In accordance with Hebrew prophecy, Jews anticipate the twelve tribes being gathered and the Temple in Jerusalem being rebuilt before the commencement of the Messianic Age. The coming of the Messiah is strongly associated with the restoration of the tribes.

Usually, the fulfillment of biblical prophecy can only be accurately gauged in retrospect, after the fact. In the matter of the gathering of Israel, however, we have been witnessing the unfolding of prophecy and are in a position to look back and assess certain historical events and tendencies, and forward to conceivable end results.

The God of Israel certainly appears to have been doing "a new thing" over the past five decades: the reestablishment of the Jewish homeland; the location of tribal groups within the geographical areas mentioned in Isaiah 11; the emergence of Messianic believers and their vibrant ministries; and the current appreciation of the Jews and their heritage by gentile Christians. There is another, more subtle, underlying dimension to the concept of restoration that warrants our attention, however.

Modern day Jews are the only clearly identifiable "remnant" of the original tribes of Israel. Even the New Testament supports the view that they are an amalgamation of the tribes and therefore represent "all Israel." Comparatively low Jewish population figures indicate, however, that they represent a relatively small percentage of the full complement of Jacob's descendants. Therefore, millions of Gentiles must, unknowingly, be of Hebrew descent! Evidently, at various points in history, due to migration, intermarriage, adoption into gentile families, or apostasy, their forebears either lost or forfeited their Hebrew identity and heritage, and were assimilated into the sea of humanity.

The term "Jew" comes from the word "Judah"; the royal line of Israel. Although the name has been used as a general appellation for the people of Israel since Old Testament times, it was originally synonymous with the southern kingdom of Judah—which consisted of the tribes of Benjamin, Simeon, Judah, and some Levites. As the biblical record does not indicate that there was a significant influx of northern Israelites into the southern kingdom of Judah at any point in their history, we will assume that the Jews are, predominantly, the descendants of the southern tribes. We will also assume that, for the most part, it was northern Israelites who were assimilated into gentile nations. The subject of who those "lost" Israelites might be is a sensitive one. Over the centuries, various groups have attempted to claim descent from the northern tribes. They have often been radical, racist, and elitist in their doctrines.

A decided transformation in attitudes between Christians and Jews has been evident in recent decades. The old deep-seated distrust and hostility between them has been dissipating. Since the restoration of the State of Israel, a rejuvenating Hebrew ambiance has been filtering into Christian worship and Messianic Jews, in ministering to Gentiles, have substantially increased their understanding of the Jewish roots of Christianity. Growing numbers of Gentiles are not only *receptive* to this new influence; they are demonstrating an intense *hunger* for the Hebrew culture. Some have even established ancestral ties with the tribes by means of genealogical research and DNA testing!

This phenomenon has refreshed numerous jaded believers and gently fanned the embers of the Faith. One now sees Hebrew images and hears Hebrew words being spoken and sung in churches, and many are professing a deep love for the Jewish people. And while millions of Jews have "made *aliyah*" ("pilgrimage" or "ascent"; the act of returning to the Holy

Land), the State of Israel has also been visited by countless *gentile* pilgrims, since its independence.

In this most unexpected manner, Messianic Jews and Christians—those whose hearts are turning back to the Hebrew fountainhead of the Faith—are being united in their love for the Jewish Messiah and their understanding of the Hebrew culture. This unparalleled gentile sensibility toward the Jews and cross-pollination of Christian and Jewish thought are noteworthy phenomena of our time.

Certain Hebrew prophets and teachers—men such as Isaiah, Hosea, Jeremiah, Ezekiel, Elijah, Zechariah, and the apostle Paul—are particularly important with regard to the concept of restoration. In one way or another, they all confirm that the tribes have never ceased to be "a people" in the eyes of the God of Israel.

> This is what the Lord says, he who appoints the sun to shine by day, who decrees the moon and stars to shine by night, who stirs up the sea so that its waves roar—the Lord Almighty is his name: "Only if these decrees vanish from my sight," declares the Lord, "will the descendants of Israel ever cease to be a nation before me." (Jer. 31:35–36)

> "I will strengthen the house of Judah and save the house of Joseph. I will restore them because I have compassion on them. They will be as though I had not rejected them, for I am the Lord their God and I will answer them. The Ephraimites will become like mighty men, and their hearts will be glad as with wine. . . . I will signal for them and gather them in. . . . Though I scatter them among the peoples, yet in distant lands they will remember me. They and their children will survive and they will return. . . . I will strengthen them in the Lord and in his name they will walk." (Zech. 10:6–12)

> When he [God] roars, his children [Ephraim] will come trembling from the west. They will come trembling like birds from Egypt, like doves from Assyria. (Hos. 11:10–11)

Ezekiel's Vision

Ezekiel was living as God's prophet among Jewish exiles in the plains of Babylonia in the sixth century B.C. when he was given the following vision of the restored nation of Israel. First, he saw a striking image of a "valley of dry bones" that was restored to life as a "great army." Then he was instructed to write the names "Judah" and "Ephraim," and the tribes associated with them, on two sticks of wood; and to unite them in one hand, forming one stick. Ezekiel was to explain to his countrymen that the Israelites would be gathered from among the Gentiles and reunited under the authority of one king—and that God's "sanctuary" would be among them forever.

> "I am going to take the stick of Joseph—which is in Ephraim's hand—and of the Israelite tribes associated with him, and join it to Judah's stick, making them a single stick of wood, and they will become one in my hand." (Ezek. 37:19)

> "I will take the Israelites out of the nations [not only Babylon] where they have gone. I will gather them from all around and bring them back into their own land. I will make them one nation in the land on the mountains of Israel. There will be one king over all of them and they will never again be two nations or be divided into two kingdoms." (Ezek. 37:21–22)

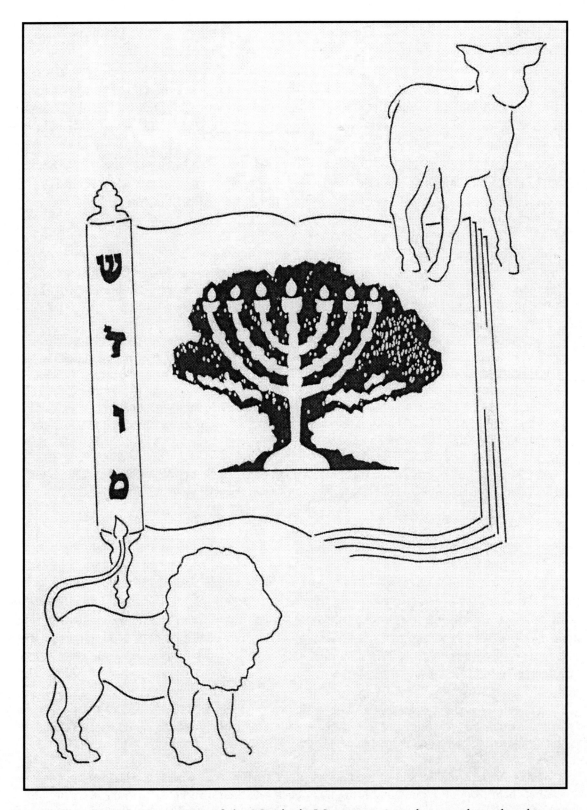

Figure 22: During the emergence of the Messianic Movement over the past three decades, many Jews and Christians have been drawn together by their love for Yeshua, the "Lamb of God," "Light of the World," and "Lion of Judah." The vertical Hebrew characters on the scroll spell *"Shalom,"* meaning "Peace"

"My servant David will be king over them, and they will all have one shepherd. . . . They will be my people, and I will be their God. . . . Then the nations will know that I the Lord make Israel holy, when my sanctuary is among them forever." (Ezek. 37:24–28)

We read in this chapter that this unified nation would be governed by King David; but David had reigned approximately four centuries *before* the time of Ezekiel. Who then was the king to whom the prophet was referring? Furthermore, the Assyrian exile of the Northern Kingdom had occurred more than two hundred years before Ezekiel's time. So if the Babylonian Jews were an amalgamation of the tribes—already "one stick"—why was a distinction made between "the stick of Joseph" and "the stick of Judah" in this vision?

Therefore, although Ezekiel's message assuredly inspired hope and encouragement among the exiles, it could not have related to that period in time. Ezekiel's vision was a picture of the gathering and uniting of the whole house of Israel prior to the eternal reign of the Messiah—the "King of Kings"—who would be a *descendant* of the royal *line of David*. Only the Messiah's reign could be *eternal*. In this context, notice the words of Gabriel to *Miryam* (Mary), Yeshua's mother:

"You will become pregnant, you will give birth to a son, and you are to name him Yeshua [Salvation]. He will be great, he will be called the Son of *HaElyon* [the Highest]. *Adonai* [the Lord: *Y-H-V-H*], God, will give him the throne of his forefather David; and he will rule the House of *Ya'akov* [Jacob] forever—there will be no end to his Kingdom." (Luke 1:31–33; JNT page 72)

Ezekiel 37:19 refers to a single stick of wood, but the Hebrew word for stick (*'etz*) can also be translated as "tree" or "wood." The term "*'etz ekhad*," can therefore be interpreted as "one stick," "one piece of wood," or "one tree." For this reason, the stick of wood representing one united nation corresponds with the concept of the restoration of the olive tree; that is, the original House of Israel. Furthermore, at this point in time, an amalgamation of all the descendants of the northern and southern tribes would certainly constitute an immense nation—comparable to a great army. Is the Spirit giving new life to the "dry bones" of ancient Israel at this time by restoring Gentiles to their Hebrew heritage and by spiritually regenerating increasing numbers of Jews through belief in the Messiah?

"Son of man, these bones are the whole house of Israel." (Ezek. 37:11)

In the Manner of Elijah

Elijah lived during the ninth century B.C. and is known to have been one of the greatest prophets of the Northern Kingdom. He was sent specifically to the idolatrous Ephraimites in order to "turn their hearts back" to the God of Israel and to restore them to their Hebrew heritage. All who have studied the Scriptures will have noticed that Elijah's name has a way of surfacing in the most unexpected places—and it is always associated with turning back to God in repentance, or preparation for a momentous event.

Does the emergence of the Messianic Movement and the unprecedented desire of many Gentiles to "return" to the Hebrew fountainhead of the Faith at this time, indicate that the era of multi-cultural gentile dominance has run its course? And does the restoration of a strong Jewish influence denote that the Jews, "the royal line of Judah," are to resume their original role as leaders in the Church? In coming years, will many more "children of Israel" (*B'nei*

Yisra'el) be restored to a common faith and heritage in preparation for the arrival of the Messiah?

> He will raise a banner for the nations and gather the exiles of Israel; he will assemble the scattered people of Judah from the four quarters of the earth. Ephraim's jealousy will vanish and Judah's enemies will be cut off. Ephraim will not be jealous of Judah, nor Judah hostile toward Ephraim. (Isa. 11:12–13)

> He answered, "On the one hand, *Eliyahu* [Elijah] is coming and will restore all things; on the other hand, I tell you that Eliyahu has come already, and people did not recognize him but did whatever they pleased to him." (Matt. 17:11; JNT page 24)

Yeshua spoke of an "Elijah" who was not recognized, and another who would come and "restore all things." As we read the Gospels, we discover that the former was John (*Yokhanan*) the Baptist. He preached repentance in the *manner* of Elijah. In so doing, he turned hearts back to God in preparation for the Messiah.

The second Elijah relates to age-old Jewish expectations regarding this prophet. Based on the following reference in Malachi, Jews believe that Elijah will return "before the great and dreadful day of the Lord," in order to prepare the way for the Messiah. Each year, a place is set aside for him at every Passover Seder table and a glass of wine poured out in anticipation of his arrival.

> "See, I will send you the prophet Elijah before that great and dreadful day of the Lord comes. He will turn the hearts of the fathers to their children, and the hearts of the children to their fathers. . . . " (Mal. 4:5, 6)

Moses and Elijah met privately with Yeshua on the occasion of his transfiguration. These two spiritual giants of Hebrew history returned, we are told, to *prepare* Yeshua for what was to come—his death, resurrection, and ascension (Luke 9:28–36).

> As he was praying, the appearance of his face changed; and his clothing became gleaming white. Suddenly there were two men talking with him—*Moshe* [Moses] and *Eliyahu* [Elijah]! They appeared in glorious splendor and spoke of his exodus, which he was soon to accomplish in *Yerushalayim* [Jerusalem]. (Luke 9:29–31; JNT page 90)

Is the Spirit presently at work *in the manner of Elijah,* "turning hearts back" and "restoring all things" in *preparation* for the Messiah? Or should we expect another Elijah?

Hosea's Symbolic Marriage
Hosea, a prophet of the decadent northern kingdom, directly prior to the Assyrian exile, was given a powerful show-and-tell message. (Hosea chapters 1-3 CJB, pages 707-709.)   *Y-H-V-H* told him to marry a prostitute—"for the land is engaged in flagrant whoring." He was told to name their first son "*Yizre'el*" (Jezreel) —"I will punish the house of Yehu for having shed blood at *Yizre'el* (Jezreel Valley); I will put an end to the kingdom of the house of *Isra'el* [Israel or Ephraim]." Hosea was told to name their second child, a daughter, *Lo-Ruchamah* (unpitied) —"for I will no longer have pity on the house of *Isra'el*." His third child, a son, would be "*Lo-Ammi*" (not my people) —"because you are not my people and I will not be your God."

He was told that these "cast away" northern tribes, scattered among the Gentiles, would be in seclusion for a *long* time and would become too numerous to be counted. Then they would return in repentance and "come trembling to *Adonai* [the Lord] and his goodness in the *acharit-hayamim* [latter days]." (3:4-5) According to this prophecy, the full period of the seclusion of the northern tribes from their ancient Hebrew heritage had to run its course. *Y-H-V-H* decreed that his original relationship with them would only be restored in the "latter days." It was never his *intention* that the "Jewishness" of the Faith be preserved by the gentile Church. Is the phenomenon of the Jewish Roots Movement and the fate of the "lost" northern tribes explained, for all to see, in the Book of Hosea?

Time Chart of Hebrew History

1900 B.C.	Abraham		
	Isaac		
	Jacob		
1300	Moses		
	Joshua		
1100	Saul		
	David		
	Solomon		
900	**Judah**	**Divided**	**Ephraim** or **Israel**
	Rehoboam	**Kingdom**	Jeroboam
			(Hosea)
734-722	(Isaiah)		Assyrian Exile
	(Micah)		
	(Jeremiah)		
605-586	Babylonian Exile	(Daniel & Ezekiel)	
534	Return	(Zechariah)	
A.D.	**Messiah**		
66-73	Jewish Revolt		
132-135	*Bar Kokhba* Revolt		
1948	State of Israel		

Sha'ul (Paul) and the Time of the Gentiles

One perennial question remains to be answered: Why did the majority of Jews *not* accept Yeshua as their Messiah in the first century? Would the New Covenant message have remained "within the camp" and not "gone out into all the world" had they acknowledged him? Paul (*Sha'ul*), in his letter to the Romans, offered a more intriguing explanation. He stated that the Jewish nation had been "hardened in part"—some had been held back from recognizing the Messiah—"until the full number of the Gentiles" had "come in."

> Israel has experienced a hardening in part until the full number of the Gentiles has come in. And so all Israel will be saved. . . . (Rom. 11:25–26)

He suggests that the Jewish rejection of Yeshua paved the way for the gracious inclusion of the Gentiles. Because many Jews were "held back," numerous Gentiles, and believers of Hebrew descent among them, received the gospel message. If this is true, a remnant of "Israel" must have been "saved" during the past sixteen centuries, while Gentiles have dominated the Faith. Does this explain Paul's words: "And so all Israel will be saved"?

The purpose of this investigation into the restoration of Israel is simply to supply food for thought in the light of recent phenomena. Needless to say, the Christian faith has always been for *all* people; regardless of culture. Salvation has never been dependent on race or bloodlines. It's dependent only on "grace"—the undeserved favor of a merciful God. However, as Messianic believers reach out to fellow Jews and nurture gentile believers, gentile Christians are encouraged to seek peace with the Jews and embrace the rich Hebrew heritage that is being redefined and offered to them at this time.

A Richly Ornamented Robe

The names of three prominent Hebrews reflect the idea of abundance: Abraham, "Father of *a multitude*"; Joseph, "*May he add*"; and Ephraim, "*Fruit*" (plural). The words in Jacob's blessing over Ephraim also mirror this concept, but introduce an element of diversity; "His descendants will become a group [or "*multitude*"] of nations. How appropriate it is then that Jacob gave Joseph, his "firstborn," a coat of *many* colors, a *richly ornamented* robe. This corresponds perfectly with the concept of a restored nation of Israel that will exhibit the cultural influences of a great *variety* of gentile civilizations.

Joseph's coat is usually associated with division among the sons of Jacob, but because the line of Joseph originally inherited the birthright of the firstborn, in this book a "richly ornamented robe," bearing the names of the Hebrew tribes, represents the restored nation of Israel. A Jewish Star of David is positioned below the name of Judah, the royal line, and above the names of Simeon and Benjamin. It is these three tribes that are most strongly associated with the ancient Jewish Southern Kingdom.

> Now Israel loved Joseph more than any of his other sons, because he had been born to him in his old age; and he made a richly ornamented robe for him. (Gen. 37:3)

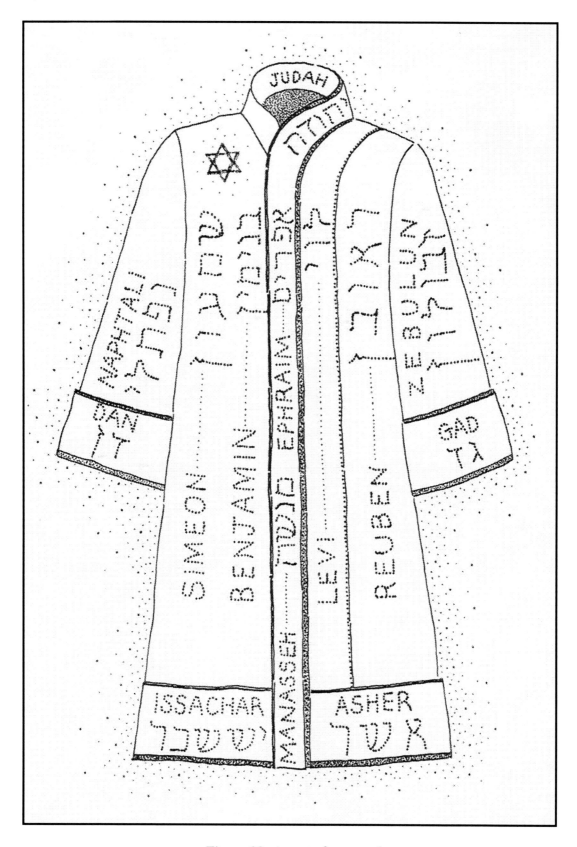

Figure 23: A coat of many colors

The Lord's ways are far higher than humanity's ways. For the gift of the prestigious coat led to Joseph being sold as a slave in Egypt

- which eventually led to his promotion as "second-in-command" to the pharaoh
- which led to his family's 430 year sojourn in Egypt
- which led to the establishment of the Hebrew nation
- which led to their persecution by a later pharaoh
- which led to God sending them a deliverer—Moses
- which led to the Exodus, their departure from Egypt
- which led to the wilderness period
- which led to the giving of the *Torah* and to the construction of the Tabernacle

When the Israelites reached the borders of the Promised Land, twelve spies were sent in to survey the countryside. Only two of them encouraged the Israelites to enter the land. They were: Joshua, from the tribe of *Ephraim*, and Caleb, from the tribe of *Judah*. However, the Israelites, as a whole, lacked the necessary faith to enter Canaan

- which led to their forty year sojourn in the Sinai desert
- which led to their occupation of the land under the leadership of Joshua
- which led to the establishment of a monarchy beginning with Kings Saul, David, and Solomon
- which led to the division of this united kingdom into the kingdoms of Ephraim (or Israel) and Judah
- which led to the corruption of the Northern and Southern Kingdoms
- which led to the fall and exile of these two kingdoms
- which led to the scattering, first of Ephraim and then of Judah, among the Gentiles
- which will lead to the restoration of the Israelites from a multitude of nations
- which will make them like a coat of many colors, "a richly ornamented robe"

"As the heavens are higher than the earth, so are my ways higher than your ways and my thoughts than your thoughts." (Isa. 55:9)

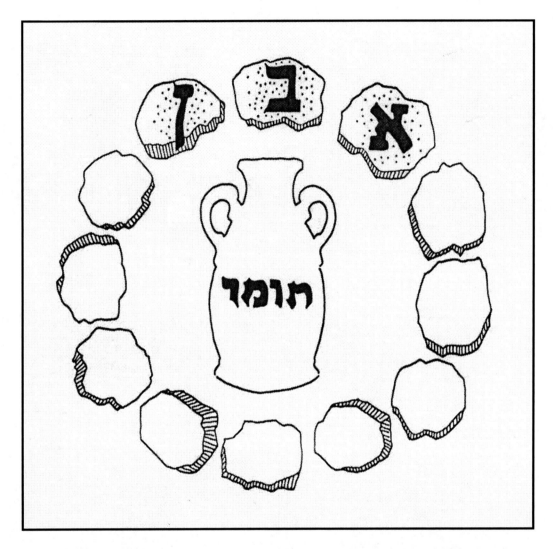

Figure 24: The Hebrew words "*even*" and "*khomer*" mean "stone" and "clay"

Part 3

Stones, Tents and Clay

Hebrew Dwellings

The very first Hebrews were semi-nomadic. They lived in goatskin tents and moved when it became necessary to find water and fresh pastures for their flocks. That lifestyle changed during their sojourn in ancient Egypt. For four centuries they lived in mud-brick houses in the fertile region of Goshen and enjoyed some semblance of permanence. After the Exodus in the thirteenth century B.C., they wandered in the Sinai desert for forty years under the leadership of Moses. At first they lived in make-shift shelters, but probably soon reverted to tents similar to those used by their forefathers.

It is not surprising, therefore, that symbolic tent images frequently appear in the Scriptures. They represent God's protection and providence, the home as a place of comfort and refuge, earthly and heavenly kingdoms, prosperity and well-being, the universe as God's creation, and the human body as the dwelling place of the soul.

> He wraps himself in light as with a garment; he stretches out the heavens like a tent. . . .
> (Ps. 104:2)

> For while we are in this tent we groan and are burdened, because we do not wish to be unclothed but to be clothed with our heavenly dwelling. . . . (2 Cor. 5:4)

Stone—in Hebrew, "*even*"—was the most commonplace permanent substance known to the ancients. The Sinai peninsular is not a shifting sandy desert. It is a stony, rugged, mountainous region dissected by *wadis*—dry riverbeds—and featuring occasional flat plains. During the time of the Exodus, the boulders and majestic unyielding peaks that surrounded the flimsy tents of the Israelites must have given them a sense of that which was impervious, constant, permanent—even protective. In the Scriptures this most universal and timeless of natural materials is therefore often equated with strength and endurance—and with their more sublime counterparts; faithfulness and eternity.

> As the mountains surround Jerusalem, so the Lord surrounds his people both now and forevermore. (Ps. 125:2)

After the conquest of Canaan, the lives of the Hebrews took on a greater permanence and security when they started to build in stone. In towns and cities, the poor lived in one-roomed, flat-roofed houses constructed of mud bricks on a stone foundation. Wealthier Israelites built their homes from the quarried bedrock of Canaan. From that time this golden quarried stone was used extensively in their architecture—particularly by the ancient Romans, who were great builders and engineers.

Moshe (Moses)

Before examining the magnificent Hebrew "dwelling place" of the Sinai desert, we will first focus on two cornerstone figures of the Old and New Testaments; *Moshe*—Moses—and Yeshua, the "prophet like Moses." In this section emphasis will also be placed on essential, but less familiar, matters of interest: the Hebrew names of God, the role of the Hebrew prophets, the Levitical priesthood, biblical covenants, the Mosaic Law and ancient symbols of stone and clay.

Because of its proximity to Canaan, the country of ancient Egypt (*Mitzrayim*) frequently features in the Scriptures. Abraham and Sarah traveled to this fruitful valley to escape a period of famine. Three generations later, Joseph was sold into slavery there. After his dramatic promotion to the position of right-hand-man to the pharaoh, Joseph's entire family, numbering seventy in all, moved to Egypt—also to escape a period of famine. Over a period of 430 years, those Hebrews grew into a sizable nation (Exod. 12:41).

A later Egyptian pharaoh, fearing that these foreigners living within his borders posed a military threat, forced them into slavery. This period in Hebrew history was foretold centuries earlier when the initial covenant was made with Abraham (Gen. 15:13–14):

> Then the Lord said to him, "Know for certain that your descendants will be strangers in a country not their own, and they will be enslaved and mistreated four hundred years. But I will punish the nation they serve as slaves, and afterward they will come out with great possessions." (Gen. 15:13–14)

> Then a new king, who did not know about Joseph, came to power in Egypt. "Look," he said to his people, "the Israelites have become much too numerous for us. Come, we must deal shrewdly with them or they will become even more numerous and, if war breaks out, will join our enemies, fight against us and leave the country." (Exod. 1:8–10)

During the thirteenth century B.C. a decree was issued in Egypt, stating that all male Hebrew babies be put to death. This was designed to arrest the rapid growth of this nation. A Levite woman by the name of Jochebed, in an effort to save her child's life, placed him in a waterproof basket and set it among the reeds in the river Nile. The crying boy was soon discovered by the pharaoh's daughter and he was promptly adopted into royalty. Because the baby was rescued, or "drawn out" of the river Nile, he was given the name "*Moshe*"; a word that sounds very much like the Hebrew term for "draw out."

Moses (*Moshe*), who would be the deliverer (*moshi'a*) of Israel, was therefore raised in the royal court of one of the most sophisticated and powerful civilizations of the ancient world. He must have wandered through majestic sunlit hallways supported by stone colonnades, read eloquent hieroglyphics that recorded Egyptian history and beliefs, delighted in elegant frescoes depicting everyday life in the fertile Nile valley, and mused about sacred statuary and amulets that immortalized numerous gods and pharaohs. Moses would have known that the cobra symbolized royalty and probably recoiled at the deification of such creatures as the hawk, ibis, jackal, and cat.

The immense sphinx and pyramids of Gizeh had been in existence for more than a thousand years before his time. Opulent rock-cut tombs had been dug into the mountainsides of the Valley of the Kings five centuries before Moses' birth. Even King Tutankhamen and beautiful Nefertiti preceded Moses. The Egyptian preoccupation with death and their custom of mummifying bodies in sacred mortuary temples—in order to provide them with a safe passage to the afterlife—would have been profoundly familiar to him. All of this was in direct opposition to the monotheism of his Hebrew forefathers.

Although Moses' privileged childhood and education in the luxurious Egyptian court separated him from the slavery to which his people were subjected, at the age of about forty, his good fortune came to an abrupt end. He accidentally killed an Egyptian guard while defending an Israelite slave who was being harshly treated. To escape retribution, Moses had to flee the country.

He would spend the next forty years in Midian. There he married Zipporah, the daughter of a Midianite priest. Moses lived the simple life of a shepherd until the God of Israel commissioned him to return to Egypt and lead his people to freedom. *Moshe* was therefore chosen to *draw* the Israelites *out* of Egypt.

> "Therefore, say to the Israelites: 'I am the Lord, and I will bring you out from under the yoke of the Egyptians. I will free you from being slaves to them, and will redeem you with an outstretched arm and with mighty acts of judgment. I will take you as my own people, and I will be your God. . . . And I will bring you to the land I swore with uplifted hand to give to Abraham, to Isaac and to Jacob. I will give it to you as a possession. I am the Lord.' " (Exod. 6:6–8)

Eighty year old Moses then found himself back in the home of his youth. Using his knowledge of Egyptian court protocol, and with his older brother Aaron (*Aharon*) as his spokesman— Moses stuttered—he approached the throne and requested that the Israelites be permitted to leave the country. The pharaoh proved unwilling to relinquish his slave nation, however. It had become too much of an asset to his economy.

The impotence of Egyptian idols, magicians, sorcerers, and even the pharaoh himself was then made plain as the God of the Hebrews demonstrated his awesome power. Ten plagues (*nega'im*) followed each other in quick succession: (1) All water supplies in Egypt were turned to blood; (2) frogs, (3) gnats, and then (4) flies covered the land; (5) a plague destroyed all Egyptian livestock; (6) festering boils broke out on people and animals; (7) hail destroyed the flax and barley crops and stripped every tree of its leaves; (8) swarms of locusts devoured all that remained after the hail; (9) total darkness covered Egypt for three days; and (10) the firstborn son of every Egyptian family died, including the firstborn son of the pharaoh. None of these plagues harmed the Hebrews in any way.

After the final calamity, a great *wail* of mourning arose from among the Egyptians. It was "the death of the firstborn" that made the pharaoh relent. It was this last plague that precipitated the Exodus (*Yetsi'ah Hamonit*) —the departure of the Israelites from Egypt.

The Hebrew nation had entered a new phase in their history. Under the leadership of Moses, they would live as nomads in the Sinai peninsular for the next forty years. And during that time the most important covenant of the *Tanakh* (OT) would be established, they would be reorganized to form an orderly community, disciplined by means of God-given laws, and given an exemplary system of worship.

> Remember how the Lord your God led you all the way in the desert these forty years, to humble you and to test you in order to know what was in your heart, whether or not you would keep his commands. (Deut. 8:2)

Their forty year sojourn in the Sinai Desert, also known as "the wilderness period," is extremely important. The foundations of Judaism, and accordingly, the Christian New Testament, were established during that period in Hebrew history. It therefore forms a perfect springboard for an examination of some crucial biblical fundamentals.

In the Scriptures the number forty is frequently associated with periods of testing or probation—followed by the commencement of a new phase in Hebrew history. During the great flood, it rained for forty days and forty nights. Moses spent forty years in Midian before being called to deliver Israel—and forty days on the mountain before presenting God's people with the Law and the design for the Tabernacle. Prior to entering the Promised Land, the Israelites wandered about the wilderness (Sinai desert) for forty years. Jonah's Ninevites were given forty days in which to repent. In the New Testament, Yeshua spent forty days being tempted in the desert, in preparation for his ministry. For forty days before his ascension, he made appearances as the resurrected Messiah.

A Prophet like *Moshe*

> The Lord your God will raise up for you a prophet like me from among your own brothers. You must listen to him. (Deut. 18:15)

Moses was not only the great deliverer of Israel. He is, undoubtedly, the most important prophet of the *Tanakh* (OT). The Hebrew word for prophet (*navi*) means "called" (by God). Their work was never easy. They were repeatedly sent to warn their people of coming judgment and destruction, and call them back to God in repentance. Following a calamity, it was also their task to comfort and encourage the nation.

Hebrew prophets were the prime instruments through whom God's will was revealed and, as such, were obligated to relay his messages. When filled with the Spirit they often involuntarily spoke words directly from God. More often, though, God spoke privately to them and his words were then passed on to the community. If a prophet failed to speak the words he'd been given, *he* was accountable for the sins of the people. In general the prophets were "forth-tellers" of God's words, rather than "foretellers" of future events.

> Then Moses went up to God, and the Lord called to him from the mountain and said, "This is what you are to say to the house of Jacob and what you are to tell the people of Israel. . . ." (Exod. 19:3)

In Figure 25 (opposite) the translation of the Hebrew writing on the *Torah* scroll reads: "The Law will go out from Zion, the word of the Lord from Jerusalem" (Micah 4:2). Yeshua's first century followers frequently referred to him as "The Living *Torah*"; hence the figure emerging from the *Torah* scroll. In the Scriptures, mountains and hills are often associated with important events or with the giving of spiritual instruction: Moses and the Law on Mt. Sinai; the sacrifice of Isaac and Hebrew worship on Mt. Moriah (the Temple Mount); the Beatitudes of Yeshua taught from a hillside; his Transfiguration on Mt. Tabor; and his crucifixion on the hill of Golgotha.

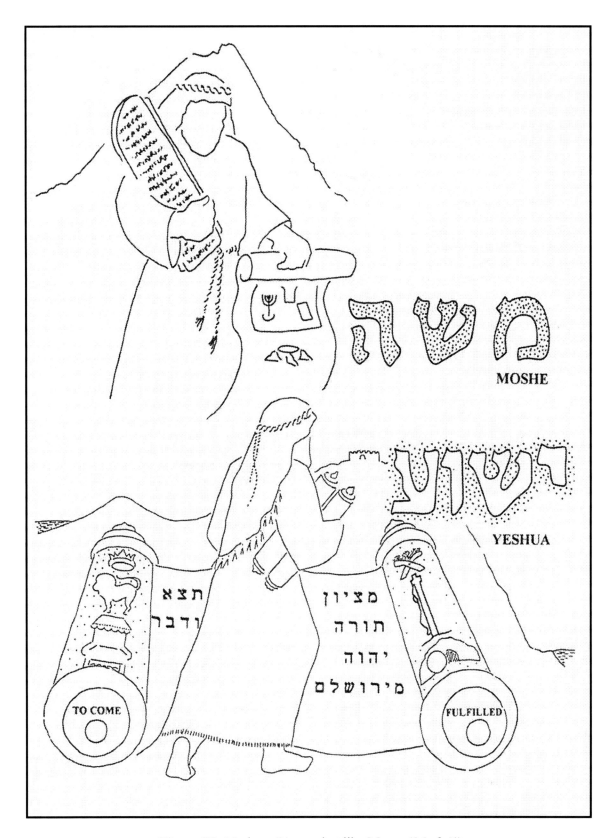

Figure 25: Yeshua: "A prophet like Moses (*Moshe*)"

Yeshua: A Prophet like Moses

- Both were born in countries ruled by ancient pagan cultures: the Egyptians (Moses) and the Romans (Yeshua).
- At birth both lives were threatened as a result of decrees issued by the rulers of these countries, relating to the slaughter of male Hebrew babies under the age of two.
- God's power was demonstrated by means of miraculous events in both lives.
- Both spoke with the authority of men sent by God.
- Moses delivered the Israelites from physical slavery. Yeshua delivers his people from subjugation to the old carnal nature; that is, "slavery to sin."
- After crossing the Red Sea, Moses' sister, *Miryam*, led the Israelite women in praising God for saving them from the Egyptians. On meeting her cousin, Elizabeth, Yeshua's mother, *Miryam* (Mary), praised God for the privilege of bearing the Messiah, the savior of humanity.
- Under the leadership of Moses, God supernaturally supplied the wandering Israelites with a type of bread called "manna." Yeshua taught that he was the "Bread of Life," the source of humanity's spiritual sustenance.
- By God's grace, Moses supplied the Israelites with "water from the rock." Yeshua supplies his people with "living water"; the Holy Spirit.
- Both taught Israel about the requirements of God's Law.
- Both displayed "righteous indignation" when the God of Israel was dishonored by his people. Moses broke the tablets of the Law and severely disciplined the Israelites when they worshipped the golden calf. Yeshua single-handedly drove the merchants and money-changers out of the Temple courtyard in Jerusalem.
- Through Moses, the Israelites received the Tabernacle; the "Dwelling Place" of God. Through Yeshua a new spiritual "Dwelling Place" was created for the Almighty; with the Messiah as the "cornerstone" and his followers, the "living stones."
- With Moses the Ten Commandments of the *Torah* were written on stone tablets. Yeshua, the embodiment of the Law, is referred to in the New Testament as the Living Stone, the Cornerstone and the Capstone. His *talmidim* (disciples) called him "The Living *Torah*."
- Moses instructed his people in the preparation of the Passover lamb. Yeshua's death coincided with the Jewish Passover. He is referred to as "the Passover Lamb" of the New Covenant.

"Surely this man is the Prophet." (John 7:40)

One thousand three hundred years after the time of Moses, another great Hebrew prophet was born. He is regarded by Christians as being the quintessential deliverer, not only of Israel, but of humankind. He initiated a more universal covenant (the New Covenant or *Brit Khadashah*) and became the one through whom God and his people would be eternally reconciled. He did not have to present God's laws on stone tablets. He himself was the embodiment of the Law—"The Word became flesh and dwelt among us." Through this man, God's *Torah*, or Law, was "written on hearts" by means of his Spirit. As seen in the above chart, many striking parallels can be drawn between Moses and Yeshua.

Because both Moses and Yeshua were permitted to enter God's presence, we find similar descriptions relating to "radiance" in the accounts of both lives. We are told that the face of Moses was radiant after speaking with God on the mountain and that Yeshua was radiant after speaking to Moses and Elijah on the occasion of his transfiguration. In the Book of Revelation, he was radiant in his appearance as the glorified Messiah.

As he was praying, the appearance of his face changed, and his clothes became as bright as a flash of lightning. (Luke 9:29)

[H]is face was like the sun shining in full strength. (Rev. 1:16; JNT page 336)

On his return from the mountain Moses' face shone so brightly, it made the Israelites fearful (Exod. 34:29). He therefore covered it with a veil. In Michelangelo's well-known marble sculpture of Moses, the massive seated figure is depicted with two horns protruding from its head. The addition of the horns causes confusion, but there *is* an explanation: The three Hebrew letters for "horn," pronounced *keren*, are identical to the Hebrew letters for "ray of light" or "radiance" (*keren*). Michelangelo's error was the result of a mistranslation in his Latin Bible.

The Hebrew Names of God

While being raised in the Egyptian court, Moses was exposed to the gods of the Egyptians—such as Osiris, the goddess of fertility; Ra, the god of the sun; and Nut, the sky-goddess. Later he was introduced to the gods of his father-in-law, who was a Midianite priest. Therefore, when God instructed him to deliver his people from slavery in Egypt, Moses pointedly asked him to identify himself.

"Suppose I go to the Israelites and say to them, 'The God of your fathers has sent me to you,' and they ask me, 'What is his name?' Then what shall I tell them?" God said to Moses, "I AM who I AM. This is what you are to say to the Israelites: 'I AM [*Hayah*] has sent me to you.' " (Exod. 3:13–14)

"This ["I Am"] is my name forever, the name by which I am to be remembered from generation to generation." (Exod. 3:15)

Who do Christians worship?—Jehovah, Jesus, Christ, the Lord, God? Over the centuries, biblical Hebrew names and their meanings have become obscured through the process of translation. The majority of believers are now uninformed—sometimes even *mis*informed—with regard to the *actual* names of their God.

Hebrew names have specific meanings and therefore special significance. The names of the first Hebrews related to the role of men and women in God's plan (e.g. *Avraham*). They related to a change of character (e.g. *Ya'akov* to *Yisra'el*). With the sons of Jacob, they related to the circumstances surrounding their births. The names of God, on the other hand, reveal something of his nature and, in the case of the Messiah, his mission.

Although many "lords" and "gods" are spoken of on this earth, only one has called himself *Hayah* ("I Am"), or the closely related and more familiar *Y-H-V-H* ("He that is"). The sacred proper name of the God of Israel and, strictly speaking, his only *personal* name is *Y-H-V-H*. These four letters are known as the "Tetragrammaton." Although sometimes translated as "*Yahveh*" or "*Yahweh*," in the Scriptures they are usually rendered simply as "Lord." According to Jewish custom, out of reverence for God, and because the original pronunciation is no longer known, this divine name is never spoken. It is substituted by the Hebrew word for "Lord" (*Adonai*) or simply the Hebrew equivalent of "The Name"

(*HaShem*). For instance, in Hebrew translations of the Twenty-third Psalm, it is "*Y-H-V-H*" who is the "Lord" and shepherd of David.

The name "Jehovah" came into use in the twelfth century A.D. It was a term employed only by Christians, never by Jews. In some Hebrew manuscripts the vowel points on the word "*Adonai*" were added under the Hebrew consonants of the Tetragrammaton, to indicate that the word "*Adonai*" was to be spoken in *the place of* God's sacred personal name. Christians erroneously *combined* these vowel points with the four letters of the Tetragrammaton; thereby forming the word "*Ya-Ho-VaH*," or *Jehovah*. This was long believed to represent the true pronunciation of the Tetragrammaton, but in reality, it is merely a hybrid transliteration of this most holy of names.

> "You shall have no other gods [*elohim*] before [besides] me . . . I, the Lord [*Y-H-V-H*] your God [*Elohim*], am a jealous God [*El*]." (Exod. 20:3 and 5)

The Hebrew word *El* means "God" in the broadest sense. "*Elohim*," its plural form, is frequently used as a title for the Almighty. It is a name that is used to express his majesty and supremacy; relating closely to the Christian concept of the Trinity—Father, Son, and Spirit, who are one in nature and purpose. Notice the use of "Lord," and a modification of the plural "*Elohim*" (*Eloheinu:* our God) in the Jewish *Shema*:

> "Hear [*Shema*], O Israel: The Lord [written as *Y-H-V-H*, spoken as *Adonai*] our God [*Eloheinu*], the Lord is one [*ekhad*]." (Deut. 6:4)

Father

In both Old and New Testaments, the God of Israel is referred to as a heavenly Father. Yeshua went so far as to refer to him as *Abba*, an intimate personal form of the Hebrew word for "father"; equivalent to the English, "dad" or "daddy" (Mark 14:36; Rom. 8:15; Gal. 4:6). Although originally an Aramaic term, "Abba" was adopted by the Jews and is still used by Israeli children today when referring to their fathers.

> Yet, O Lord, you are our Father. We are the clay, you are the potter; we are all the work of your hand. (Isa. 64:8)

> "I do nothing on my own but speak just what the Father has taught me." (John 8:28)

> Father [*Abba*],
> May your name be kept holy.
> May your Kingdom come. (Luke 11:2; JNT page 93)

Son

The *Tanakh* (OT) was written in Hebrew and Aramaic. The New Testament, or *Brit Khadashah*, which centers on the Jewish Messiah, was originally written in Greek—the universal language of the Roman Empire at that time. The name "Jesus" is therefore derived from the Greek "Iesous." Because the Scriptures have been translated into most of the earth's languages, numerous derivations of "Iesous" are in use today.

> "You will become pregnant, you will give birth to a son, and you are to name him Yeshua." (Luke 1: 31; JNT page 72)

Barukh HaShem: Blessed be the Name

> God: *El*   Almighty God: *Elohim*   Lord: *Adonai*
> Lord our God: *Adonai Eloheinu*   "I AM": *Hayah*
> "He that is": *Y-H-V-H*   The Name: *HaShem*
> The Holy One: *HaKadosh*   Father: *Abba*
> The Holy Spirit: *Ruach HaKodesh*
> Messiah: *Mashiach*   Christos   Christ   Anointed One
> Jesus: *Yeshua*   Savior   Redeemer   Emmanuel   God with Us
> Son of Man   Son of God   Lamb of God   Atoning Sacrifice: *Korban*
> Cornerstone   Capstone   Stumbling Stone   Living Stone   Spiritual Rock
> The True Vine   The Way   The Truth   The Life   The Bread of Life
> The Good Shepherd   Teacher: *Rabbi*   High Priest: *Cohen HaGadol*
> Almighty God   Counselor   Prince of Peace   Righteous One
> Lion of Judah   King of Kings   Lord of Lords
> King of the Universe: *Melekh Ha'Olam*
> Ruler of the Universe: *Ribbon Ha'Olam*
> The First and the Last   The Beginning and the End
> The Alpha and the Omega

The Hebrew term "*Mashiach*," translated into English as "Messiah" or "Christ," means "Anointed One." Jesus' Hebrew name was Yeshua; meaning "*Y-H-V-H* saves" (Luke 1: 31). Yeshua can also mean "salvation," the masculine form of the Hebrew word *yeshu'ah.* The name "*Yeshua*" is closely associated with the name *Y'hoshu'a* (Joshua), meaning "*Y-H-V-H* saves, *Y-H-V-H* delivers." (Joshua foreshadowed the Messiah. He led the children of Israel out of the wilderness and into the Promised Land; Yeshua leads his children out of a spiritual "wilderness," into the promised kingdom of God.)

Throughout this book the name "Yeshua" is used in place of the more familiar "Jesus." How gratifying it is that Yeshua's true name has *not* been common knowledge over the centuries. Blasphemers and skeptics have been unable to use it in their efforts to discredit the Faith!

Yeshua was a relatively popular name among the Jews in the first century. It later fell into disuse because of its association with "the god of the Christians" and anti-Semitism. To this day, the name "Jesus," as with the Christian cross, is offensive to many Jews.

Spirit
The Hebrew term for the Spirit of God is "*Ruach HaKodesh*." Surely the name "Holy Ghost" is redundant? The word "ghost"—associated with dead bodies, graveyards, ghouls and specters—is completely at odds with the concept of the life-giving Spirit of God.

"Not by might nor by power, but by my Spirit," says the Lord Almighty. (Zech. 4: 6)

The Holy Spirit is the third person of the Trinity and should be referred to accordingly; as "he" or "him," not as "it." Notice too that in 2 Corinthians, the term *Y-H-V-H*—the personal name of God—is used with reference to the Spirit:

111

Now the Lord [*Y-H-V-H*] is the Spirit. . . . (2 Cor. 3:17)

God the Father, Son, and Spirit may be likened to the Hebrew patriarchs: Abraham, "the father of a multitude," to God the Father; Isaac, offered as a sacrifice, to the Son; and Jacob, who wrestled with the ways of God versus the ways of the world, to the Spirit who enables God's people to succeed in this struggle each day.

The Levitical Priesthood

In the wilderness, the tribe of Levi, to which Moses and his brother Aaron belonged, was designated by God as the priestly tribe. Aaron was appointed as the first high priest (*cohen hagadol*) and his sons served under him as priests (*cohanim*). Aaron's line officiated in the Tabernacle and taught the people "all the decrees" of God. The line of Moses assisted the Aaronic priesthood. They were permitted to handle the "holy things" only when the Israelites moved camp. It was their task to dismantle, transport, and assemble the Tabernacle structures and furnishings.

Cohen Hagadol: The High Priest

Traditionally, the ministry of the high priesthood was passed down from father to son through the line of Aaron. Approximately eighty men served in this office over a period of 1,370 years. During the Roman occupation of Palestine, high priests were appointed by the Roman authorities and often complied with their demands in order to maintain their positions; thereby forfeiting their credibility among the Jews. For instance, it was the high priest Caiaphas and his *father-in-law,* Annas—the former high priest—who supervised the trial of Yeshua.

The ancient Israelite system of worship, characterized by blood sacrifice, came to an abrupt end with the destruction of Herod's Temple in A.D. 70. But Aaron's line of *cohanim* continues among the Jews to this day. It is still passed down from father to son. The name "*Cohen,*" and its derivations, such as *Kogan, Hogan, Katz* and *Kaganovitch* are indicative of this priestly lineage.

An "anointed one." A Hebrew high priest was an "anointed" priest. His head was anointed with sacred olive oil at the commencement of his ministry. Other priests had oil sprinkled only on their garments. Although a high priest could perform any of the priestly duties, his main function was to act as his people's representative before God. He offered sacrifices on Sabbaths, new moons, and feast days.

The high priest's attire. The high priest's clothing was extraordinary, befitting his station before the Almighty. Across his forehead was a gold plate inscribed with the words "HOLINESS TO *Y-H-V-H.*" This was attached to a blue and white double turban that covered his head. He wore several layers of clothing: a long-sleeved, white undergarment; a shorter, sleeveless blue undergarment; an embroidered "ephod"; and a breastplate embellished with gemstones. A row of decorative pomegranates and small gold bells were attached to the hem of his blue undergarment. The front and back panels of the ephod were clasped at the shoulders with two engraved onyx stones; each one inscribed with the names of six of the tribes of Israel. However, the crowning glory of the high priest's vestments was undoubtedly his ornate breastplate (*khoshen*).

The breastplate. The breastplate backing was made from the same materials as the ephod. It was a gold, blue, purple, and scarlet square of finely twisted linen that formed a pouch. Four gold rings at its corners kept it in place. They were fastened to the onyx shoulder stones by means of two gold cords, and to the ephod girdle by means of two blue bands. The breastplate pouch contained two stones called the Urim and Thummin. Their function is not entirely clear. They are thought to have been used in the deciphering of the will of God; indicating "Yes" or "No." For this reason, the breastplate is sometimes referred to as the "breastplate of judgment" or the "breastpiece of decision."

> Fashion a breastpiece for making decisions. . . . Make it like the ephod: of gold, and of blue, purple and scarlet yarn, and of finely twisted linen. . . . It is to be square and folded double. Then mount four rows of precious stones on it. (Exod. 28:15–17)

> Whenever Aaron enters the Holy Place, he will bear the names of the sons of Israel over his heart on the breastpiece of decision as a continuing memorial before the Lord. (Exod. 28:29)

Twelve precious gemstones featured on the breastplate. Each was inscribed with one of the names of the sons of Jacob. The high priest therefore "wore the sons of Israel across his heart" when he entered the presence of God. It is believed that these stones were arranged from right to left in birth order (Exod. 28:10). Various translations of the Bible differ in their interpretations regarding the classification of the gemstones. The New International Version lists them as a ruby, topaz, beryl, turquoise, sapphire, emerald, jacinth, agate, amethyst, chrysolyte, onyx, and jasper.

> There are to be twelve stones, one for each of the names of the sons of Israel, each engraved like a seal with the name of one of the twelve tribes. (Exod. 28:21)

The stone of the priestly tribe of Levi was a garnet; deep red in color and oval in shape. Garnets were regarded as symbols of abundance, because they resembled the succulent seeds of the pomegranate fruit, or *rimon*. (Similarly, the Latin name for garnet is "granatum," meaning "pomegranate.") Therefore the decorative pomegranates on the fringe of the ephod undergarment probably related to the fact that the high priests were *Levites*. The tinkling bells (*pa'amonim*), on the other hand, announced their approach to God's private chamber in the Tabernacle tent—the Most Holy Place.

Yeshua: Eternal Priest of the Highest Order

Mashiach: "Anointed One." The name Messiah, or *Mashiach*, means "Anointed One." The ancient anointed Levitical high priests therefore prepared the ground for the ministry of the Messiah. The New Testament teaches that after the destruction of the Temple and the demise of the Levitical priesthood in A.D. 70, Yeshua alone continued the ministry of the high priesthood. He became the only mediator between the God of Israel and his people. In the Book of Hebrews, Yeshua is repeatedly referred to as an eternal high priest; one who pleads the cause of his people at the right hand of his heavenly Father.

Figure 26: The Levitical high priests' attire: turban, ephod, breastplate, and undergarments

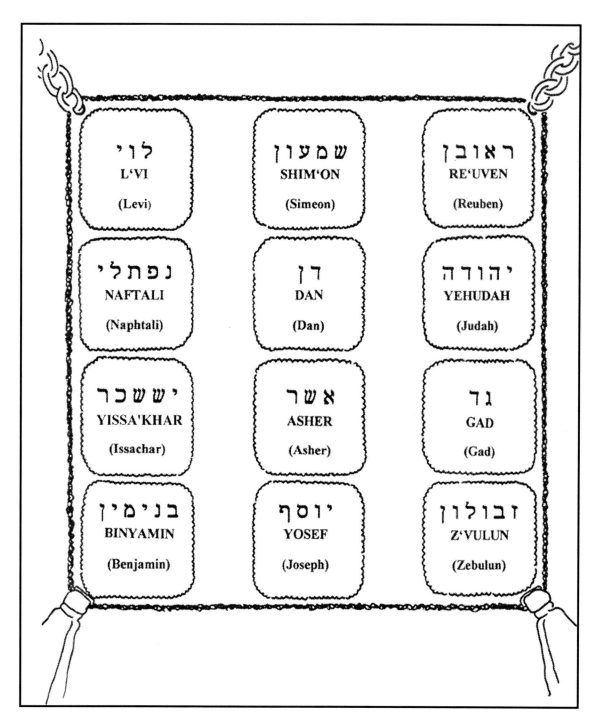

Figure 27: The breastplate gemstones inscribed with the names of the twelve sons of Jacob; including Hebrew transliterations and English translations of the names. (Read from right to left)

Figure 28: The breastplate as a symbol of God's love for his "treasured possession"—drawn from "a multitude of nations."

A Treasured Possession

> 1. "you are a *chosen people*" (1 Pet. 2:9)
>
> 2. "you will be *my treasured possession*" (Exod. 19:5)
>
> 3. "you will be for me a *kingdom of priests*" (Exod. 19:6)
>
> 4. "you will be for me a *holy nation*" (Exod. 19:6)
>
> 5. "Let the *beloved of the Lord* rest secure in him" (Deut. 33:12)
>
> 6. "How delightful is your love, my sister, *my bride*! (Song of Songs 4:10)
>
> 7. "Here am I, and the *children the Lord has given me*" (Isa. 8:18;   Heb. 2:13)
>
> 8. "He [Yeshua] said to him [Peter], 'Feed *my lambs*' " (John 21:15; JNT page 151)
>
> 9. "I know *my sheep* and *my sheep* know me" (John 10:14)
>
> 10. "Greater love has no-one than this, that he lay down his life for *his friends*" (John 15:13)
>
> 11. "you yourselves, as *living stones*, are being built into a spiritual house" (1 Pet. 2:5; JNT page 317)
>
> 12. "These are *they who have come out of the great tribulation*; they have washed their robes and made them white in the blood of the Lamb" (Rev. 7:14)

"They will be mine," says the Lord Almighty,
"in the day when I make up my *treasured possession*"
[or jewels: AV] (Mal. 3:17)

But because he lives forever, his position as *cohen* [priest] does not pass on to someone else; and consequently, he is totally able to deliver those who approach God through him; since he is alive forever and therefore forever able to intercede on their behalf. This is the kind of *cohen gadol* [high priest] that meets our needs—holy, without evil, without stain, set apart from sinners and raised higher than the heavens; one who does not have the daily necessity, like the other *cohanim g'dolim* [high priests], of offering up sacrifices first for their own sins and only then for those of the people; because he offered one sacrifice, once and for all, by offering up himself. (Heb. 7:24–27; JNT page 301)

A priest like Malki-Tzedek. In the Book of Hebrews, Yeshua is also equated with the mysterious priest-king Melchizedek or *Malki-Tzedek*. This man lived during the time of Abraham, centuries before the establishment of the Levitical priesthood. *Malki-Tzedek* of Salem, or Shalem (probably Jerusalem), is described as being a priest of the Most High God. There is evidence to suggest that he was an eternal priest of the highest order (Heb.7:3).

Other than that, we know little about him. There is no mention of his ancestry, birth or death. Abraham gave him "a tenth of everything" and received a blessing from him.

> This Malki-Tzedek, king of Shalem, a *cohen* [priest] of God *HaElyon* [the Most High], met *Avraham* [Abraham] . . . and blessed him. . . . (Heb. 7:1; JNT page 300)

The name "*Malki-Tzedek* of Shalem" is rich in meaning. *Malki* is the Hebrew for "king of"—the root word *melekh*, meaning "king." *Tzedek* means "righteousness" or "justice." S*halem* is equivalent to the Hebrew word *shalom*, meaning "peace." "*Malki-Tzedek* of *Shalem*" therefore describes the Messiah and his coming reign. It means, "My king is righteous (or just)" or "king of righteousness (or justice)." Add to this the names Yeshua ("Salvation") and *Mashiach* ("Anointed One") and a picture emerges of a divinely appointed Savior who will rule as a just and righteous king in the city of peace (Jerusalem).

> "You [Yeshua] are a *cohen* [priest] forever, to be compared with Malki-Tzedek." (Heb. 5:6; JNT page 299, Ps. 110:4)

A priesthood of believers. In the first letter of Peter in the New Testament, the title "royal priesthood" is used to describe Yeshua's followers:

> But you are a chosen people, a royal priesthood, a holy nation, a people belonging to God, that you may declare the praises of him who called you out of darkness into his wonderful light. (1 Peter 2:9)

The role of the New Covenant priesthood would be more universal than that of the Levitical priesthood. They would bear witness to Yeshua, not only among the Israelites, but throughout the world. They would care for God's people among the nations of the earth; bring their needs before him in prayer; and lead millions to worship the God of Israel "in Spirit and in truth." Certain individuals were certainly acknowledged as teachers and leaders in first century messianic communities, but this early "priesthood of believers" was always corporate. *All* sincere believers were regarded as being Yeshua's *cohanim*. No individual was elevated above the rest by the adoption of such titles as "priest." Similarly, the word "saints," used frequently in more traditional translations of the Bible, referred to all believers; not to a spiritual elite. The Jewish New Testament's translation of this term as "God's people" is more appropriate.

> "[A]t the cost of blood you ransomed for God persons from every tribe, language, people and nation. You made them into a kingdom for God to rule, *cohanim* [priests] to serve him; and they will rule over the earth." (Rev. 5:9–10; JNT page 339)

A treasured possession. Abraham was singled out to become the founding father of a holy *nation*; a nation that would become God's treasured possession. Add to this the allusion to the Gentiles—"all people"—in the making of the Abrahamic covenant, and a larger picture comes into focus:

> The Lord your God has chosen you out of all the peoples on the face of the earth to be his people, his treasured possession. (Deut. 7:6)

"[A]ll peoples on earth will be blessed through you." (Gen. 12:3)

Because Yeshua is viewed as the eternal high priest of the New Covenant, the stones of the breastplate, worn "across the heart" of the high priest, may be linked to his priestly ministry. As with Joseph's richly ornamented robe, they can be seen to symbolize the cultural *variety* of God's people: Jews and Gentiles drawn from a multitude of nations, all of great worth—like precious jewels. In the breastplate drawing on page 116, images of multi-cultural believers illustrate the inestimable value of God's people in his eyes; as do the twelve terms of endearment. (Italics added by author.)

Biblical Covenants

After the Israelites' exodus from Egypt, God renewed the covenant he'd made with Abraham. At Mt. Sinai it was expanded to become deeper and more meaningful, however. Many centuries later, in approximately 30 A.D., a new covenant was established between God and *all* of humanity. This was the New Covenant. The Abrahamic, Sinai, and New Covenants tower above all other biblical covenants.

Five Major Covenants

1. God promised Noah that the earth would never be flooded again. He set his rainbow in the sky as a sign of this covenant.
2. God promised the land of Canaan to Abraham and his descendants. Sacrificial offerings, a change of names, and the performance of circumcision affirmed this covenant.

"Leave your country, your people and your father's household and go to the land I will show you. I will make you into a great nation and I will bless you; I will make your name great, and you will be a blessing. I will bless those who bless you, and whoever curses you I will curse; and all peoples on earth will be blessed through you." (Gen. 12:1–3)

3. At Sinai God called the Israelites to be a nation demonstrating allegiance to him alone. He would be their God and they his people. His presence among them in the Tabernacle ratified this agreement.
4. God promised David that his royal line would endure forever. The Messiah would come from David's line. The Jews continue this royal line to this day.
5. God promised the Israelites that he would establish a new covenant with them: "I will put my law in their minds and write it on their hearts. . . " (Jer. 31:33). The entire New Testament (*Brit Khadashah*) points to Yeshua as the Jewish Messiah. It traces the transition from obedience to an externally imposed set of laws, the Mosaic Law, to obedience to the teachings of Yeshua through the promptings of the Spirit.

A covenant, or *brit*, is a binding contract made between two parties; both of which accept the terms of the agreement. In the Scriptures, God alone determines the requirements and individuals are beneficiaries in so far as they adhere to them. Most biblical covenants therefore took the form of one-sided decrees given by God, with his people agreeing to the conditions. From the beginning, the God of Israel also granted humanity the gift of free will.

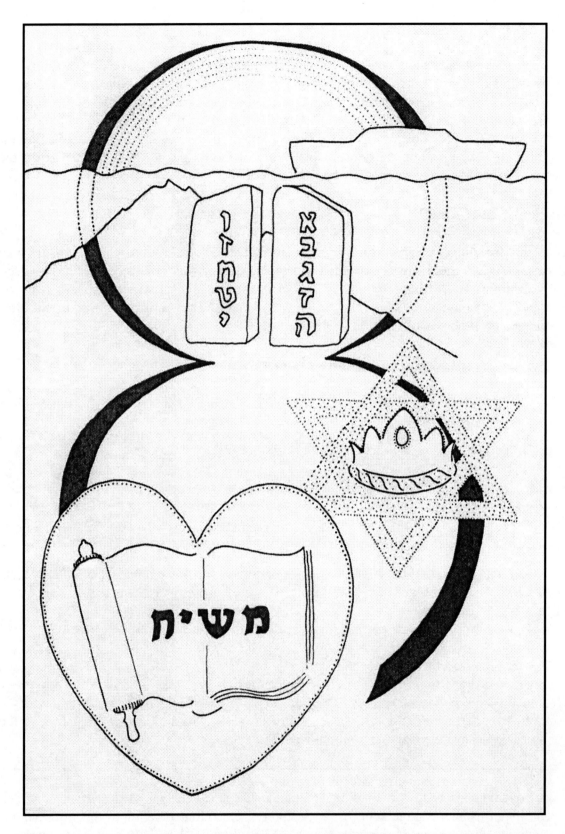

Figure 29: Images of biblical covenants that relate to Noah, Moses, King David, and Yeshua. The ten Hebrew numerals on the tablets of the Law represent the Ten Commandments, and the Hebrew letters on the scroll and Bible image read "*Mashiach*," meaning "Messiah"

The series of divine contracts made with the Israelites were an expression of God's *love* for them. Those "covenants" have served as anchors and signposts for his people throughout the ages; providing a sense of direction and purpose, and also encouragement during times of hardship. Moses was God's mediator in initiating and establishing the Sinai Covenant—the most all-embracing covenant of the *Tanakh* (OT)—but the New Covenant, or *Brit Khadashah*, was made without mankind's participation. The deliverance from a weak and imperfect nature was outside of humanity's jurisdiction.

Covenant Blood

In ancient times, a solemn agreement, or covenant, was often sealed in a ritual act that involved the shedding of the life-blood of animals. The animals were sometimes slaughtered and cut in half, and the pieces laid side-by-side. The two parties then proceeded to walk between the pieces, describing a figure eight, until they met in the center. There they recited and confirmed the terms of their agreement. In this book, a figure 8 therefore appears in several drawings that relate to covenants.

The killing and dissection of animals indicated that the penalty for breaking the agreement was death. In ancient times, God was always regarded as being the chief witness in solemnizing these binding agreements. Abraham was put to sleep while the Abrahamic Covenant was being made; the divine granting of the land was entirely beyond his control. Notice how the parts of the sacrificed animals were positioned.

> "Bring me a heifer, a goat and a ram, each three years old, along with a dove and a young pigeon. Abram brought all these to him, cut them in two and arranged the halves opposite each other. . . . As the sun was setting, Abram fell into a deep sleep and a thick and dreadful darkness came over him. When the sun had set and darkness had fallen, a smoking firepot with a blazing torch appeared and passed between the pieces. On that day the Lord made a covenant with Abram and said, "To your descendants I give this land, from the river of Egypt to the great river, the Euphrates. . . ." (Gen. 15:9–18)

In the making of the Abrahamic, Sinai, and New Covenants the shedding of blood was crucial. The first two were sealed with the blood of animals. The latter was sealed with the blood of the "Lamb of God"; the Messiah.

> Then he [Moses] took the Book of the Covenant and read it to the people. They responded, "We will do everything the Lord [*Y-H-V-H*] has said; we will obey." Moses then took the blood, sprinkled it on the people and said, "This is the blood of the covenant that the Lord [*Y-H-V-H*] has made with you in accordance with all these words." (Exod. 24:7–8)

> For if sprinkling ceremonially unclean persons with the blood of goats and bulls and the ashes of a heifer restores their outward purity; then how much more the blood of the Messiah, who, through the eternal Spirit, offered himself to God as a sacrifice without blemish, will purify our conscience from works that lead to death, so that we can serve the living God! (Heb. 9:13–14; JNT page 303)

Circumcision

The Abrahamic covenant was also marked by a change of names—*Avram* became *Avraham*, *Sarai* became *Sarah*—and by the act of circumcision. Abraham was instructed that *every* male in his household had to be circumcised as a sign of this covenant.

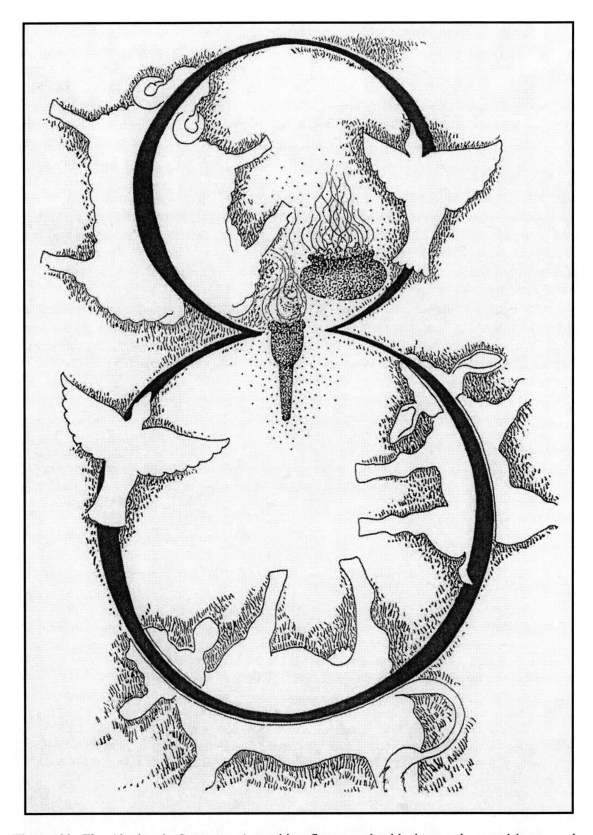

Figure 30: The Abrahamic Covenant. A smoking firepot and a blazing torch passed between the pieces, signifying the presence and approval of God

The ritual of circumcision often featured in ancient initiation rites; it signaled the entry of a male child into adulthood. With the Israelites it was different. Because they were set apart to be the people of God, circumcision was an outward mark of ownership. It was the sign that they belonged to *Y-H-V-H*; that they were people with whom he'd made an exclusive contract. To this day male Jewish babies are circumcised on the eighth day after birth in a special ceremony known as the *Brit Milah*, or "Covenant of Circumcision." The removal of the foreskin indicates that the child is a descendant of Abraham, a member of the Hebrew race.

> "Every male among you shall be circumcised. You are to undergo circumcision, and it will be the sign of the covenant between me and you." (Gen. 17:10–11)

Circumcision: Abraham, Moses, and Yeshua

With Abraham, physical circumcision was the outward sign that a man was set apart and consecrated to God. At Sinai the Israelites were further "circumcised" by the Law; a code of conduct that "circumcised their hearts," effectively removing their old pagan ways.

> "The Lord your God will circumcise your hearts and the hearts of your descendants, so that you may love him with all your heart and with all your soul, and live." (Deut. 30:6)

Early in the first century A.D., this same God went one step further. By means of a powerful offering—a *korban*—he resolved the problem of sin once and for all when he sacrificed his son. Fifty days later, at the Feast of *Shavu'ot* (Pentecost), God's people were "circumcised" not only by the Law, but by his Spirit. "He put his law in their minds and wrote it on their hearts." The old inner life, like a worthless foreskin, was replaced by the priceless holy things of God. This *inner* transformation became the confirmation that a person belonged to God.

> "The time is coming," declares the Lord, "when I will make a new covenant with the house of Israel and with the house of Judah. It will not be like the covenant I made with their fore-fathers when I took them by the hand to lead them out of Egypt, because they broke my covenant, though I was a husband to them. . . . I will put my law in their minds and write it on their hearts. I will be their God, and they will be my people. No longer will a man teach his neighbor, or a man his brother, saying, 'Know the Lord,' because they will all know me, from the least of them to the greatest." . . . "For I will forgive their wickedness and will remember their sins no more." (Jer. 31:31–34)

Three types of circumcision are therefore associated with the three most significant covenants. With Abraham, it was the physical circumcision of all Hebrew males. At Sinai, it was behavioral circumcision by means of an outwardly imposed set of laws. On the day of Pentecost, it was the spiritual circumcision of the old carnal life.

Fire, Smoke, and Darkness

In the Scriptures, fire, smoke, and darkness are often associated with the presence and approval of God—and with the establishment of major covenants. *Y-H-V-H* sent fire to consume the offering on Elijah's altar. In Midian, God spoke to Moses from a *burning* bush. A smoking firepot and a blazing torch "in the thick and dreadful darkness" confirmed his presence in the making of the Abrahamic covenant. Fire, smoke, and darkness on Mt. Sinai indicated that God was there. The cloud by day and pillar of fire over the Tabernacle each night confirmed that he was among them in the wilderness camp.

The New Testament records that an unnatural *darkness* fell over the land of Palestine as Yeshua Messiah underwent his crucifixion. On the day of Pentecost, as the first New Covenant believers were anointed with God's Spirit, tongues of *fire* appeared above their heads.

> The people remained at a distance, while Moses approached the thick darkness where God was. (Exod. 20:21)

> To the Israelites the glory of the Lord [*Y-H-V-H*] looked like a consuming fire on top of the mountain. Then Moses entered the cloud as he went up on the mountain. (Exod. 24:17–18)

> It was now about the sixth hour, and darkness came over the whole land until the ninth hour, for the sun stopped shining. (Luke 23:44)

> Then they saw what looked like tongues of fire, which separated and came to rest on each one of them. They were all filled with the *Ruach HaKodesh* [Holy Spirit] and began to talk in different languages, as the Spirit enabled them to speak. (Acts 2:3–4; JNT page 154)

> The God who answers by fire—he is God. (1 Kings 18:24)

The Terms "Old Covenant" and "New Covenant"

In the Book of Jeremiah, God promised to make a "new covenant" and not a "new testament" with his people. The term "testament" is derived from a Greek word meaning either covenant or testament—as in a last will and testament. "New Testament" would therefore have been more accurately translated as "New Covenant"; the former does not reflect the promise made to God's people through the prophet Jeremiah. The Hebrew term *Brit Khadashah*, on the other hand, actually *means* "New Covenant." It is therefore self-explanatory. Similarly, "Old Covenant," as opposed to "Old Testament," would have been a more appropriate equivalent for the Hebrew *Tanakh*—although we should be sensitive to the fact that Jews dislike the term "Old Testament." For them it is not "old" or irrelevant. It is revered as a series of holy writings given to their nation by the God of Israel.

The term "*Tanakh*" is an acronym—a combination of the first letters of several words, thereby forming a new word. Tanakh is derived from three words: *Torah* (Teaching), *Nevi'im* (Prophets), and *K'tuvim* (Writings).

Figure 31: (opposite) "Heart circumcision," showing the *barzel*, a traditional Jewish instrument of circumcision. The top section relates to infant circumcision, the lower section to the Mosaic Law and New Covenant spiritual circumcision

The Mosaic Law

After their prolonged sojourn in ancient Egypt, the Israelites needed to be welded into a self-respecting nation and to be reintroduced to the very concept of monotheism itself. They had grown far too accustomed to the Egyptian worldview and to idols such as the golden calf. The Jewish *Tanakh* (OT) teaches that there is one Almighty God who is both creator and ruler of the universe, and that he revealed himself to the nations of the earth through the Hebrew race—because humanity did not know him. It shows that he is actively involved in the affairs of mankind and presents him as one who is merciful and constant; a *personal* God full of love, power, and wisdom. All other gods are viewed as being idols or merely figments of the imagination.

In the first five books of the Bible—known as the Pentateuch, Five Books of Moses, or the *Torah*—we learn that God made himself known to the Israelites and supplied them with a moral code of conduct. No distinction was made between civil and sacred laws: *Y-H-V-H* governed every aspect of their lives. He was their God, King, Captain, and Lawgiver. He directed their religious practices, social conduct, health, and hygiene.

The Law, strongly associated with Moses and Mt. Sinai, was, in essence, the method by which an extraordinary agreement was fulfilled. The Covenant of Sinai set the Hebrews apart from other nations to become God's "treasured possession," "a people belonging to him." The Law served as *Y-H-V-H*'s chisel and mallet in the sculpting of his "holy nation."

> "You yourselves have seen what I did to Egypt, and how I carried you on eagles' wings and brought you to myself. Now if you obey me fully and keep my covenant, then out of all nations you will be my treasured possession. Although the whole earth is mine, you will be for me a kingdom of priests and a holy nation." (Exod. 19:4–6)

The Hebrew term *kadosh*, or "holiness," means "setting apart." The tribes were commanded to separate themselves from the practices of their polytheistic neighbors and were severely admonished when they indulged in pagan divinatory practices. Sorcery, mysticism, and necromancy—consulting the spirits of the dead—were strictly prohibited. Their religious practices also did not include orgies, prostitution, fertility rites or human sacrifice. To this day, according to the Judeo-Christian worldview, spiritism, astrology, tarot-card, and palm reading constitute corrupt substitutes and untrustworthy alternatives to reliance on the Almighty God. We read in Deuteronomy 18:9–12 that such things are an "abomination" to the Lord.

The Law served to protect, discipline, and unite the nation. But its principles were so ethically sound that they led to a state of moral refinement that was unprecedented in the ancient Middle East. The Mosaic Law was exceptionally pure and just—and more beneficial to the Israelites than they could possibly have realized.

The Ten Commandments

In the ancient world, at the time of the Exodus, stone tablets measuring approximately 12 x 18 inches were frequently used for royal, commemorative, legal or religious texts. It could have been tablets similar to these on which the Ten Commandments (*'Aseret HaDibrot*) were "written with the finger of God."

These ten divine commands were based on the principles of loving and respecting both

God and one's neighbor. The first four related to the Israelites' relationship with their God; the last six, to their relationships with each other. They were later summarized by Yeshua in the following words:

"Love the Lord your God with all your heart, and with all your soul and with all your mind" . . . [and] . . . "Love your neighbor as yourself." (Matt. 22:37 and 39)

To the ancient Israelites, the concept of "religion," as we know it, would have been quite foreign. They saw each individual as a single entity and did not distinguish between the body, mind, and soul, as most do today. They believed that on dying, the whole person went to *Sheol*—a resting place devoid of experience, deep within the earth—where he or she awaited resurrection. They accepted that God orchestrated all aspects of their daily lives and simply measured their conduct in terms of their obedience, or disobedience, to the laws they'd been given.

The Law provided a sense of security and well-being. Because it was so very *exacting*, it also humbled individuals by exposing the moral weaknesses of human nature; highlighting the need for compensating for improper conduct. Because a state of holiness was, and still is, the ultimate aim in God's plan for his people, and because this cannot be achieved by an individual's own efforts, a system of sacrifice had to be provided.

The Ten Commandments

1. You shall have no other gods before me.
2. You shall not make for yourself an idol in the form of anything in heaven above or on the earth beneath and in the waters below.
3. You shall not misuse the name of the Lord your God.
4. Remember the Sabbath day by keeping it holy. Six days you shall labor and do all your work, but the seventh day is a Sabbath to the Lord your God.
5. Honor your father and your mother.
6. You shall not murder.
7. You shall not commit adultery.
8. You shall not steal.
9. You shall not give false testimony against your neighbor.
10. You shall not covet [desire, lust for] your neighbor's house . . . wife . . . manservant or maidservant . . . ox or donkey . . . or anything that belongs to your neighbor. (Exod. 20:1-17)

The Jewish *Torah*

For religious, non-Messianic Jews, the Sinai Covenant and Mosaic Law are still paramount. In studying Judaism, we are therefore able to obtain a sense of the ancient Hebrew worldview. The following information relating to the Jewish *Torah*, their traditional religious attire, symbols of the Sabbath, and ancient food laws, reflects something of the mindset of the original tribes of Israel.

Torah can be loosely translated into English as "instruction" or "teachings." It includes not only the Ten Commandments, or Decalogue, but information relating to creation, pre-

Hebrew history, the patriarchs, the Hebrew feasts, priestly offerings, the Sabbath, and legal matters in general.

From the time of the Babylonian exile in the sixth century B.C., synagogues were built by Jews in major centers. One of the most precious symbols of Judaism, the *Torah* scroll, was central to synagogue worship and remains so to this day. These scrolls are considered to be sacred objects and are treated with utmost respect; having pride of place in each synagogue in a special cabinet called the "Holy Ark." As the Hebrew words are read from right to left, a pointer—in the shape of a small hand—is used, in order avoid physical contact with the surface of the scroll. This pointer is known as a "*yad*," meaning "hand." When making a new scroll, each one is meticulously copied by a trained scribe with a quill pen and specially prepared ink. On completion, it is rolled onto two pins. During synagogue services the scroll is rolled back, from the end of Deuteronomy to the beginning of Genesis, on the last day of each sacred year. This ceremony is known as "*Simkhat Torah*"—"The Rejoicing of the *Torah*."

Much discussion as to the meaning of the words of the *Torah* took place among rabbis over several centuries. Their findings were compiled into holy books called the *Mishna*, or Rabbinic Law (interpretations of the Law); and the *Talmud*, meaning "to study" (commentaries on the *Mishna*). The *Tanakh*, on the other hand, is the name given to the complete Hebrew Bible (the Old Testament). It is a record of Israelite history, extending from the creation account to the sixth century B.C.

The *Torah* scroll is important in various other contexts. It is studied by Jewish children from an early age and, on the occasion of a thirteen year old boy's birthday, he becomes *bar mitzvah*; "a son of the commandment." A Jewish girl, on the other hand, becomes *bat mitzvah*, "a daughter of the commandment," on her twelfth or thirteenth birthday. On the Sabbath following their birthdays, the *Torah* is read by these young Jews—always by the boys, not always by the girls—signifying their graduation into adulthood and their acceptance of personal responsibility in following God's Law.

Jewish phylacteries contain excerpts from the *Torah* (Deut. 6:8, 11:18; Exod. 13:9, 13:16). These small boxes, called *t'fillin*, are strapped to both the forearms—upper left arm, "near the heart"—and foreheads of Orthodox Jews during times of prayer. This ritual is performed on all days, except for the Sabbath and Jewish holidays. The word *t'fillin* is derived from the Hebrew word for prayer: "*t'fillah*." Another ritual object, the *mezuzah*, meaning "doorpost," also contains verses from the *Torah* (Deut. 6:4–9, 11:13–21). It is often seen on Jewish doorposts. On the back, the Hebrew letter "*shin*" is visible through a small slit. It stands for *Shaddai*, meaning "Guardian of the doors of Israel."

In these ways Jews bind themselves to God: The *Torah* is strapped to their bodies, fastened to their entrance doors, and read on a regular basis—"lest they should forget" to honor the God of Israel.

> Tie them as symbols on your hands and bind them on your foreheads. Write them on the doorframes of your houses and on your gates. (Deut. 6:8–9)

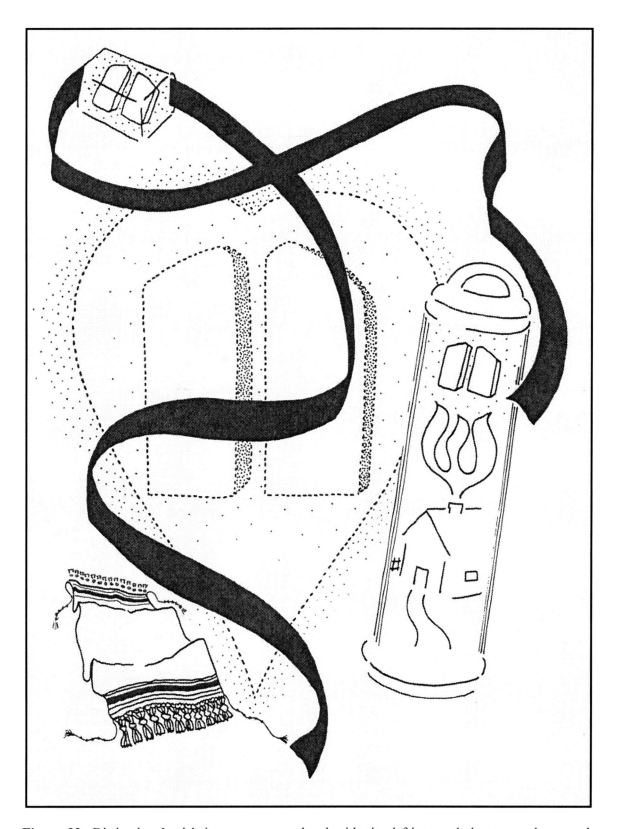

Figure 32: Distinctive Jewish images: prayer shawl with ritual fringes, phylactery, and *mezuzah*. The stone tablets represent the laws of the *Torah*

Shabbat—the Jewish Sabbath

The keeping of the Saturday *Shabbat* in obedience to the fourth commandment remains the most important holy day in the lives of observant Jews. In their homes, the symbols of *Shabbat* include a wine goblet, two loaves of fine white *khallah* bread, straight and braided candles, and a spice box.

The straight candles are lit by the mother of the household each Friday evening in order to "welcome the Sabbath." The two loaves relate to the double portion of manna collected before the Sabbath during the wilderness period. The aroma of spices delights family members as they have delighted in the Sabbath. The double wicked and braided *Havdalah* candle symbolizes the separation of the six week-days from the seventh day of rest.

During times of morning worship, rabbis, cantors, and many Jewish worshipers wear skull caps (Hebrew: *kippah*; Yiddish: *yarmulka*) and a prayer shawl, or *talit*, in obedience to God's command in Numbers (15:37–39). Orthodox Jews go so far as to wear a small talit (*talit katan*) as an undergarment on a daily basis.

> Throughout the generations to come you are to make tassels on the corners of your garments, with a blue cord on each tassel. You will have these tassels to look at and so you will remember all the commands of the Lord, that you may obey them and not prostitute yourselves by going after the lusts of your own hearts and eyes. (Num. 15:37–39)

The most important features on the *talit* are the *tzitziyot* or ritual fringes. These are made with four long white cords that are passed through holes at the corners of the shawl and then knotted together. Traditionally, each white *tzitzit* (fringe) had to contain one blue strand—white symbolizing purity and blue symbolizing heaven—but this is no longer required. A Jew's *talit* accompanies him throughout his life and, in the end, often becomes his burial shroud. Although women are not specifically barred from wearing a *talit*, they are usually worn only by the men. Many Messianic Jews have retained the use of this attire in worship.

The blue and white striped Israeli flag is based on the design of the Jewish *talit*.

Mosaic Food Laws

The ancient Mosaic laws relating to diet reveal the mind of an all-wise Creator. Many Jews still comply with these kosher, or *kasher*, food laws today. A "clean" mammal is one that chews the cud and is cloven-hoofed. A "clean" fish has scales and fins—no scavenging crustaceans. All birds of prey, reptiles, and rodents are considered to be "unclean." The only "clean" insects, according to Mosaic Law, are those from the grasshopper family. The humane *kasher* slaughter of meat is also still enforced: animals have to be slit at the throat, completely drained of blood, and stripped of fat. Other more specific laws relate to the prohibition of the combination of meat (excluding fish) and dairy products; and eating the sinews of the thigh of an animal. The latter relates to the injury Jacob sustained while wrestling with the angel on the banks of the River Jabbok. (Gen. 32:32). Jewish kosher kitchens feature several sets of cookware, crockery, and cutlery in order to fully comply with the requirements of the Law.

> "You must not eat any fat or any blood." (Lev. 3:17) "Do not cook a young goat in its mother's milk." (Exod. 34:26)

Eating scavenging creatures, such as crustaceans, often results in food-poisoning. The pig, another scavenger, carries several parasites that are harmful to humans. To this day, Jews are also careful not to eat the meat of any diseased or injured animals.

Laws relating to washing and quarantine served to prevent the spread of bacteria and disease among the Israelites. Only in the last century, with giant strides made in the medical field, have these laws proven to be necessary prerequisites to a society's physical health. We are now also well aware of the problems that are caused by disease-carrying animals, such as rats and predatory birds—Jews were persecuted during the period of Europe's bubonic plague in the fourteenth century, because their strict compliance with the Mosaic health laws halted the spread of the disease among them.

At this point in history, it is abundantly clear that many of these laws correlate directly with the principles that govern nature itself; making them beneficial to all individuals at any time. The ancient Israelites did not have scientists to educate and guide them in these matters. They had a more reliable authority—the Creator of the natural order.

The "Jewishness" of the Christian Savior

The *Tanakh* (OT) is principally the story of the Israelites and the *Brit Khadashah* (NT), written by Jews, focuses on a Jewish Messiah. Furthermore, the Scriptures clearly state that "Salvation is from the Jews" (John 4:22) and that the New Testament was written "first for the Jew, then for the Gentile" (Rom. 1:16). The fundamental concepts of a messiah, a vicarious sacrificial atonement, the Passover, and water-baptism, are all distinctly Hebrew. It is therefore appropriate that gentile believers come to terms with the "Jewishness" of their Savior. In the following description, Hebrew words will appear first, with their English equivalents in parenthesis, in order to emphasize this cultural legacy.

The Messiah was a descendant of *David* and *Shlomoh* (Solomon), the Hebrew kings of Judah. He was born in *Bet-Lekhem* (Bethlehem), in the land promised to the *'Ivrim* (Hebrews). He died in the Jewish capital of *Yerushalayim* (Jerusalem).

As a newborn, he was circumcised on the eighth day (his *Brit Milah*) and given a Hebrew name; "Yeshua." As required by the *Torah* (Mosaic Law), after thirty-three days he was presented at the Temple and an offering of a pair of doves or two young pigeons was made—because he was *Miryam's* (Mary's) firstborn son.

During his boyhood, Yeshua would have attended the local synagogue school in *Natzrat* (Nazareth) where, in order to study the Scriptures, he would have learned to read (but not necessarily *write*) in *'Ivrit* (Hebrew). At age thirteen, he would have become *bar mitzvah*—"a son of the covenant." On that occasion, he would have read publicly (right to left) from a *Torah* scroll.

While growing up, his family would have "welcomed *Shabbat*" (the Sabbath) each Friday evening. On the following morning, led by the *rav* (rabbi), he would have worshipped *Adonai* (Y-H-V-H: the Lord) in the synagogue—wearing his *talit* (today a prayer shawl, but in the first century a four cornered robe) with its *tzitziyot* (ritual fringes). To him, the *Magen David* (Star of David), the twelve tribal blessing symbols, and blasts of the *shofar* (ram's horn trumpet) would have been profoundly familiar.

In keeping with Jewish tradition, Yeshua would have eaten *kasher* (kosher) food and celebrated the *mo'adim* (seven feasts of Israel) —which were regulated by Hebrew numerals

131

on a Hebrew lunar calendar. While reclining at the Passover Seder table, he would have enjoyed *matzot* (unleavened Passover bread) and Jewish *yayin* (wine) as he listened to the story of the Exodus of his ancestors from ancient Egypt. Each year, following the olive harvest, he would have made the journey to Jerusalem in order to participate in the *Yamim Nora'im* (High Holy Days) of the Jews.

In accordance with the Hebrew birthright custom, Yeshua naturally assumed leadership of his family on the death of *Yosef* (Joseph), and later *Yokhanan* (John), the son of a Levitical priest, officiated at Yeshua's Jewish ritual cleansing in the river *Yarden* (Jordan) —the event that marked the commencement of his ministry.

The overwhelming majority of his first followers were Jewish and his twelve *talmidim* (disciples) were chosen within the context of a tradition where the number twelve had always been associated with God's earthly government. And let us not forget that the greatest of his emissaries was *Sha'ul* (Paul), who was originally a Jewish *Parush* (Pharisee).

At the wedding in *Kanah* (Cana), before turning water into good Jewish wine, he presumably witnessed the marriage ceremony of a Jewish bridegroom and his bejeweled bride, under their Jewish *khuppah* (wedding canopy). Yeshua might even have joined in a traditional Jewish circle dance—like the *Horah*—to the animated rhythms of ancient Hebrew melodies.

He frequently taught at the Jewish Temple with its altars, laver, showbread, and *menorah* and, as the Son of God, performed astounding miracles and spoke with absolute authority. But the Scriptures record that he also often exhibited the *khutzpah* (audacity) —from the perspective of the religious authorities'—sharp wit, and tenacious vigor of a Galilean Jew.

Messianic Believers and the Law

For Messianic believers, the New Testament is the fulfillment of all that preceded it and is the most important, all encompassing covenant. Although they acknowledge that "faith without works is dead" (James 2:17), they tend to rely more on the internal promptings of the Spirit than on legalistic compliance with an externally imposed set of laws. Messianic Jews certainly trust in the guidance of God's Word for their salvation; but for them, the atoning work of the Messiah and the undeserved favor of a merciful God are paramount.

> "For it is by grace you have been saved, through faith—and this not from yourselves, it is the gift of God—not by works, so that no one can boast." (Eph. 2:8–9)

We should note that Yeshua showed utmost respect for the Mosaic Law at all times and that the Scriptures clearly indicate that he came not to abolish them, but to complete them. He took these laws to a far deeper level, however; encouraging his followers to obey the *spirit* rather than the letter of the Law. He stated, for example, that we violate the law against killing when we hate our fellowman; and that we commit adultery in our hearts when we harbor lustful thoughts. He promoted ideals of love and peace, and the abandonment of self-righteousness and self-centeredness. The Law was used as the basis for all of his teachings.

> "You have heard that our fathers were told, 'Eye for eye and tooth for tooth.' But I tell you not to stand up against someone who does you wrong. On the contrary, if someone hits you on the right cheek, let him hit you on the left cheek too!' " (Matt. 5:38–39; JNT page 7)

132

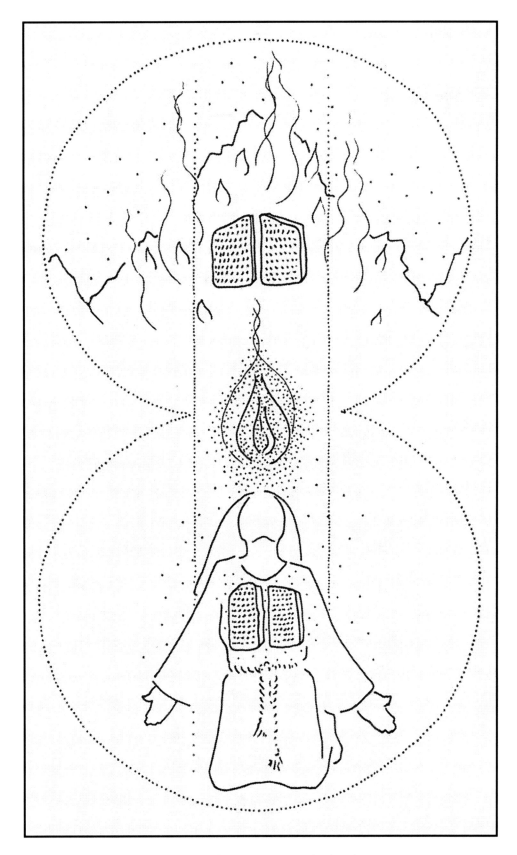

Figure 33: Fire and the Law on Mt. Sinai and at Pentecost

"You have heard that our fathers were told, 'Love your neighbor—and hate your enemy.' But I tell you, love your enemies! Pray for those who persecute you! Then you will become children of your Father in heaven." (Matt. 5:43–45; JNT page 7)

The moral principles at the heart of the Law remain absolute for New Covenant believers. And the Ten Commandments will forever retain their power; simply because they are so good, so sound, so absolutely right. But the New Covenant goes one step further. It offers mankind an everlasting atoning sacrifice and the unprecedented assurance of present and eternal reconciliation with the Ruler of the Universe—our *Ribbon Ha'Olam*—through his son.

"Take my yoke upon you and learn from me, because I am gentle and humble in heart, and you will find rest for your souls. For my yoke is easy, and my burden is light." (Matt. 11: 29–30; JNT page 16)

Stones and Clay

We will now examine the use of stone and clay as symbolic images in the Scriptures. Because of its association with permanence and eternity, stone is strongly associated with the God of the Bible and with his kingdom. Clay is associated with "malleable" humanity.

In the second chapter of Daniel, an image appears that is seldom emphasized. When this prophet interpreted King Nebuchadnezzar's dream, he indicated that the different materials comprising the statue in the king's dream represented powerful kingdoms that would rule the earth. The giant *stone* that struck and destroyed this statue, becoming a huge mountain that filled the earth, heralded the establishment of an eternal kingdom that would crush and supersede all previous manmade kingdoms (verses 24 to 45). The permanence of God's kingdom was exemplified in an image of stone.

"In the time of those kings, the God of heaven will set up a kingdom that will never be destroyed. . . . It will crush all those kingdoms and bring them to an end, but it will itself endure forever." (Dan. 2:44)

The foundations of this "Stone Kingdom" are recorded in the *Tanakh* (OT): The twelve tribes worshipped the Almighty One—the "Stone of Israel" (Gen. 49:24). His irrevocable and eternal commandments, inscribed on stone tablets, remain absolute—"written in stone" (Exod. 20:1–17; Josh. 8:30–35). This "holy nation" was represented by means of a dozen gemstones (*even tovah*) on the high priest's breastplate. The Israelites set up piles of twelve river stones that memorialized important events in the Lord's dealings with them (Exod. 24:4; Josh. 4:1–9).

When the whole nation had finished crossing the Jordan, the Lord said to Joshua, "Choose twelve men from among the people, one from each tribe, and tell them to take up twelve stones from the middle of the Jordan." . . . These stones are to be a memorial to the people of Israel forever. (Josh. 4:1–3 and 9)

Figure 34: Images of stone in the *Tanakh* (OT): the tablets of the Law, the breastplate, and a monument comprised of twelve river stones

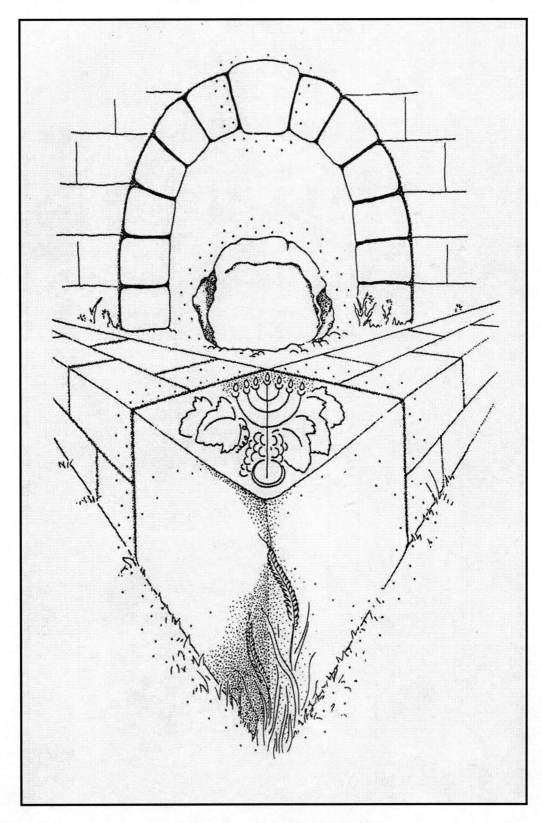

Figure 35: Stones as symbols of Yeshua: A capstone or keystone (upper-most), a stumbling stone (middle), and a cornerstone (lower)

But his bow remained steady, his strong arms stayed limber, because of the hand of the Mighty One of Jacob, because of the Shepherd, the Rock [or Stone] of Israel. . . . (Gen. 49:24)

The Lord said to Moses, "Come up to me on the mountain and stay here, and I will give you the tablets of stone, with the law and commands I have written for their instruction." (Exod. 24:12)

The New Testament records that Yeshua built on those ancient Hebrew foundations. His people, the "living stones" (1 Peter 2:4–5) are held in place by the Messiah: the great "cornerstone," "the stone the builders rejected," "the capstone," and "stumbling stone." But God's kingdom will only be fully established once Yeshua has returned to govern his people from Jerusalem, the city of golden stone.

A Cornerstone

The chief cornerstone (*even pinnah*) is a massive foundation stone that anchors one corner of a new building in place. It binds together two or more courses of building stones, giving great strength and permanence to the entire structure. This was certainly an appropriate symbol for the Messiah. Once in place as the great foundation stone of the New Covenant, his presence became the source of his people's staying power and strength.

You have built on the foundation of the emissaries [apostles] and the prophets, with the cornerstone being Yeshua the Messiah himself. In union with him, the whole building is held together, and it is growing into a holy temple in union with the Lord. Yes, in union with him, you yourselves are being built together into a spiritual dwelling-place for God! (Eph. 2:20–22; JNT page 259)

The Messiah, the "rock of our salvation," finished his atoning work in Zion (*Tziyon*). ("Zion," the name of the ancient Jebusite fortress captured by King David, later became Jerusalem, his capital city.) In the eighth century B.C., several centuries before the birth of the Messiah, Isaiah, one of the four major prophets, wrote the following words relating to "a precious cornerstone" laid in Jerusalem:

See, I lay a stone in Zion, a tested stone, a precious cornerstone for a sure foundation; the one who trusts will never be dismayed. (Isa. 28:16)

The Stone the Builders Rejected

The stones used in the construction of Solomon's Temple were prepared *away* from the building site, so that the noise of the iron tools did not disturb this sacred precinct. They were only positioned once they had been perfected. In the same way, the rejected Messiah underwent his brutal crucifixion *outside* of the ancient city gates of Jerusalem. Like this most valuable of stones, quarried by God himself, the followers of Yeshua are also prepared for service and then, at the appointed time, positioned by God to commence their designated work.

A Capstone and Keystone

The writers of the *Tanakh* (OT) envisaged the capstone as a large horizontal slab that was placed on top of a stone structure, serving to complete and unify the whole. The word *capstone* is also sometimes used with reference to the central keystone of a Roman arch, however. Early Jewish believers would have been familiar with the Roman building methods of the time and might very well have linked the word *capstone* to the image of a keystone.

Roman arches were made up of wedge-shaped stones that were locked together by the last stone to be put into place; the large, central keystone. This was the most essential component of an arch. It prevented the arch from collapsing once the temporary wooden supports had been removed. Although the Jewish authorities of the time failed to recognize him, Yeshua the Messiah, like a central keystone, was the *last* and most *essential* "stone" to be lovingly positioned by God. He fulfilled and completed all that had preceded him. "The stone the builders rejected" became the quintessential cornerstone, capstone, and keystone of the new order.

> The stone the builders rejected has become the capstone; the Lord has done this, and it is marvelous in our eyes. (Ps. 118:22)

A Stumbling Stone

This stone symbol is different. Here we find the image of a common stumbling stone (*even negef*); an object that would be passed by unnoticed, if it didn't constitute such a hindrance to the-man-in-the-street. This common stumbling stone relates to Yeshua's humanity.

> The Word became a human being and lived with us, and we saw his *Sh'khinah* [Glory], the *Sh'khinah* of the Father's only Son, full of grace and truth. (John 1:14; JNT page 118)

He was a man, but was no ordinary man. The circumstances surrounding his birth were extraordinary. His life, the fulfillment of numerous messianic prophecies in the Hebrew Scriptures, was extraordinary. His death, resurrection, and ascension were extraordinary. Yeshua also cannot be regarded merely as a prophet or great teacher. His miracles and teachings do not leave us with that option. His "I Am" statements, found in the Gospel of John, left no doubt in the minds of Jewish teachers that he was claiming equality with Almighty God.

> "I tell you the truth" . . . "before Abraham was born I am!" (8:58) . . . "I am the bread of life." (6:48) . . . "I am the light of the world." (8:12) . . . "I am the good shepherd." (10:11) . . . "I am the resurrection and the life." (11:25) . . . "I am the way and the truth and the life." (14:6) . . . "I am the true vine and my Father is the gardener."(15:1)

Yeshua also cannot be viewed as a man who was simply deluded. Too many supernatural occurrences confirmed and underscored his unique vocation. Yeshua cannot be ignored. He is abhorred or adored—an unavoidable stumbling stone, or an unshakable refuge in a changing world.

> [A]nd he will be a sanctuary; but for both houses of Israel he will be a stone that causes men to stumble and a rock that makes them fall. (Isa. 8:14)

Approximately forty years after Yeshua's ascension, the Temple in Jerusalem was destroyed: "Not one stone was left standing upon another." For nearly two thousand years, the poor in spirit, the broken-hearted, and those who hunger and thirst for the living God have found in this *Messiah* a sacred and precious precinct, a hiding place from the storms of life. Yeshua, the foundational cornerstone, central keystone, and finishing capstone—and his people, the "living [building] stones"—have been joined together to form a dwelling place for the Almighty. They have become the New Covenant priesthood of God's "Stone Kingdom" (Matt. 21:42; Ps. 118:22; 1 Peter 2:4).

> As you come to him, the living stone, rejected by people but chosen by God and precious to him, you yourselves, as living stones, are being built into a spiritual house to be *cohanim* [priests] set apart for God. . . . (1 Pet. 2:4–5; JNT page 317)

The Master Potter and His Clay

The Bible reveals not only the immutable nature of the God of Israel, but the malleable nature of humankind. God's people are represented as precious gemstones on the breastplate and as enduring "living stones," or building blocks, in God's Kingdom. But in the Books of Isaiah and Jeremiah, they are also portrayed as clay (*khomer*) in the hands of a master potter.

> O Lord, you are our Father. We are the clay, you are the potter; we are all the work of your hand. (Isa. 64:8)

Man's nature is clearly imperfect. Because human failings corrupt every life, and therefore every nation on Earth, it is a very unpredictable world in which we live. God's people are therefore inwardly rebuilt by his Spirit. Much like malleable clay in the hands of a potter, the old "vessel" needs to be broken down—even shattered—before it can be remodeled. In the Scriptures, this process of rebuilding is illustrated by means of the compelling image of a potter shattering and then refashioning his clay pots, as seems best to him.

> Shall what is formed say to him who formed it, "He did not make me"? Can the pot say of the potter, "He knows nothing"? (Isa. 29:16)

In the wilderness, the God of Israel disciplined and "rebuilt" the Israelites by means of the Law. Similarly, followers of Yeshua must be recreated to become precious and useful vessels in his kingdom. God therefore draws individuals to himself and then rebuilds them. His Spirit breaks down old preoccupations, attitudes, and habits—and replaces them with the "holy things of God," rejuvenating insights, and a clarity of purpose.

> "No one can come to me unless the Father who sent me draws him and I will raise him up at the last day." (John 6:44)

> When I consider your heavens, the work of your fingers, the moon and the stars, which you have set in place, what is man that you are mindful of him, the son of man that you care for him? (Ps. 8:3–4)

All sincere believers are therefore "reborn" in the sense they are given a fresh start, filled with the Spirit, and renewed in such a way as to develop their natural God-given potential.

All are prepared in some respect for the privilege of becoming productive members of God's *cohanim*—his priesthood. A recent convert all too often appears "fanatical" as this dramatic inner transformation spills over in an "unnatural" exuberance—but how momentous this time is for the newly regenerated soul.

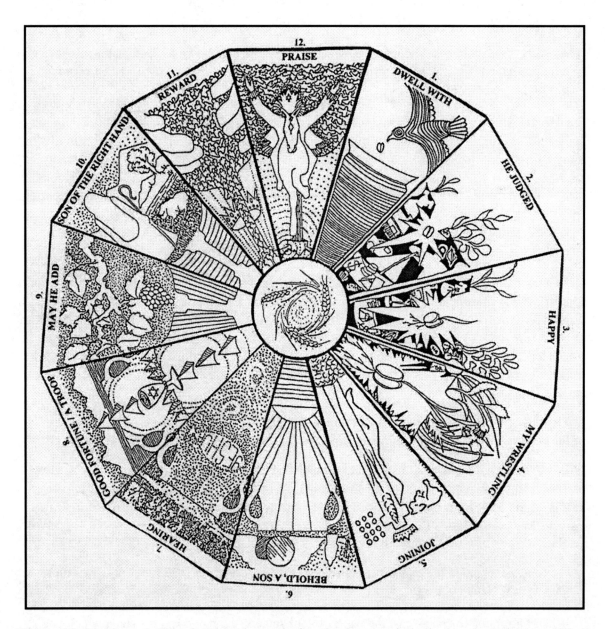

Figure 36: The Potter's Wheel. When the seed of truth takes root in believers, the Spirit proceeds to transform them from "common clay pots" into "vessels of honor"

The Potter's Wheel Prayer

Zebulun or *Z'vulun* (Dwell with):	O Lord, you are the potter I am the common clay pot You are the sower, my soul is the soil Come, dwell with me
Dan (He judged):	Let your Spirit reveal my true nature For despite my failings, you have accepted me
Asher (Happy):	May your truth take deep root Pushing aside the old useless self I long for the peace that surpasses understanding
Naphtali or *Naftali* (My wrestling):	Give me the strength to prevail As the vestiges of my old life Wrestle against your Spirit
Levi or *L'vi* (Joining):	Until my old life lies shattered At the foot of the stake And I am truly joined to you
Reuben or *Re'uven* (Behold, a son!):	I will surely rise from this death As a newly rebuilt child of God
Simeon or *Shim'on* (Hearing}:	And by your Spirit, will be given eyes to see Ears to hear
Gad (Good fortune or A troop):	During times of testing I trust that you will help and sustain me
Joseph or *Yosef* (May he add):	Transforming me into a vessel of honor Making my life increasingly fruitful
Benjamin or *Binyamin* (Son of the right hand):	And when my end comes Lord, let me rest in you
Issachar or *Yissa'khar* (Reward):	Until you gather up and reward your people
Judah or *Yehudah* (Praise}:	How we will praise you on your return O king of all nations

(Not in birth order)

141

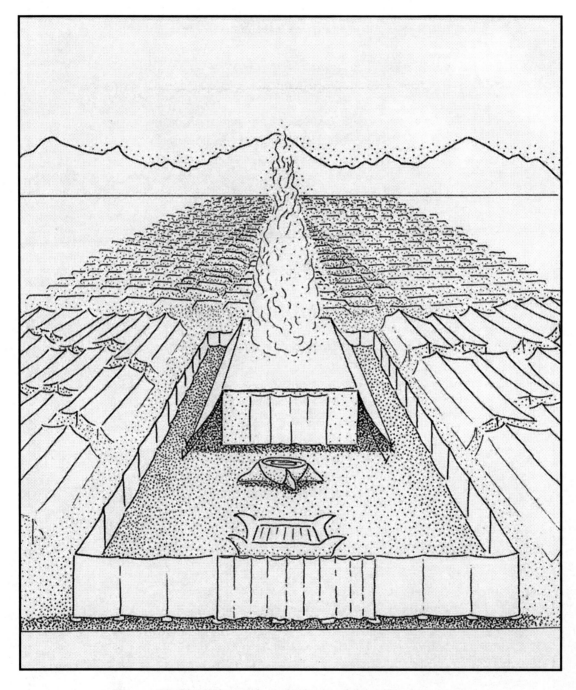

Figure 37: The Tabernacle at the heart of the wilderness camp

Part 4

The Dwelling Place

The Wilderness Camp

After 430 years, to the day, God freed his people from Egypt. He provided them with a means of crossing the Red Sea—thereby escaping Pharaoh's armies—and supplied them with food and water in the Sinai desert. The migrating Israelites soon became discontent, however. It appears that they were initially extremely disoriented.

After their extended period of slavery the tribes of Israel (*Sh'vatim Yisra'el*) needed to be welded together, given a sense of identity and worth. They also needed order and routine in their new nomadic way of life. Therefore, early in the second year after the Exodus, the Lord commanded Moses to take a census of the people and to consolidate the tribes into an efficiently organized camp. The census figures recorded in the Book of Numbers indicate that there were approximately two million Israelites at that time.

The camp would resemble a vast army compound, with the Tabernacle as its majestic headquarters—notice the use of military terms such as "Israel's army," "divisions," "standards," "banners," "rearguard," and "units" in the Book of Numbers. An aerial view might have revealed a cruciform plan, with the priestly tribe of Levi camped around the Tabernacle and the tents of the other tribes extending outward in four triad groups from the center. But in terms of the logistics of moving such a massive number of people and finding large enough sites in which to set up camp, it's more likely that they were arranged in a square or rectangular formation—as indicated in the illustration. Furthermore, the Scriptures speak of the tribes being "next to" each other, not "behind" each other.

The Levites were positioned on all four sides of the Tabernacle, forming a buffer zone between God's holy dwelling place and the encampments of the other tribes. Pride of place was given to the families of Moses and Aaron, who were situated opposite the eastern entrance to the Tabernacle enclosure. The arrangement of the rest of the tribes was designed to correspond with their marching order.

Family groups were consolidated into tribal groups, each of which was united under a tribal banner—Jewish tradition suggests that the colors of the banners correlated with the colors of the gemstones on the high priest's breastplate.

When moving, four triad tribal groups followed the standards of the four chief tribes: Judah, Reuben, Ephraim, and Dan. The royal tribe of Judah always took the lead and camped to the northeast of the Tabernacle, "toward the sunrise"; while the division of Dan formed the rearguard of this migrant nation. By this time, the descendants of Joseph were split into the two tribal groups of Ephraim and Manasseh.

> The Israelites are to camp around the Tent of Meeting some distance from it, each man under his standard with the banners of his family. (Num. 2:2)

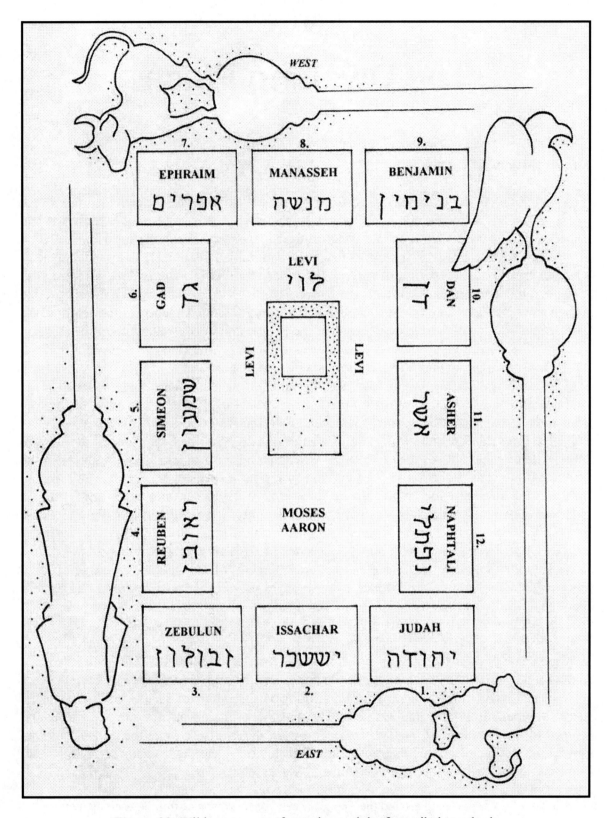

Figure 38: Wilderness camp formation and the four tribal standards

144

The Levites, however, are to set up their tents around the tabernacle of the Testimony so that wrath will not fall on the Israelite community. (Num. 1:53)

On the east, toward the sunrise, the divisions of the camp of Judah are to encamp under their standard. . . . The tribe of Issachar will camp next to them. . . . The tribe of Zebulun will be next. . . . They will set out first. (Num. 2:3–9)

On the south will be the divisions of the camp of Reuben under their standard. . . . The tribe of Simeon will camp next to them. . . . The tribe of Gad will be next. . . . They will set out second. (Num. 2:10–16)

Then the Tent of Meeting and the camp of the Levites will set out in the middle of the camps. They will set out in the same order as they encamp, each in his own place under his standard. (Num. 2:17)

On the west will be the divisions of the camp of Ephraim under their standard. . . . The tribe of Manasseh will be next to them. . . . The tribe of Benjamin will be next. . . . They will set out third. (Num. 2:18-24)

On the north will be the divisions of the camp of Dan, under their standard. . . . The tribe of Asher will camp next to them. . . . The tribe of Naphtali will be next. . . . They will set out last. (Num. 2:25–31)

The four standards, when held up high, would have been visible from a distance. They might therefore have been used as signaling devices; a means of controlling the enormous divisions more efficiently—a system later used by the Roman legions. Jewish tradition suggests that the standard of Judah bore the image of a lion; Reuben, the image of a man; Ephraim, the image of an ox; and Dan, the image of an eagle—thereby conforming with the "four living creatures" described in the Books of Ezekiel and Revelation. Although some Gentile traditions teach that these four creatures represent the Gospel writers—Matthew (man), Mark (lion), Luke (ox), and John (eagle) —Hebrew tradition indicates that they symbolize the tribes of Israel.

Each of the four had the face of a man, and on the right side each had the face of a lion, and on the left side the face of an ox; each also had the face of an eagle. (Ezek. 1:10)

The first living creature was like a lion, the second was like an ox, the third had a face like a man, the fourth was like a flying eagle. (Rev. 4:7)

Some of the most precious symbols of Judaism and the Hebrew culture were initiated during the wilderness period. Tabernacle rituals, including the celebration of the feasts, were introduced; and the hierarchy and duties of the Levitical priesthood were established. A journey through the ancient Tabernacle will therefore reveal the foundations of Judaism and, consequently, Christianity.

A Journey through the Tabernacle

Because the entire system of Israelite worship was centered in the Most Holy Place, the biblical account of the Tabernacle design begins in this small, sacred chamber with its ark and mercy seat; not with the brazen altar at the courtyard entrance. We, however, will put ourselves in the sandals of a Levite priest and begin our journey by entering the courtyard of the *Mishkan* through its eastern entrance. As we shall see, the power of biblical symbols often lies in their utter simplicity: the *fire* of the brazen altar and menorah, the *water* of the laver, the *incense* of the Holy Place altar, the *bread* of the table of showbread and the *wings* of cherubim over the Ark of the Covenant.

Mishkan: The Tabernacle

Moses was given two sets of information during his forty day meeting with God "within the cloud" on the mountain. The first was a code of conduct, written on stone tablets, which formed the basis of an effective system of government. The second was a detailed design for a place of worship. Moses' disoriented people were given *tangible* objects that would educate, inspire, and unite them.

The Hebrew word *Mishkan*, equivalent to the English term "Tabernacle," means "dwelling place." Two tabernacles are, in fact, referred to in the Scriptures. The original Tabernacle, or "Tent of Meeting" (*Ohel Mo'ed*), was a small portable tent that was situated on the outskirts of the Israelite camp. It served as a meeting place for Moses and the God of Israel, exclusively. When Moses entered this tent, a cloud (*ha'anan*), signifying the presence of God, came down and covered its entrance.

The second Tabernacle, although also a portable "tent of meeting," was very different. It was much more magnificent than the first and was situated at the heart of the wilderness camp. This birthplace of Israelite worship served as a meeting place for God and the entire community of Israel. This Tabernacle's tent "clothed" the Most Holy Place (*Kodesh Kodashim*) —God's earthly throne room—the most sacred of chambers. The Most Holy Place, in turn, contained the tablets of the Law (*Lukhot HaBrit*), the basis of God's government. It was there that Israel's high priests met with the Almighty.

The essential significance of the Tabernacle lies in the fact that the God of Israel came to dwell among his people. It would foreshadow later "holy dwelling places": the Jerusalem temples, the Messiah as the incarnation of God, and spirit-filled believers. On completion, a cloud, or dense mist—according to Josephus—covered the Tabernacle and the *Sh'khinah* glory of *Y-H-V-H* filled his "dwelling place." (Exod. 40:34–35; Lev. 16:2). When night fell, the cloud resembled a "pillar of fire" above the tent. This cloud and fire would become the means by which God would lead his people through the desert. As long as the cloud remained over the Tabernacle, the Israelites remained settled. When it lifted, they broke camp and followed it. Wherever the cloud came to rest, they set up camp again.

> Then the cloud covered the Tent of Meeting, and the glory of the Lord filled the tabernacle. . . . In all the travels of the Israelites, whenever the cloud lifted from above the tabernacle, they would set out; but if the cloud did not lift, they did not set out—until the day it lifted. So the cloud of the Lord was over the tabernacle by day, and fire was in the cloud by night, in the sight of all the house of Israel during all their travels. (Exod. 40:34–36)

God's wilderness dwelling place is given several different names in the Scriptures, but it is usually referred to as "the Tabernacle" by the Gentiles and as "*Mishkan*" by the Jews. Its different names are relevant in that they help to explain its functions.

The Names of the Tabernacle

- *Mishkan*: Dwelling Place
- *Mishkan Y-H-V-H*: Dwelling of *Y-H-V-H*
- *Mishkan Ha'edut*: Dwelling of the Covenant Terms
- *Mishkan Ohel Mo'ed*: Dwelling of the Tent of Meeting
- *Ohel Mo'ed*: Tent of Meeting
- *Kodesh*: Holy Place
- *Mikdash*: Sanctuary
- *Bet Y-H-V-H*: House of *Y-H-V-H*

Materials. A full ten chapters of Scripture describe the design and contents of the Tabernacle. Its exact dimensions, costly materials, colors, and decorative motifs were all stipulated by God. Although the description is very detailed, the biblical account is not a *complete* blueprint. Some practical information is missing. We are not told, for example, whether the roof of the tent was flat, or pitched to allow for drainage.

Many of the materials used in the building and furnishing of the Tabernacle came from Egypt. By the time the Israelite slaves were set free, the Egyptians were more than happy to see them go. Dreading the prospect of more plagues, they actively *encouraged* the "*Habiru*" to leave by giving them silver, gold, and clothing. It was these treasures, and various other materials, that were later offered for the construction of the Tabernacle.

All who were willing, men and women alike, came and brought gold jewelry of all kinds: brooches, earrings, rings and ornaments. They all presented their gold as a wave offering to the Lord. Everyone who had blue, purple or scarlet yarn or fine linen, or goat hair, ram skins dyed red or hides of sea cows brought them. Those presenting an offering of silver or bronze brought it as an offering to the Lord, and anyone who had acacia wood for any part of the work brought it. . . . And all the women who were willing and had the skill spun the goat hair. The leaders brought onyx stones and other gems to be mounted on the ephod and breastpiece. They also brought spices and olive oil for the light and for the anointing oil and for the fragrant incense. (Exod. 35:22–28)

Significance of Colors and Materials

- gold (*zahav*): deity
- silver (*kesef*): salvation
- bronze or copper (*nekhoshet*): judgment
- wild acacia (shittim) wood ('*etz*): mortal man
- white linen (*pishtan lavan*): purity and righteousness
- scarlet (*shani*): sacrifice
- purple (*argaman*): royalty
- blue (*kakhol*): heaven

147

Design. The Tabernacle consisted of two rectangular structures: an open courtyard measuring 150 x 75 feet (45.7 x 22.9 meters) and an elaborate tent measuring 45 x 15 feet and 10 feet in height (13.7 x 4.6 x 3 meters). This tent, in turn, was divided into two sections: the Holy Place and Most Holy Place. The smaller innermost sanctuary, the Most Holy Place, formed a perfect square that measured 15 x 15 feet (4.6 x 4.6 meters).

The tent was supported on a framework of acacia wood and strengthened by a series of gold-plated wooden boards that lined the south, west, and north sides of the structure. There were four tent coverings; the first of which was a set of ten curtains made of linen (*pishtan*) that was embroidered with figures of cherubim (*kruvim*) in blue, purple, and scarlet yarn. It seems probable that this set of curtains hung down on the inside of the gold boards, forming a gorgeous tapestried interior. In the strictest sense, the term *Mishkan*, or Dwelling Place, related exclusively to these inner curtains that formed a screen around the God of Israel's "earthly throne room."

A separate linen curtain, also embroidered with cherubim, separated the tent's two chambers. It formed a division between the Holy Place (*HaKodesh*) and Most Holy Place (*Kodesh Kodashim*). This curtain was called the veil, or *parokhet*. As with ancient Middle Eastern women's wedding attire, the veil hid the most precious picture—the purest personage—from the eyes of the community. To "enter within the veil" was to enter into the most private dwelling place of a most holy God. This was prohibited to all except the high priests of Israel—and even they were permitted to enter this most sacred of chambers on only one day of the year. A less elaborate linen curtain—also embroidered in blue, purple, and scarlet yarn—was drawn across the eastern entrance to the Tabernacle tent.

Tabernacle Design and Ritual Objects

The Courtyard:
1. The bronze- (or copper-) plated altar of burnt offering
2. The solid bronze (or copper) laver or wash basin

The Holy Place:
3. The gold-plated table of showbread
4. The gold-plated altar of incense
5. The solid gold seven branched candelabra or *menorah*

The Most Holy Place or Holy of Holies:
6. The gold-plated Ark of the Covenant
7. The solid gold mercy seat with its two cherubim

The second tent covering consisted of a set of curtains made from goat hair. They were longer than the inner embroidered linen curtains, and one of them formed an external "door" hanging on the east side of the tent. This was made to fall down on the outside of the linen entrance curtain when necessary. The goat hair covering was overlaid with two more weatherproof coverings of ram skins—dyed red—and seal or porpoise skins. The open courtyard enclosure was defined by a fence consisting of linen hangings supported on movable supports.

148

We are familiar with the names of the Tabernacle craftsmen—Bezalel and Oholiab—from the biblical account. They would not have *signed* their sculptural "furnishings," however. The objects were created solely for the purpose of serving and glorifying *Y-H-V-H.*

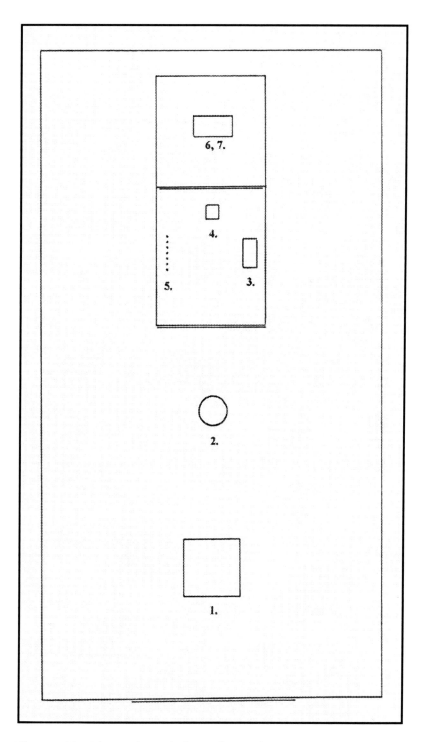

Figure 39: Floor plan of the Tabernacle tent and enclosure. It included seven very distinctive ritual objects, as well as carrying poles and utensils

The Courtyard

1. Sacrifice and the Brazen Altar

> "Build an altar of acacia wood, three cubits high; it is to be square, five cubits long and five cubits wide. Make a horn at each of the four corners, so that the horns and the altar are of one piece, and overlay the altar with bronze." (Exod. 27:1–2)

The first object of Tabernacle ritual was positioned at the eastern end of the courtyard enclosure. It was the brazen altar (*mizbe'akh ha'olah*); so called because it was built of acacia wood and overlaid in bronze (or copper). It measured about 4½ feet (1.4 meters) in height and about 7½ feet (2.3 meters) in length and width. Four horn shapes (*keren*) extended from its top corners. Halfway up its outer surface, a horizontal projection formed a narrow ledge. It's possible that the priests used this ledge in order to elevate themselves while performing their sacrificial duties. The altar was hollow. It is therefore supposed that when in use, it was filled with earth and stones or simply used as an incinerator.

The Life-Blood
The wilderness Tabernacle was made from the finest materials, exquisitely decorated, handled with the utmost reverence—and was splattered with blood. Blood was sprinkled on the brazen altar's four horns, on the priests' garments, on the horns of the altar of incense, and before the *parokhet* in the Holy Place. Once a year, on the Day of Atonement, it was also splattered before and on the mercy seat in the Most Holy Place. Animal sacrifices were repeatedly offered by individual worshippers and by the priests. We recoil at the thought.

In technologically advanced countries, we rarely see blood in the quantities that the ancients saw it. Our world is far more clinical. Meat comes from abattoirs and warfare is usually conducted from a "safe" distance. We have to make a real effort to grasp the significance of the life-blood.

As in primitive societies today, the ancients saw blood flow every time they slaughtered an animal, every time they engaged in a bloody hand-fought battle. They observed that when it flowed, it drained the life from the body. It appeared to contain "the spark of life"; the human life-force. Some cultures also believed that drinking the blood of a "noble" person was a means of gaining the attributes of his character; the inner life of that person.

Blood sacrifice, perceived to be the most costly offering that could be made to the various gods, was a common practice in the ancient world. Sometimes the blood alone was offered. At other times, it was the entire body of the person or animal. The Phoenicians are known to have offered their babies to the god Molech.

The Levitical Sacrificial System
The Israelites practiced only animal sacrifice and it is clearly stated that their rituals were given to them by God for a specific purpose.

> For the life of the creature is in the blood, and I have given it to you to make atonement for yourselves on the altar; it is the blood that makes atonement for one's life. (Lev. 17:11)

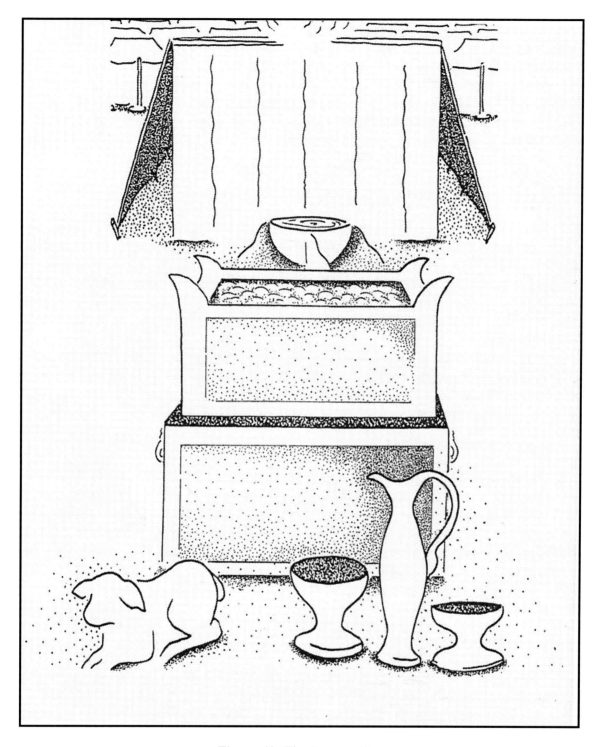

Figure 40: The Brazen Altar

The God of Israel is utterly holy. Humanity is utterly fallible. Therefore, individuals cannot simply enter his presence; in much the same way as light and dark, midday and midnight, cannot co-exist. Our sullied natures separate us from the Giver of Life—which ultimately results in spiritual death. Because the Israelites were bound to fall short of the holiness of God and the perfection of his Law, a sacrificial system was provided as a means of being reconciled to *Y-H-V-H,* the source of Life.

With the Hebrews, the precious blood of animals was not offered to appease an angry God. It served as a means of "covering sin," of "paying the price" for a guilt-stained life—in order to secure oneness with *Y-H-V-H.* The blood of an animal was proof that a life had been taken, so that another, the life of the worshipper, could be restored. In this way, pardoned Israelites regained full membership into the holy community of Israel. The differences between Israelite sacrifices and those of other ancient cultures lay not so much in the objects themselves, as in the underlying motive.

Four types of sacrifice were performed at the brazen altar or "altar of burnt offering":

1. Burnt offerings. An Israelite selected a male animal "without blemish" from his herd as an offering. A bird was permissible for the poor. Before sacrificing the animal in the forecourt of the Tabernacle, he laid his hand on it, thereby identifying himself with the sacrifice (*korban*) —indicating that the animal represented himself. He then slit the animal's throat and a Levite priest caught the blood (*dam*) in a bowl before sprinkling it on the horns and sides of the brazen altar. The animal was then cut up and the pieces laid on the burning wood of the altar.

Levite priests had to ensure that the fire (*esh*) burnt continuously. The offering remained on the hearth throughout the night and its ashes were deposited at a ceremonially clean site outside the camp in the morning. The distinctive feature of this ritual was that the whole animal was burnt on the altar, signifying the total dedication of the worshipper to God.

It is a burnt offering, an offering made by fire, an aroma pleasing to the Lord. (Lev. 1:13)

2. Sin and guilt offerings. The procedure for sin and guilt offerings was the same as the burnt offerings, except that only a specified part of the animal was burnt. The rest of the animal was eaten by the priests or by the priests and their families—at times, even by the worshiper. The difference between the sin and guilt offerings is not entirely clear, but the significance of the atoning life-blood was emphasized in both rituals. It appears that the first was made in order to make restitution for offenses against God, whereas the guilt offerings related more to social offenses against fellow Israelites. In the larger context, all forms of wrongdoing were seen as being offenses against God. It is worth noting that both sacrifices dealt with *unintentional* or unavoidable breaches of the Law. No ritual was provided for deliberate violations of God's Law.

3. Peace offerings. These animal offerings were not used as a means of atonement, but as a means of maintaining sound relationships between individuals and God—and between people and their neighbors. The Hebrew name for this ritual implies peace and well-being. Part of this offering was burnt on the altar, while the rest was shared by the Levite priests and the worshipper and his family. These offerings might also have been used as thank offerings.

4. Cereal or meal offerings. Flour, olive oil, and incense were used in the cereal, or meal, offerings. They were sometimes baked beforehand by the worshipper and presented as cakes or wafers. In this instance, the Israelites were instructed to include salt, but not yeast or honey. The latter were considered to be "unclean" because of their association with fermentation. Part of the offering was burnt on the altar, except when given as a firstfruit offering. The rest belonged to the priests. Any grain offering presented by a member of the priesthood was not permitted to be eaten. It had to be completely burned. The essential meaning of this sacrifice is also unclear, but its Hebrew name suggests that, in general, it was used to pay homage to God and to express thankfulness. This offering often accompanied a burnt or peace offering.

> When someone brings a grain offering to the Lord, his offering is to be of fine flour. He is to pour oil on it, put incense on it and take it to Aaron's sons, the priests. (Lev. 2:1)

The Levitical sacrificial system could easily have become a meaningless ritual; an external procedure with little or no effect on personal attitudes. Therefore, in the case of a sin offering, a confession had to be made in the presence of a priest at the time of sacrifice, and an attempt had to be made to "right the wrong." Priestly duties included declaring God's acceptance or rejection of the offerings.

Although this system of worship constituted a giant leap forward in terms of civilized standards and practices, it fell short of fully resolving the problem of sin. Nevertheless, it is extremely significant in that it enables us to grasp the true meaning of the ultimate offering; the sacrifice of *God's* Lamb. In A.D. 70, during the first Jewish Revolt, the Levitical system of animal sacrifice came to an abrupt halt with the destruction of Herod's Temple.

Yeshua as the Lamb of God

Two important examples of human sacrifice feature in biblical history: The (near) sacrifice of Isaac, the son of Abraham, and the sacrifice of Yeshua. The first foreshadowed the second—except that Isaac's life was spared; whereas God allowed his son to die for the greater good.

> For the *cohen hagadol* [high priest] brings the blood of animals into the Holiest Place as a sin offering, but their bodies are burned outside the camp. So too Yeshua suffered death outside the gate, in order to make the people holy through his own blood. (Heb. 13:11–12; JNT page 310)

Soon after the Exodus, the Israelites, frustrated with their desert wanderings, started to complain bitterly. Their defiant attitude toward Moses and, therefore, *Y-H-V-H*, separated them from God's providence. When they found venomous snakes infesting their camp, they hastily repented of their rebellion and pleaded for the snakes' removal. It was then that God instructed Moses to make a brazen serpent and elevate it on a pole. We are told that all who had been bitten were miraculously healed when they looked up at it.

This image of a serpent entwined on a vertical support is reminiscent of the blessing symbol of the tribe of Dan; a serpent supported on the vertical axis of the scales of justice. In fact the Hebrew word "*dan*" means "judge"—and this son of Jacob was appointed as the judge of Israel.

The abovementioned serpents were therefore associated with rebellion, judgment and justice. Christians would not equate the Messiah with a biblical symbol for evil, but three images of serpents relate to his sacrificial death: the serpent of Eden, the serpent in the blessing symbol of the tribe of Dan, and Moses' brazen serpent on the pole. (Num. 21:4–8)

When Yeshua was elevated on a Roman crucifixion stake, he sank to the level of the serpent of Eden. He took upon himself the burden of humanity's corruption and "became sin." In fact, the magnitude of humankind's sin so completely separated him from his holy Father, that he cried out; *"Eli! Eli! L'mah sh'vaktani?"* ("My God, my God, why have you deserted me?" Matt. 27:46; JNT page 42; Ps. 22:1). But, like the brazen serpent on the pole, he became humanity's source of salvation. The crucifix serves as a powerful reminder that by means of his sacrifice believers are rescued from sin, the judgment of God, and spiritual death.

Believers: An Offering Made by Fire
In terms of the making of covenants, fire, smoke, and darkness marked God's presence and approval. In terms of sacrificial offerings, *fire* alone signified the purging of the soul. As precious metals are refined in a fiery furnace, so God frequently refines and rebuilds his people through hardship and suffering.

> "God is a consuming fire." (Heb. 12:29; Deut. 4:24)

Believers do not enter God's kingdom nonchalantly, with self-righteous confidence. They often enter with a broken and contrite spirit; humbled by pain, distress, or hardship of some kind. This is usually acknowledged only in retrospect as being a work of "grace." The old nature is broken down to make way for the new regenerated soul—just as the Messiah had to suffer and die in order to be filled with resurrection life. In this sense all sincere believers share in the Messiah's crucifixion experience.

At times, the conversion of a family member, particularly among the Jews, causes dissension and creates deep divisions. It frequently triggers a raging battle, a family "civil war," as the group attempts to restore the new convert to the old status quo. Therefore believers in Yeshua do not necessarily enjoy domestic peace, but an incomparable *inner* peace "which passes understanding." When God's messengers, "the heavenly host," appeared to the shepherds of Bethlehem on the night of the Messiah's birth, they didn't proclaim that there would be peace on Earth. They announced the coming of peace "to men on whom his [God's] favor rests."

> "Glory to God in the highest, and on earth peace to men on whom his favor rests." (Luke 2:14)

> "I have come to bring fire on the earth, and how I wish it were already kindled. . . . Do you think I came to bring peace on earth? No, I tell you, but division." (Luke 12:49)

> How good and pleasant it is when brothers live together in unity! (Ps. 133:1)

Following Yeshua is therefore not necessarily the easy choice, but it is the *only* choice for those who are drawn to him. For them the ancient Levitical system of animal sacrifice has forever been replaced by the offering of "sacrifices of praise."

> Therefore, let us go out to him who is outside the camp and share his disgrace. For we have no permanent city here; on the contrary, we seek the one to come. Through him, therefore, let us offer God a sacrifice of praise continually. For this is the natural product of lips that acknowledge his name. (Heb. 13:13–15; JNT page 310)

Figure 41: Levitical animal sacrifices replaced by a "sacrifice of praise"

2. Washing and the Brazen Laver

"Make a bronze basin, with its bronze stand, for washing. Place it between the Tent of Meeting and the altar, and put water in it. Aaron and his sons are to wash their hands and feet with water from it. Whenever they enter the Tent of Meeting, they shall wash with water so that they will not die. Also, when they approach the altar to minister by presenting an offering made to the Lord by fire, they shall wash their hands and feet so that they will not die." (Exod. 30:17–21)

The second ritual object, positioned between the brazen altar and the entrance to the Tabernacle tent, was the laver (*kiyor*). This was a bronze (or copper) wash basin supported on a base of the same material. The Scriptures do not describe its dimensions, design, or ornamentation; but we are told that it was made from the primitive burnished mirrors of the Israelite women who served at the entrance to the Tabernacle.

Figure 42: A Levitical priest washes at the brazen laver. (Exod. 30:21, 29:1–4, 30:17–21, 38:8)

The Laver and the Priesthood

Israelite worshipers who entered the courtyard enclosure to offer sacrifices were not permitted to go beyond the brazen altar. The laver was used only by the priesthood for the ritual cleansing of hands and feet prior to offering sacrifices or entering the tent's Holy Place. Levitical priests had to purify themselves before ministering to members of the community. They even offered sacrifices for personal sins before attending to their priestly duties. These men were not above the Law. On the contrary, they had to be careful to comply with *all* of its requirements in order to enjoy the privilege of serving the living God.

Purification and the Priesthood of Believers

Members of the New Covenant priesthood of believers are also cleansed in preparation for the privilege of serving God. They undergo water baptism, are baptized in the Holy Spirit, and are "washed in the waters of the Word." In New Testament writings, the symbol of water (*mayim*) is therefore often linked to the purging and regenerative activities of the Spirit.

Water baptism. When John the Baptist performed the act of ritual cleansing by immersing people in the river Jordan, he was obeying Jewish Law. However, with him, baptism took on additional meaning. He was preparing the Jews for the ministry of the Messiah.

Water baptism continues to constitute a major turning point in the life of believers. It is a public act demonstrating an individual's earnest desire to turn from the meaningless confused old life, to the spiritual abundance of the new. In baptism by immersion, the complete submersion of the believer in water symbolizes the burial of the old life. The reemergence from the water represents the resurrection to a new life. Believers are provided with the opportunity for a fresh start; a means of having the bitterness, pain, and regrets of the past washed away. How comforting and necessary this is for the new convert.

Some churches no longer practice infant baptism. They have replaced this sacrament with a dedication service. For them, infant baptism is viewed as meaningless and ineffectual; merely a gratification of social expectations and antiquated church traditions. They point out that infant baptism it is not an outward show of a conscious decision, on the part of a believer, to become a follower of Yeshua. The decision is made by someone *other* than "the convert." It negates the directive; "Repent and be baptized." (Acts 2:28)

> Through immersion into his death we were buried with him; so that just as, through the glory of the Father, the Messiah was raised from the dead, likewise we too might live a new life. (Rom. 6:4; JNT page 205)

Early Messianic communities sometimes used the stag as a symbol for water baptism. Because intense thirst can drive this animal to travel for hundreds of miles in search of water, it was used to represent the restlessness and intense thirst of new believers for the waters of baptism.

> As the deer pants for streams of water, so my soul pants for you, O God. My soul thirsts for God, for the living God." (Ps. 42:1–2)

The Spirit: a spring of water. When Yeshua spoke to the Samaritan woman at the well, he compared the Spirit (*Ruach HaKodesh*), who would be sent to quench the yearnings of the human soul, to a spring of fresh water:

> Yeshua answered, "Everyone who drinks this water will get thirsty again, but whoever drinks the water I will give him will never be thirsty again! On the contrary, the water I give him will become a spring of water inside him, welling up into eternal life!" (John 4:13–14; JNT page 123)

Every person is born with a natural soul, but because God is Spirit, each new believer must be inwardly reborn—given a new spiritual sensitivity and intelligence. We are told to earnestly pray for this baptism or anointing of the Spirit—a gift bestowed on individuals as a sovereign act of God. The "spring of water" then wells up inwardly, making intimate communion with a holy God possible; giving believers a heightened awareness of spiritual realities; giving them the capacity to worship "in Spirit and in truth."

> "I tell you the truth, no one can enter the kingdom of God unless he is born of water and the Spirit. Flesh gives birth to flesh, but the Spirit gives birth to spirit." (John 3:5–6)

In the Scriptures, the Spirit is referred to as the Counselor, Spirit of Truth, and Comforter. His role in the Trinity is to be humanity's helper as he cleanses, rebuilds, comforts, heals, strengthens, guides, and teaches. He reveals the very mind of God. The anointing of the Spirit is the crowning glory of God's plan for humankind. The sacrifice of Yeshua, and his resurrection and ascension, would all have been meaningless and ineffectual without the gift of the Spirit.

Each new convert has useless inner baggage. Like the superfluous foreskin, it needs to be discarded. The indwelling Spirit therefore severs believers from the old life in stages, so as not to further damage the soul, and the things of this world are gradually replaced by the holy things of God. Although believers feel the pain of the spiritual surgery, they are always astonished and delighted by the transformation—by the beauty and strength of the new inner life. This New Covenant "heart circumcision," instituted on the Day of Pentecost, is subtle and thorough.

> "The Lord your God will circumcise your hearts and the hearts of your descendants, so that you may love him with all your heart and with all your soul, and live." (Deut. 30:6)

> "For whoever wants to save his life will lose it, but whoever loses his life for me will find it." (Matt. 16:25)

The purging power of the Word. Man's natural conscience is often regarded as being a source of wisdom. But just as the Israelite women looked into their primitive burnished bronze mirrors and saw only their own vague and imperfect reflections, so human conscience reflects only the rationale of a confused and imperfect nature within the context of social norms. It is weak and unreliable without the illumination of Scripture.

> For now we see obscurely in a mirror, but then it will be face to face. Now I know partly; then I will know fully, just as God has fully known me. (1 Cor. 13:12; JNT page 233)

The Bible, on the other hand, is a source of immense wisdom. When people look into the "mirror" of the Word, they sense not only the reflection of their sullied souls, but the face of the Messiah and the presence of *Y-H-V-H*. The true nature of both humanity and the Ruler of the Universe are revealed. It is the Spirit that makes God's Word ring true in our hearts.

> So all of us, with faces unveiled, see as in a mirror the glory of the Lord; and we are being changed into his very image, from one degree of glory to the next, by *Adonai* [*Y-H-V-H*] the Spirit. (2 Cor. 3:18; JNT page 240)

Figure 43: Images that reflect the Spirit as mankind's helper: "Listen to me . . . you whom I have upheld since you were conceived, and have carried since your birth. Even to your old age and gray hairs I am he, I am he who will sustain you. I have made you and I will carry you; I will sustain you and I will rescue you. (Isa. 46: 3–4) . . . "I will never leave you or forsake you." (Josh. 1:5)

The Holy Place

The Holy Place (*HaKodesh*) in God's *Mishkan* featured three articles of ritual. In the middle, in front of the veil, or *parokhet*, was a small-horned altar; the altar of incense (*mizbe'akh ha-ketoret*). On the south side of the tent was the only source of light (*or*); solid gold seven-branched candelabra (*menorah*). On the north side was the table of showbread (*shulkhan lekhem*).

The Priests in the Holy Place

The priests entered the Holy Place daily. They offered incense at the altar during morning and evening prayers. They also replenished the olive oil in the *menorah*, ensuring that it remained lit. Once a week, on the Sabbath, they replaced the twelve loaves of showbread on the table with fresh bread. They were then permitted to eat the old bread. In this cool quiet interior, away from the bustle and activity of the outer courtyard, the aroma of the incense and showbread, and the flickering light of the *menorah*, must have created an atmosphere of sanctity and tranquility.

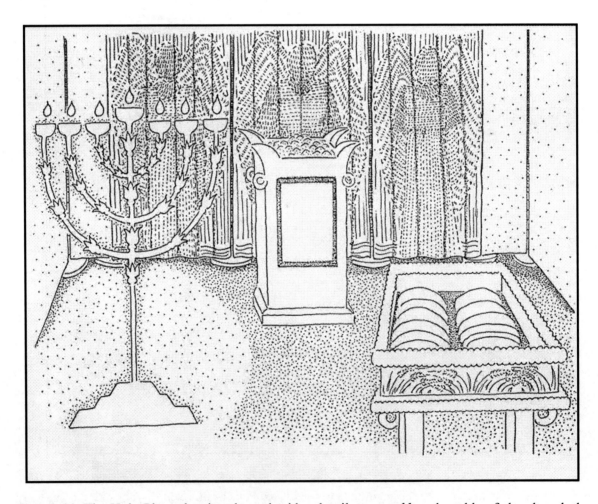

Figure 44: The Holy Place showing the embroidered veil, or *parokhet*, the table of showbread, the altar of incense, and the solid gold candelabra or *menorah*

A Priesthood of Believers and the Holy Place
For believers, "the Holy Place" can be the bank of a tranquil stream, the privacy of a bedroom or office, a majestic cathedral. . . It is any place in which God's people meet with him, enjoy his presence, and enter into deeper, more intimate fellowship with him. These are places of stillness and quietness when he is the only one with whom his people communicate; where he is the only source of spiritual food and light.

"Be still, and know that I am God; I will be exalted among the nations, I will be exalted in the earth." (Ps. 46:10)

"Come near to God and he will come near to you." (James 4:8)

I will praise the Lord who counsels me; even at night my heart instructs me. (Ps. 16:7)

In this exploration of the Holy Place, we will move in the Hebrew manner—right to left—from the table of showbread, to the altar of incense, and then to the *menorah*.

3. Fellowship and the Table of Showbread

"Make a table of acacia wood—two cubits long, a cubit wide and a cubit and a half high. Overlay it with pure gold and make a gold molding around it. Also make around it a rim a handbreadth wide and put a gold molding on the rim. . . . Put the bread of the Presence on this table to be before me at all times." (Ex. 25:23–30)

Bread (*lekhem*) was the staple diet of the ancient Israelites. In the *Tanakh* (OT), it appears as manna, leavened or unleavened bread, and as showbread. Among the Jews today it is prepared in various distinctive ways: as bagels, rye bread, sweet *khallah* bread for the Sabbath and as unleavened *matzot* at the time of Passover.

The Bread of the Presence
The table of showbread measured 3 feet (.9 meters) in length, 1½ feet (.5 meters) in width, and 2¼ feet (.7 meters) in height. It was constructed of acacia wood and overlaid with gold. The word showbread (*lekhem ha-panim*), literally translated, means "bread of the faces." On the table, twelve unleavened loaves were arranged in two rows—with six in each row—and placed on a blue cloth. Because the bread was situated in front of the Most Holy Place and was, therefore, continually before the Lord, the loaves were also referred to as "the Bread of the Presence."

Symbolism Relating to Bread
The twelve loaves of showbread obviously represented the twelve tribes of ancient Israel, but they may also be linked to those who have been "grafted into the Olive Tree of Israel" by means of their acceptance of the Jewish Messiah.

Breaking bread together. The most meaningful times of fellowship often take place while sharing a meal. This was especially true in the ancient world. To "break bread together" signified a time of special communion, a time of sharing not only food, but also the wealth of the human spirit. The showbread in the Holy Place can therefore be equated with times of precious fellowship with the God of Israel.

Unleavened bread. The fact that the showbread was unleavened is significant. At that time, yeast or "leaven" (*khametz*) was made by setting aside a portion of the old dough and allowing it to ferment. Because this fermented dough rendered the fresh batch "unclean," it was never added to bread that was to be used in worship. Sacred bread had to be *unleavened*, because leaven was linked to the concept of impurity.

"Be on your guard against the yeast [or leaven: impure teaching] of the Pharisees, which is hypocrisy." (Luke 12:1)

Manna and the Bread of Life. Yeshua said, "*I am* the way, the truth and the life." He didn't say "I will show you the way," as have other great prophets and teachers. Similarly, he didn't say "I will give you the bread of life." He said "I *am* the bread of life." For forty years in the wilderness, the God of Israel fed his people with manna, but he has since provided them with this "Bread of Life"; a lifelong source of spiritual food. Christians believe that Yeshua was as pure and as "unleavened" as the manna and showbread; that he was "without sin."

"I am the living bread that came down from heaven. If a man eats of this bread, he will live forever. This bread is my flesh, which I will give for the life of the world." (John 6:51)

"It is written: 'Man does not live on bread alone, but on every word that comes from the mouth of God.' " (Matt. 4:4)

4. Prayer and the Altar of Incense

Make an altar of acacia wood for burning incense. It is to be square, a cubit long and a cubit wide, and two cubits high—its horns of one piece with it. Overlay the top and all the sides and the horns with pure gold, and make a gold molding around it. Put the altar in front of the curtain that is before the ark of the Testimony. . . . Aaron must burn fragrant incense on the altar every morning when he tends the lamps. He must burn incense again when he lights the lamps at twilight so that incense will burn regularly before the Lord for generations to come. (Exod. 30:1–8)

The small altar of incense was constructed of acacia wood and overlaid with gold. It measured 3 feet in height (.9 meter) and 1½ feet (.5 meters) in length and breadth, and was positioned directly in front of the entrance to the Most Holy Place. This article of ritual was in closest proximity to the Ark of the Covenant.

The priests burnt incense "before the Lord" twice a day during times of morning and evening prayer. A special blend of ground up spices and gum resins was used in the making of this incense; and its unique formula was reserved exclusively for this application. Hot coals were taken from the brazen altar in the courtyard and placed on this smaller altar. The incense was then sprinkled on the coals. As it slowly burned, the tent was filled with its fragrant aroma. *Ketoret*, the Hebrew word for incense, means "set on fire."

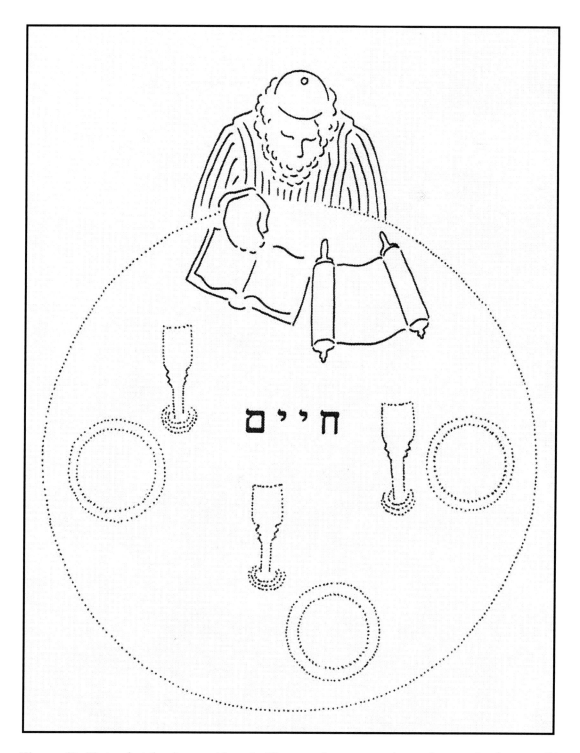

Figure 45: "I stand at the door and knock. If anyone hears my voice and opens the door, I will come in and eat (or "sup": AV) with him, and he with me." (Rev. 3:20) The Hebrew word in the center of the table is pronounced "*khayim,*" meaning "life"

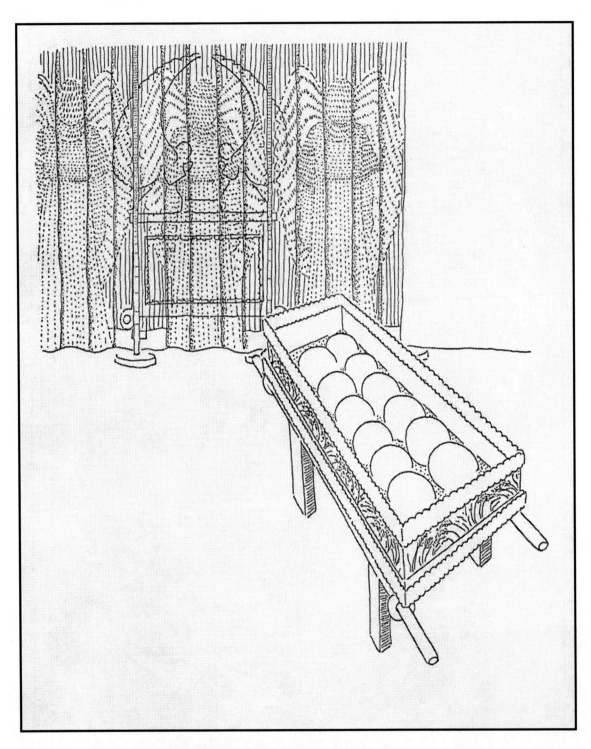

Figure 46: Table of showbread in the Holy Place. The position of the ark behind the veil is indicated by means of superimposed images. (The veil was not transparent)

"Take fragrant spices—gum resin, onycha and galbanum—and pure frankincense, all in equal amounts, and make a fragrant blend of incense, the work of a perfumer. It is to be salted and pure and sacred. Grind some of it to powder and place it in front of the Testimony in the Tent of Meeting, where I will meet with you." (Exod. 30:34–35)

Prayer and Incense in the Scriptures

Because Levite priests burnt incense during times of prayer, it is typically mentioned in the Scriptures in the context of prayer (*t'fillah*). In Revelation 5:8 it is golden bowls of incense that are the "prayers of the saints." The words, "May my prayer be set before you like incense," appear in Psalm 141:2

The altar of incense can be seen to represent a place in which we can stand before God and be warmed by his Spirit. We are told in 1 Thessalonians 5:16, that to gain the "peace that passes understanding," like ancient Levitical priests, we need to come *repeatedly* before *Y-H-V-H* in prayer. Furthermore, as the Tabernacle incense had a specific formula, so he seeks those who are willing to pray in a particular way—"in Spirit and in truth." He requires his praying people to be utterly sincere and honest before him. This to *Y-H-V-H* is like the fragrant aroma of incense in the Holy Place.

The Lord's Prayer

> Our Father in heaven!
> May your Name be kept holy.
> May your Kingdom come, your will be done on earth as in heaven.
> Give us the food we need today.
> Forgive us what we have done wrong, as we too have forgiven those who have wronged us.
> And do not lead us into hard testing, but keep us safe from the Evil One.
>
> (Matt. 6:9–13; JNT page 8)

"But when you pray, go into your room, close the door and pray to your Father, who is unseen. . . . And when you pray, do not keep on babbling like pagans, for they think they will be heard because of their many words. Do not be like them, for your Father knows what you need before you ask him." (Matt. 6:6–8)

How should we pray? When the Messiah prayed, he withdrew to a place of *solitude* and instructed his followers to do the same. Because the God of Israel "inhabits the praises of his people" (Ps. 22:3 AV), by first acknowledging his preeminence and praising him, "the gates are opened wide for the King of Glory to come in" (Psalm 24:7). This priority is shown in the first two lines of The Lord's Prayer: "Our Father in heaven! May your name be kept holy."

Notice the last line of the Lord's Prayer; "keep us safe from the Evil One." As believers draw closer to *Y-H-V-H,* they become aware of the battle that is raging for the possession of their souls. This, as with the concept of sin, is usually scornfully dismissed in our modern world. More "primitive" cultures have a far greater awareness of the unseen forces at work among us.

To the non-believer, the question, "Are you saved?" is no more than a trite phrase. Many are tempted to flippantly respond, "Saved from what?" Believers in Yeshua are rescued, or "saved," from the debilitating effects of sin, including separation from the living God, and from the malevolent influences of the Evil One. The last line in the Lord's Prayer should not be taken lightly. It *is* necessary to pray for God's protection. The Adversary, Deceiver, or "Accuser of the Brethren," is constantly attempting to discourage believers and undermine God's work. The Scriptures therefore teach us that our battle is not against *others*—"flesh and blood"—but against this unseen enemy who demoralizes and confuses God's people, thereby making them ineffective members of his *cohanim* (priesthood). C.S. Lewis, the great English apologist, once suggested that Satan's greatest deception has been to convince us that he doesn't exist.

The Lord's Prayer also stresses the importance of forgiving others: "Forgive us what we have done wrong, as—to the extent that—we forgive those who have wronged us." This is not always easy; particularly when "offenders" show absolutely no signs of remorse. A few words can sometimes clear up a misunderstanding. Failing that, matters have to be left in the hands of the Lord. In his great wisdom, and in his time, he remedies all things. Nursing a grudge harms none but the unforgiving soul. Furthermore, the New Testament instructs us to support others in prayer—including our enemies.

Because the Almighty ruler of the universe is our heavenly Father, and his Spirit our helper, prayer is our most effective defense. The odds are always in a believer's favor when distressing circumstances are committed to God in prayer.

This principle was powerfully illustrated by the prophet Elisha. An Aramean king sent an army of men to the city of Dothan in order to capture him. When Elisha's servant saw the enemy, he was overcome with fear; but Elisha remained calm and confident. He knew he was safe. He could see that they were being protected by the heavenly hosts of the God of Israel:

> "Don't be afraid," the prophet answered. "Those who are with us are more than those who are with them." And Elisha prayed, "O Lord, open his eyes so that he may see." Then the Lord opened the servant's eyes, and he looked and saw the hills full of horses and chariots of fire all around Elisha. (2 Kings 6:16–17)

When we are overwhelmed by hardship or pain and are unable to pray, the Scriptures encourage us to simply wait on the Lord; "Be still and know that I am God" (Ps. 46:10). Only he understands the true nature of each person. Only he can determine the long term consequences of the events in our lives. We are also told that as the high priests of Israel interceded "before the Lord" on behalf of the nation at the altar of incense, so the Messiah and the Spirit plead on behalf of God's people before the heavenly Father. (Heb. 9:24 and Rom. 8:26–27)

> Don't worry about anything; on the contrary, make your requests known to God by prayer and petition, with thanksgiving. Then God's *shalom* [peace], passing all understanding, will keep your hearts and minds safe in union with the Messiah Yeshua. (Phil. 4:6–7; JNT page 267)

Figure 47: The altar of incense before the Most Holy Place. Incense was sprinkled on the hot coals twice a day, but the veil was opened only once a year on the Day of Atonement—*Yom Kippur*

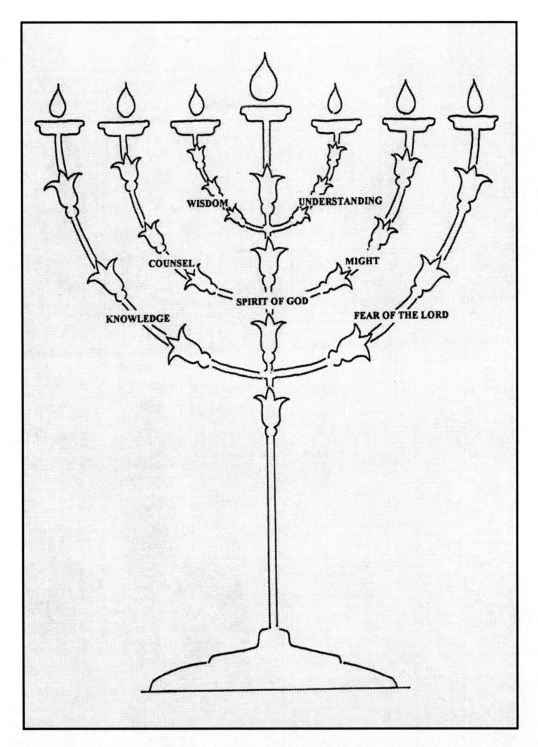

Figure 48: The *menorah* as a symbol of the seven attributes of the Messiah as described in the Book of Isaiah: "A shoot [descendant] will come up from the stump [remnant] of Jesse [father of King David]; from his roots [David's royal line, the Jews] a Branch [the Messiah] will bear fruit [believers]. The Spirit of the Lord will rest on him [1]—the Spirit of wisdom [2] and of understanding [3], the Spirit of council [4] and of power [5], the Spirit of knowledge [6] and of the fear of the Lord [7]—and he will delight in the fear of the Lord." (Isa. 11:1–3; Exod. 25:31–40; Col. 1:19; Rev. 4:5)

5. Revelation and the *Menorah*

Make a lamp stand of pure gold and hammer it out, base and shaft; its flowerlike cups, buds and blossoms shall be of one piece with it. Six branches are to extend from the sides of the lamp stand—three on one side and three on the other. (Exod. 25:31–32)

The *menorah* was a solid gold seven-branched candelabra; the only source of light (*or*) in the cool dark interior of the tent. Its form was hammered out of one piece of pure gold. Together with its accessories, it weighed about 75 pounds. It appears to have been intricately sculptured, featuring "cups shaped like almond flowers with buds [or calyxes] and blossoms." In contrast to the Israelites' small pottery bowl lamps, fueled with coarse olive oil or fat and used only at night, the menorah was replenished daily by the priests with pure olive oil. It was kept burning continuously "before the Lord."

"Command the Israelites to bring you clear oil of pressed olives for the light so that the lamps [of the *menorah*] may be kept burning." (Exod. 27:20)

Symbolism Relating to Lamps and their Light
For mortal man, fire is the closest visual equivalent to the majesty and power of the living God. In the Scriptures, his presence is manifested in a firepot in Abraham's vision; fire on Mt. Sinai; the pillar of fire above the Tabernacle; an all consuming fire on Elijah's altar; chariots of fire in Elisha's vision; and tongues of fire at Pentecost. Lamps and their light, on the other hand, are symbols of joy, prosperity, guidance, and the revelation of God's truth.

Yeshua as the light of the world. The New Testament reveals Yeshua as being the one in whom the fullness of God dwelt in physical form. (Col. 2:9; JNT page 270) His humble, yet glorious birth; his ministry, miracles and teachings; his sacrificial death, his resurrection and ascension; and his final return to the earth—all correspond with scriptural foundations established for him by the Hebrew prophets. He fulfilled "what was written."

Yeshua Messiah is also the only name given through whom individuals can be effectively rescued from the carnal "self" and from the Evil One. He is the one strong clear light that can be followed with confidence.

"I am the light of the world. Whoever follows me will never walk in darkness, but will have the light of life." (John 8:12)

Yeshua as the light of the Word. The Bible itself is also described as being a lamp and a light. It explains the history, culture, and worship of an ancient people; and it provides a record of the life and teachings of the Jewish Messiah. Throughout its pages, it also reveals the involvement of the Creator in the affairs of humankind. The Scriptures remain the most important means by which God guides and instructs his people.

Your word is a lamp to my feet and a light for my path. (Ps. 119:105)

Yeshua as the oil of anointing: The *menorah* was fueled with pure olive oil. This oil (*shemen*) is often associated with the concept of holiness and with the work of the Spirit. Sacred anointing oil—a blend of liquid myrrh, cinnamon, cane, cassia, and olive oil—was used in the sanctification of the Tabernacle tent and its furniture. It was used also in the consecration of priests and, later, in the consecration of the kings and prophets of Israel. As with the incense, this "oil of anointing" was reserved specifically for these applications.

The anointing of leaders signified that they were being set apart and empowered to do God's work. It indicated that they would be given God's Spirit in a special measure; enabling them to guide the Israelites with wisdom, knowledge, understanding, counsel, might, and "in the fear of [or in awe of] the Lord." This same Spirit is given to Yeshua's New Covenant people, equipping them with the necessary attributes to do his work (1 Cor. 12:7–11). The seven flickering flames of the *menorah* can therefore be seen to symbolize, not only the Messiah, but God's power that is made accessible by means of his Spirit.

To this day the *menorah* remains one of the most distinctive symbols of Judaism. The Jews use not only the seven-branched menorah, however. During the eight-day holiday of Hanukkah, a nine-branched menorah serves as an annual reminder of the oil in the temple menorah that lasted for a full eight days, instead of only one day, during the successful Jewish Maccabean revolt against Syrian rule and Greek cultural influences in Palestine in 165 B.C. The four-sided top that is spun by Jewish children during this holiday bears one Hebrew letter on each of its sides. These are the first letters of each word in the proclamation; *"Nes gadol hayah sham!"*—"A great miracle happened there!"

The Most Holy Place

The Lord's *sh'khinah* glory was manifested in the Most Holy Place, or Holy of Holies (*Kodesh Kodashim*). It was there, "between the wings of the cherubim," that he met with the high priests of Israel on the Day of Atonement (*Yom Kippur*) each year. This sacred inner chamber contained one piece of furniture consisting of two parts: a chest and its lid. The chest was referred to as the "Holy Ark" (*Aron HaKodesh*), the "Ark of the Covenant," or the "Ark of the Testimony." The lid, crowned with two cherubim, was referred to as the "atonement cover" or "mercy seat" (*kapporet*). The ark and the mercy seat formed an earthly equivalent to God's heavenly throne (*kes malkhut*) surrounded by winged celestial beings:

> I saw the Lord seated on a throne, high and exulted, and the train of his robe filled the temple. Above him were seraphs, each with six wings. . . . (Isa. 6:1–2)

> In the center, around the throne, were four living creatures. . . . Each of the four living creatures had six wings. . . . (Rev. 4:6–8)

6. God's Providence and the Ark of the Covenant

> Have them make a chest of acacia wood—two and a half cubits long, a cubit and a half wide, and a cubit and a half high. Overlay it with pure gold, both inside and out, and make a gold molding around it. (Exod. 25:10–11)

The ark was a wooden rectangular chest overlaid with gold. Its dimensions were 3 ¾ feet in length (1.1 meters) and 2¼ feet (.7 meters) in height and width. It was carried by means of poles that remained permanently in the rings at its four corners.

Figure 49: The ark containing the bowl of manna, Aaron's rod, and the tablets of the Law. The Hebrew word between the cherubim is pronounced "*khayim,*" meaning "life." (Exod. 25:10–22; Heb. 9:4)

Within the gold-plated chest lay the two stone tablets that Moses received from God on Mt. Sinai; hence the names "Ark of the Covenant" and "Ark of the Testimony." In the Book of Hebrews reference is also made to a bowl of manna and to Aaron's almond rod (9:4) within the ark. The jar of manna served as a reminder that God satisfied the physical needs of his people; the almond rod, that he had provided leadership.

When Yeshua "gave up his spirit" on the crucifixion stake, the veil in Herod's Temple is said to have torn in two—thereby revealing the Most Holy Place. The atoning death of the Messiah opened the way into the supreme "Holy of Holies," the heavenly throne room of the God of Israel, for all humanity. This event brought the need for the ancient Levitical system of worship to an end. By offering the blood of his own unblemished Lamb for the forgiveness of humanity's sins, God personally removed the veil that had previously barred his people from his presence. (Bear in mind that the Ark of the Covenant disappeared from Solomon's Temple at the time of the Babylonian exile. The Most Holy Place in *Herod's* Temple was empty.)

At that moment the curtain of the temple was torn in two from top to bottom. (Matt. 27:51)

Unlike the other high priests, he does not need to offer sacrifices day after day, first for his own sins, and then for the sins of the people. He sacrificed for their sins once for all when he offered himself. (Heb. 7:27)

Although it is often cathartic for believers to confess their sins before a priest or minister, it is no longer essential for them to enter God's presence through mediators. Individuals "covered by Yeshua's blood" are now permitted to approach *Y-H-V-H's* heavenly throne and commune directly with him. The wings of the cherubim overshadowed a seat of mercy—not judgment.

Let us then approach the throne of grace with confidence, so that we may receive mercy and find grace to help us in our time of need. (Heb. 4:16)

7. Eternal Life and the Mercy Seat

Make an atonement cover of pure gold—two and a half cubits long and a cubit and a half wide. And make two cherubim out of hammered gold at the ends of the cover. Make one cherub on one end and the second cherub on the other; make the cherub of one piece with the cover, at the two ends. The cherubim are to have their wings spread upward, overshadowing the cover with them. The cherubim are to have their wings spread upwards, overshadowing the cover with them. The cherubim are to face each other, looking toward the cover. Place the cover on top of the ark and put in the ark the Testimony, which I will give you. There, above the cover between the two cherubim that are over the ark of the Testimony, I will meet with you and give you all my commands for the Israelites. (Exod. 25:17–22)

The ark was crowned with a solid gold lid, at either end of which was a sculptured winged cherub. The wings of these cherubim overshadowed the mercy seat. Although the cherubim are sometimes rendered as winged lions with human heads, in the tradition of the ancient Assyrians, in the illustrations in this book, they are depicted as angelic beings. In the Scriptures, the Hebrew word "*kruvim*," (cherubim), is used in two other contexts: They are mentioned in Genesis, where they are said to have guarded the Tree of Life. They are also Ezekiel's "living creatures"—described as having four wings and four different faces (Ezek. 10:20–21).

In the Scriptures, we are told that God met with the high priests of Israel "between the wings of the cherubim." It was there that they made atonement for the sins of the priesthood and the community of Israel.

Two Angels in the Tomb

In the resurrection account in the Gospel of John, we find a picture of two angels in the Messiah's tomb. This is strikingly similar to the image of the ark with its cherubim and the heavenly throne of God with its winged creatures. Mary Magdalene saw the angels seated at either end of the slab on which Yeshua's body had lain:

> As she cried, she bent down, peered into the tomb, and saw two angels in white sitting where the body of Yeshua had been, one at the head and one at the feet. (John 20:11–12; JNT page 150)

They framed an empty space that was bursting with significance; that disclosed a staggering reality. Yeshua was alive. As prophesized, he had overcome physical death. Others had been known to rise from the dead, such as Jairus' daughter and Lazarus, but Yeshua's resurrection body was different. He presented himself to the twelve and ate food to prove that he was flesh and blood, but during the next forty days he appeared and disappeared at will. Finally, he rose physically from the earth and "ascended into heaven." Yeshua was not the first to be brought back to life. He was the first to rise to *eternal* life.

Figure 50: Two angels in the tomb of Yeshua. The Hebrew word between the angels is pronounced "*khay*," meaning "living" or "alive." (Exod. 25:18–20; John 20:12)

In earlier times, when the mortality rate was much higher and the dispensing of dead bodies less clinical, people were more exposed to the reality and, sometimes, the horror of physical death. The ultimate destination of the soul has always been the great unknown factor; it is assuredly the *fear* of death that has spawned the majority of our world's religions.

On the day of the Messiah's resurrection, this quandary was addressed in a tangible manner. When he died, he resolved the problem of sin. When he *rose*, he resolved the problem of death. Yeshua opened the way into God's presence—and to eternal life. From that time, all who have been "covered by his blood" have been able to "journey through the Tabernacle" into the very presence of God.

When the perishable has been clothed with the imperishable, and the mortal with immortality, then the saying that is written will come true: "Death has been swallowed up in victory." "Where, O death, is your victory? Where, O death, is your sting?" (1 Cor. 15: 54–55)

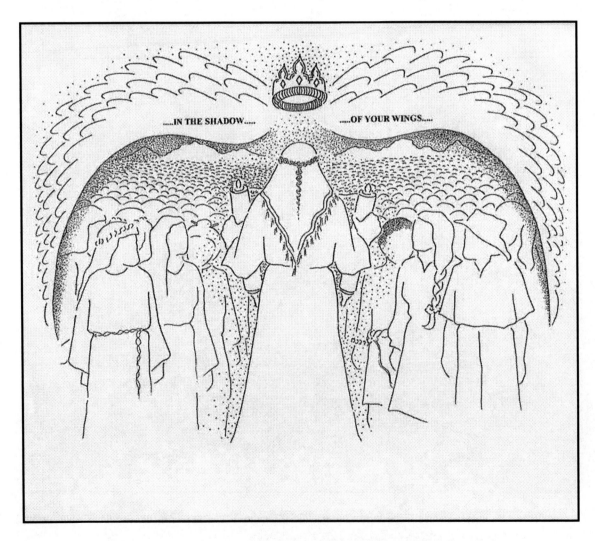

Figure 51: "I will take refuge in the shadow of your wings" (Ps 57:1)

174

The Wings of the Cherubim
Images of wings appear on several occasions in the Scriptures. They symbolize the comfort, providence, and protection that come from God. In Isaiah 40:31, the faint and weary will renew their strength and soar on wings like eagles. In the Psalms, refuge and shelter are found "in the shadow of his wings." In Luke 13:34, the wings of a hen gathering her chicks reflect Yeshua's longing to gather and protect the Jews. Similarly, the wings of cherubim, overshadowing a seat of mercy, form a picture of gentle protectiveness.

I will take refuge in the shadow of your wings. (Ps 57:1)

Now, it is a spiritual journey and fellowship with God; but in the Book of Revelation (7:9) we find a vivid description of those who are assembled in the actual presence of the Almighty—in his heavenly throne room. Eternal life is a new satisfying *quality of life*. It begins with repentance and the anointing of God's Spirit in this world. It continues, beyond physical death, into eternity.

Figure 52: The Lord our Righteousness. *Y-H-V-H*, the living God (between the wings of the cherubim), has made a loving eternal covenant (heart within the figure eight) with his people by means of a Righteous Branch (the Messiah), enabling them to become effective members of his holy kingdom. (Exod. 25:22; Isa. 11:1; Jer. 23:5–6) "The Lord our Righteousness" prayer is based on the meanings of the names of the twelve sons of Jacob. They are in birth order

175

The Lord our Righteousness: A Prayer of Thanksgiving

"The days are coming," declares the Lord, "when I will raise up to David [or "from David's line"] a righteous Branch, a King who will reign wisely and do what is just and right in the land. In his days Judah will be saved and Israel will live in safety. This is the name by which he will be called: The Lord Our Righteousness." (Jer. 23: 5-6)

Reuben or *Re'uven* (Behold, a son!)
Behold, the Son of God!

Simeon or *Shim'on* (hearing)
The "One who hears" has sent the long awaited Messiah

Levi or *L'vi* (joining)
So that we may be restored to our God.

Judah or *Yehudah* (praise)
How we praise you, O Lord,

Dan (he judged)
You have made a judgment in our favor;

Naphtali or *Naftali* (my wrestling)
For you saw our struggle and provided a Savior.

Gad (good fortune, or a troop)
O what good fortune for your people!

Asher (happy)
Now we are able to go forward with confidence

Issachar or *Yissa'khar* (reward)
Knowing that we will receive a great reward;

Zebulun or *Z'vulun* (dwell with)
For we will dwell with you eternally.

Joseph or *Yosef* (may he add)
May you continue to add more to this number

Benjamin or *Binyamin* (son of the right hand)
Through the Son of your right hand,
Yeshua HaMashiach.

I will establish his [King David's] line forever, his throne as long as the heavens endure. (Ps. 89:29)

176

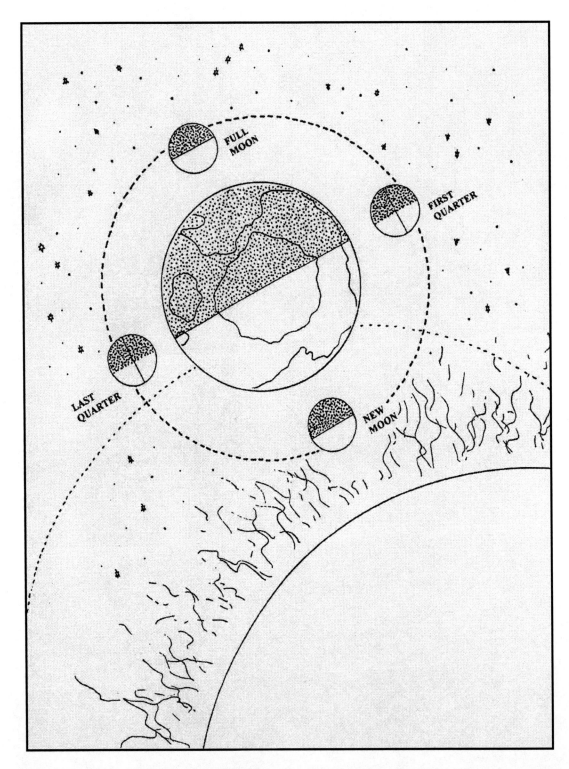

Figure 53: The lunar month. The earth takes just over 365 days to revolve around the sun. As the moon orbits the earth once a month its appearance slowly changes, resulting in a cycle of phases. Only the moon's *sunlit* side is visible from the earth. The completely dark "new moon" gives way to ever increasing crescent-shaped reflections, until the whole lunar surface glows on the night of the "full moon." This process is then slowly reversed, until the night of the dark "new moon" marks the beginning of a new month.

Part 5

Stars and Seasons

Astronomy and the Hebrews

> And God said, "Let there be lights in the expanse of the sky to separate the day from the night, and let them serve as signs to mark seasons and days and years." (Gen. 1:14)

During the early biblical period, time was reckoned solely by means of astronomical observations: the apparent movement of the sun, from sunrise to sunset, determined the time of day; the phases of the moon, regulated months; and the position of the stars, indicated the time of year and the seasons.

The ancient Israelites perceived the world to be a flat disc supported on pillars and surrounded by water. Although this concept was erroneous, it's clear that many of the heavenly constellations were known to biblical writers—and that the God of Israel was recognized as the ruler of the universe (*Ribbon Ha'Olam*). He was also acknowledged as the creator of its suns, moons, and planets; as the one who knows their numbers and names (Job 38:31; Ps. 147:4, 19:1–6). The sublime order of the heavenly cycles was viewed as being a manifestation of his supreme authority and wisdom.

> "It is I who made the earth and created mankind upon it. My own hands stretched out the heavens; I marshaled their starry hosts." (Isa. 45: 12)

> "Can you bind the beautiful Pleiades? Can you loose the cords of Orion?" (Job 38: 31)

The pseudoscience of astrology, attributing the stars (*kokhim*) with the power to influence human behavior and the events of people's lives, was widely practiced from the earliest times. But this, as with all other forms of mysticism, superstition, and necromancy, was strictly forbidden to the Israelites. Instead, they were taught to seek the Most High (*HaElyon*) exclusively, and to heed the warnings and instructions of the priests and prophets who served as his spokesmen.

> Let no one be found among you who sacrifices his son or daughter in the fire, who practices divination or sorcery, interprets omens, engages in witchcraft, or casts spells, or who is a medium or spiritist or who consults the dead. Anyone who does these things is detestable to the Lord. . . . You must be blameless before the Lord your God. (Deut. 18:10–13)

The most familiar reference to astronomy in the *New* Testament is the star of Bethlehem which miraculously led the Magi to Yeshua, the infant Messiah. Evidently, these men witnessed a unique event in the night skies that heralded the arrival of this "King of the Jews."

Magi from the east came to *Yerushalayim* [Jerusalem] and asked, "Where is the newborn King of the Jews? For we saw his star in the east and have come to worship him." (Matt. 2:1–2; JNT page 2)

The Ancient Hebrew Calendar

Millennia. The modern form of the Jewish calendar dates back over 2,300 years. Hebrew years (*shanim*) are counted "since creation"; which, in terms of our Gregorian calendar, is believed to have occurred in 3761 B.C. The year 2000 A.D. was therefore the Hebrew year 5760; becoming 5761 on the day of the Jewish New Year, *Rosh HaShanah*. For "Gregorian years," Jews use the abbreviation B.C.E. (Before the Common Era) in the place of B.C. (Before Christ), and C.E. (Common Era) in the place of A.D. (Anno Domini). *Hebrew years*, on the other hand, are followed by the abbreviation A.M.—Anno Mundi—meaning "Year of the World."

Because over 2,000 years have elapsed since the birth of Yeshua, some believers are expectantly preparing for his return and for the millennium of rest and peace. It is interesting to note, however, that counting from the year 2000 A.D., 240 years remain before the Hebrew year 6000—that is, the commencement of the Jewish seventh millennium.

Days, weeks, months, and years. The Hebrew month (*khodesh*) is lunar. It is based on the cycles of the moon (*levanah*). Each month starts and ends with the new moon—the full moon occurring midway through the month. These months are twenty-nine or thirty days in length, with an additional month occurring approximately every third year—seven times in a cycle of nineteen years. This thirteenth month serves to adjust the lunar to the solar year, producing a leap year. The addition of the extra month creates the two months of *Adar Alef* (*Adar* One), which is thirty days in length, and *Adar Bet* (*Adar* Two), which is twenty-nine days in length.

Because Hebrew dates relate to the moon, their days begin in the evening with the appearance of the first stars. For this reason, all Hebrew dates begin on the evening that precedes the date and extend from sundown to sundown.

Hebrew months (*khodashim*) are divided into four seven day weeks (*shavu'ot*), each of which culminates in a day of rest—*Shabbat* (the Sabbath). This practice is Semitic in origin and relates directly to the creation account. Contrary to English tradition, the days of the week are not given names. With the exception of *Shabbat*, the seventh day, they are designated by ordinal numbers: from Day One to Day Six.

In biblical times, every *seventh* year was a sabbatical year of rest for landlords, slaves, beasts of burden, and for the land itself. In that year, Hebrew slaves were also offered their freedom. Every *fiftieth* year was a Year of Jubilee (*Yovel*); family reunions took place, mortgages and debts were canceled, and land was returned to its original owners. This was a time of celebration and renewal. The above traditions and the repeated occurrence of specific numbers in Scripture, have led scholars to examine the symbolic significance of biblical numbers.

Numbers in Scripture

# 1	Unity or beginning.
# 2	Witnesses: "A matter shall be established by two or three witnesses."
# 3	Divine perfection: Father, Son, and Holy Spirit.
# 4	Creation of material things such as the earth, cities, etc.
# 5	Grace: God's divine undeserved favor added to his creation (4+1).
# 6	Man—who falls short of spiritual perfection (7–1).
# 7	Spiritual perfection and the Sabbath day of rest.
# 8	Abundance (7+1).
# 9	The conclusion of a matter (3x3, the last of the single digits).
# 10	Divine order: for example, the Law.
# 11	Disorder, imperfection, disintegration (10+1 or 12–1).
# 12	Earthly government of God: twelve sons, tribes, disciples. Measurement of time: twelve months in a year, twenty-four hours in a day (2x12), sixty minutes in an hour (5x12).
# 21	Divine completion of God's work (3x7).
# 24	Heavenly government (12x2).
# 30	Perfection of divine order (3x10).
# 40	The beginning of new phase in God's plan of salvation; following a period of probation, trial, or chastisement.
# 50	Jubilee: deliverance, celebration, renewal, and rest.

Two Calendars: Civic and Sacred

The ancient Hebrew calendar consisted of *two* calendars that ran concurrently: the twelve month *civic* calendar, which was based on the agricultural cycle; and the seven month *sacred* calendar, which incorporated the seven Feasts of Israel. Before the time of Moses, *Tishrei* was regarded as the first month of the Hebrew calendar; coinciding with the beginning of the agricultural year. Later, when the system of Hebrew feasts was instituted, Moses was instructed by God to regard *Nissan*, the month in which the first spring feasts were celebrated, as the beginning of the year (Exod. 12:2). Today, the Jewish New Year is once again celebrated in the month of Tishrei. (See Figure 54.)

The agricultural cycle started with the ploughing season in *Tishrei* (September/October) and culminated in the olive harvest during the month of *Elul* (August/September). The Feasts of the Lord fell within a shorter seven month period—starting with the Feast of Passover (*Pesakh*) in the month of *Nissan* (March/April) and culminating in the Feast of Tabernacles (*Sukkot*) in Tishrei (September/October). The first four feasts were therefore celebrated in the spring and the last three in the autumn.

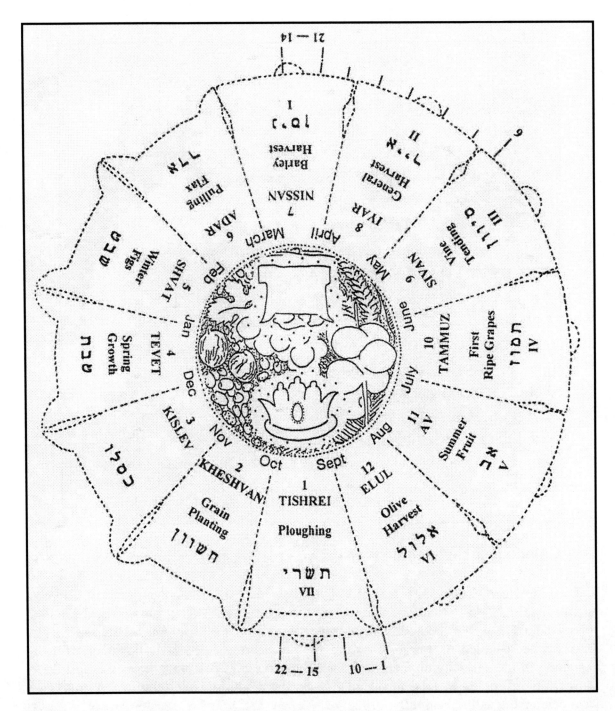

Figure 54: The Hebrew lunar calendar. Ordinal numbers (1–12) and Roman numerals (I–VII) distinguish the agricultural from the sacred calendar. Horned altar shapes represent the blood sacrifice of the Old Covenant; whereas bells (*pa'amonim*)—associated with the celebration of important events—represent the "Good News" of the New Covenant. Because *Tishrei* begins the agricultural year and closes the sacred year, it features both an altar and a bell. *Nissan* is the month of Passover—hence the sacrificial lamb on the altar above this segment. Messianic Jews believe that Yeshua will return to rule the earth during the sacred month of Tishrei—hence the crown

182

Hebrew Months: Civic (1–12) and Sacred (I–VII)

1/VII	*Tishrei*	Sept./Oct.
2	*Kheshvan*	Oct./Nov.
3	*Kislev*	Nov./Dec.
4	*Tevet*	Dec./Jan.
5	*Shvat*	Jan./Feb.
6	*Adar (Alef)*	Feb./March
	(*Adar Bet:* leap year)	
7/I	*Nissan*	March/April
8/II	*Iyar*	April/May
9/III	*Sivan*	May/June
10/IV	*Tammuz*	June/July
11/V	*Av*	July/Aug.
12/VI	*Elul*	Aug./Sept.

*The three most important sacred months.

The Seven Feasts of Israel

In the year A.D. 325, Constantine, the Emperor of Rome, banned the celebration of the ancient Hebrew feasts; asserting that they were too specifically Jewish in nature. From that time, the Resurrection was commemorated by Christians on the first Sunday after the spring equinox each year—not at the time of the Jewish Passover. Gentiles also changed the name of this celebration to "Easter"; derived from the name of an ancient pagan spring festival that occurred at about the same time as the Jewish Passover.

The Hebrew word *mo'adim* means "my feasts." It refers to seven "appointed times" in the sacred Hebrew calendar. They were all regarded as holy days on which people turned from their normal activities to honor God, but the Feasts of Passover (*Pesakh*), Weeks (*Shavu'ot*), and Tabernacles (*Sukkot*) were national celebrations —pilgrim festivals (*shalosh regalim*). All men were required to celebrate *these* three feasts in the capital city of Jerusalem.

The feasts affirm the activities of God in Hebrew history. They also have powerful messianic overtones. The four spring feasts coincided with key first century New Testament events: the death, burial, and resurrection of the Messiah; and the birth of the Church. The last three have yet to be fulfilled.

These "*mo'adim*" may be viewed from various perspectives: (1) as they were celebrated in Old Testament times, (2) as they are commemorated by the Jews today, and (3) their messianic overtones. The ancient Hebrew marriage tradition also provides clues regarding the overall sequence of Messianic events.

The Feasts of Israel

Spring Feasts

                                          Hebrew Terms (Italics)

1. Passover: *14 Nissan*   *Pesakh*

2. Unleavened Bread: *14–21 Nissan*   *Khag HaMatzot*

3. Firstfruits: *21 Nissan*   *HaBikkurim*

Forty-nine days between the second day   *Sfirat Ha'Omer*

of Passover and Pentecost (*Shavu'ot*)   or Counting of the Sheaves

4. Pentecost: *6 Sivan*   *Shavu'ot* or Weeks

Autumn Feasts

Days of Awe: *1–10 Tishrei*   *Yamim Nora'im*

5. Trumpets: *1 Tishrei*   *Yom Teru'ah* or Day of Blowing

6. Atonement: *10 Tishrei*   *Yom Kippur* or Day of Covering

7. Tabernacles: *15–22 Tishrei*   *Sukkot* or Booths

Great Day of the Feast: *22 Tishrei*   *Hoshana Rabbah*

The Rejoicing of the *Torah*: *22 or 23 Tishrei*   *Simkhat Torah*

The Feasts and the Hebrew Marriage Tradition

Ancient marriage customs. Zola Levitt, the American Messianic writer and teacher, has explained how the ancient Hebrew marriage tradition relates to the Feasts of Israel.

A unique series of events characterized this tradition; some of which took place a year or more before the wedding day (*yom nisu'im*). Marriage partners were selected by the parents and all were obliged to wed. As women were valuable working assets, a bride had to be paid for (Gen. 34:12; 1 Sam. 18:25). Therefore, when the marriage contract (*ketubah*) was drawn up, it contained a statement of the "bride price." This agreement was sealed in the drinking of a cup of wine by both parties.

The following illustration, Figure 55, depicts aspects of Yeshua's earthly ministry: He was born in a stable, raised in a middle-class Jewish home, debated spiritual matters in the Temple with the Jewish elders. After he was baptized, he taught and performed miracles. Before being arrested in the Garden of Gethsemane, he entered Jerusalem "in triumph" on a donkey. He was then crowned with a ring of thorns, struck in the face, and had his beard hairs pulled out. He was whipped, crucified, and buried. Finally, he was resurrected and ascended to heaven to become an eternal high priest. A small Star of David *(Magen David)* on the earth segment in the lowest section of the drawing indicates the location of the Holy Land.

184

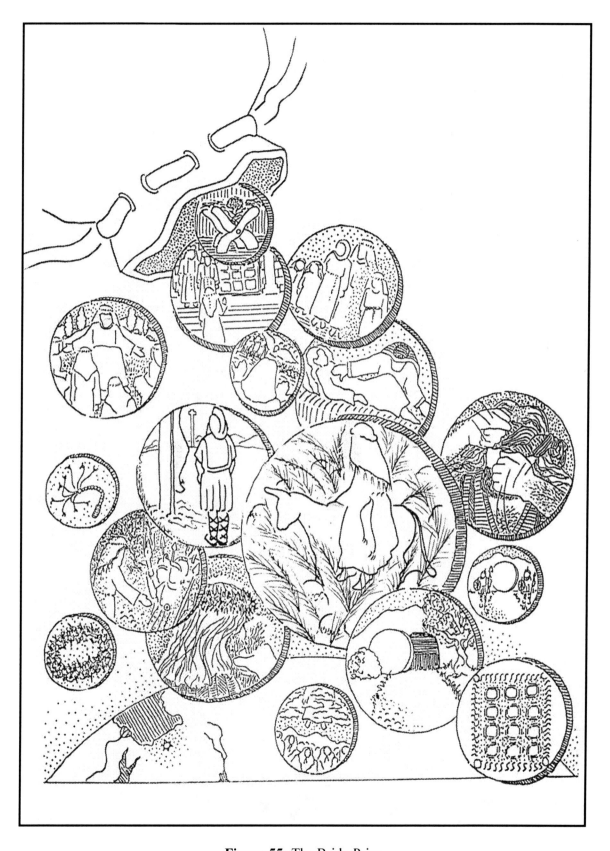

Figure 55: The Bride-Price

From that time, the girl remained veiled—indicating that she was set apart and waiting for her bridegroom (*khatan*). The young man, on the other hand, returned to his father's house and, according to custom, set about building a bridal chamber. Before he could return to claim his bride (*kalah*), his father had to approve of the chamber. Therefore, he could not state with any certainty when the wedding would take place. This was determined solely by his father (*ab*).

On the evening of the wedding day, the bridegroom, accompanied by his friends, planned a surprise arrival at the home of the bride—like "a thief in the night." They signaled their approach by shouting and with blasts on a ram's horn trumpet, a *shofar*.

After the couple had received a blessing from the girl's parents, the groom, bride, and the bridesmaids—with sufficient oil in their lamps—were led through the village toward the groom's home. Invited guests lined the streets, forming a joyful torchlight procession. The bride was then presented to the groom's parents and a week-long celebration ensued. The wedding culminated in a grand feast called the "marriage supper."

The marriage was consummated in the bridal chamber during the "bridal week." News of this was relayed to a friend of the groom who was waiting at the door. He, in turn, informed the wedding guests. References are made to these events in John 3:29, Joel 2:16, and in the account of the marriage of Jacob and Leah.

> "The bride belongs to the bridegroom. The friend who attends the bridegroom waits and listens for him, and is full of joy when he hears the bridegroom's voice." (John 3:29)

> Let the bridegroom leave his room and the bride her chamber. (Joel 2:16)

> So Laban brought together all the people of the place and gave a feast. But when evening came, he took his daughter Leah and gave her to Jacob, and Jacob lay with her. . . . "Finish this daughter's bridal week; then we will give you the younger one also. . . ." (Gen. 29:22–27)

A Jewish wedding. The modern Jewish wedding ceremony still consists of the betrothal before the marriage; and the groom still gives the bride a *ketubah*, a binding marriage contract. They are married by the rabbi under a canopy, the *khuppah*, which is said to symbolize the home—their "dwelling place." The wedding ceremony itself is called *khuppah ve-kidushin*, which means "canopy and holiness." This, as in Christian marriage, relates to the concept of *holy* matrimony; a marriage sanctified by God. The couple share wine under the canopy and, at the end of the ceremony, the groom crushes a wineglass underfoot. This is said to symbolize the destruction of the Temple in A.D. 70; an event that shattered and dispersed the Jewish people. It also serves as a reminder of the fragility of life. Therefore, when the sound of the breaking glass is heard, the wedding guests exclaim, "*Mazel Tov!*" meaning "Good Luck!"

Yeshua as the Jewish bridegroom. It is the *ancient* Hebrew marriage tradition that presents us with a picture of the *divine* contract, betrothal, and marriage. That is, the contract between the Messiah and his believing bride; the spiritual consummation of this union; and the "wedding of the Lamb." Yeshua is the Jewish Bridegroom. The "bride price" has been paid—he gave his life for his bride. The divine contract, or covenant (*brit*), was sealed in his costly blood (*dam*): "He drank the cup of suffering."(Luke 22:20) However, the betrothal, or period of waiting for the return of the Bridegroom, is not yet complete. His believing bride remains "veiled"—set apart for her Bridegroom.

The Hebrew Calendar as a Blueprint of History

When the sacred calendar is combined with the agricultural calendar, some interesting parallels with Church history emerge. The agricultural months from *Tishrei* to *Adar* will represent the period of the Old Covenant; the sacred months (*Nissan* to *Tishrei*), in combination with their harvest times, the New Covenant.

1. Tishrei: **a time of ploughing.** The agricultural cycle of ancient Israel started with a season of ploughing; a time of preparation for the seeds that were to be scattered. During the Israelite sojourn in ancient Egypt they were humbled, through suffering, in preparation for becoming God's covenant people. They were "harrowed" in readiness for the seeds, or teachings, of the *Torah*.

2. Kheshvan: **a time of planting.** At Sinai God initiated a new phase in Israel's history. He met with Moses on the mountain for forty days and proceeded to establish a unique covenant with his people. He declared that he would be their God and they his people. He gave the Israelites the Law, a righteous code of conduct; and the Tabernacle, a portable worship center that also served as God's "dwelling place."

3. Kislev: **a time of waiting.** Despite the unique privileges extended to them, the Israelites lacked the necessary faith to enter the Promised Land and were made to *wait* in the desert for another forty years. It was the following generation of Hebrews that entered the land, under the leadership of Joshua.

4. Tevet: **a time of spring growth.** Spring growth is rapid and vigorous. This new nation entered, occupied, and then quickly spread across Canaan; putting down roots and thriving under God's guidance.

5. Shvat: **time of winter figs.** Fig trees were indigenous to Canaan and grew in abundance. Their rich winter fruit appeared before their leaves. Figs (*te'enah*) were the first fruit crop of the agricultural year; a foretaste of good things to come. During the golden age of King David and Solomon's reigns, David established Jerusalem (*Yerushalayim*) as his capital city. Solomon built a magnificent temple to the God of Israel. Both were a foretaste of good things to come. The Scriptures indicate that Jerusalem will eventually be established as the magnificent capital city of the royal Messiah and become the eternal dwelling place of Almighty God.

6. Adar: **time for the pulling of flax.** The blue-flowered flax plant (*pishtan*) is the oldest of the textile fiber plants. When harvested, it was *uprooted* and the stem fibers *separated* by immersing them in water. The flax was then left to dry, often on flat rooftops, before being combed into threads. Linseed oil was produced from the plants' seeds. The dried fibers were used in the making of linen, string, nets, and lamp-wicks. This process relates to the division of the Hebrew nation: first, into the Northern and Southern Kingdoms and later, as they were uprooted and scattered among the Gentiles.

187

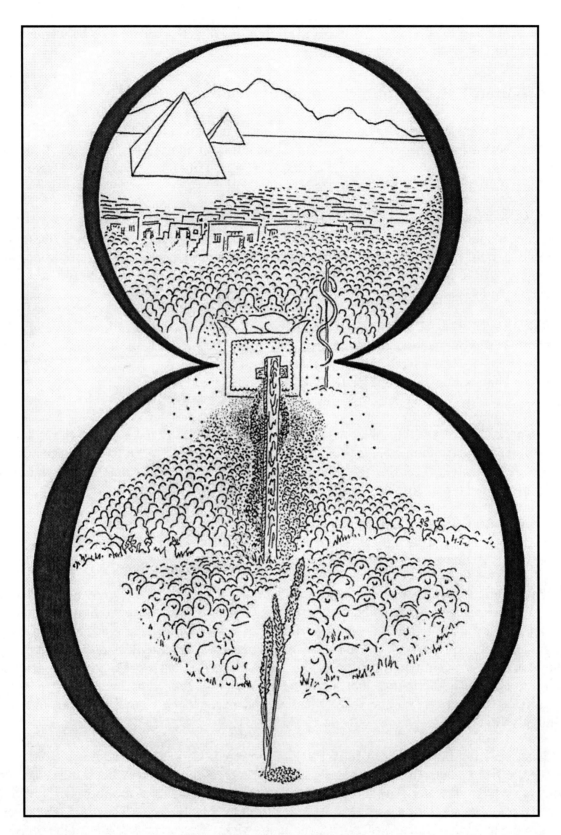

Figure 56: Passover or *Pesakh*: *Nissan* was the month of Passover and the barley harvest. In this illustration, the concept of the Passover lamb is linked to Yeshua—who is both the "Lamb of God" and the "Good Shepherd"

Figure 57: The bride-price paid in full. Yeshua becomes the High Priest of a New Covenant priesthood of believers

Spring Feasts

7. Nissan: **Barley Harvest and First Spring Feasts.** The three spring feasts of Passover, Unleavened Bread, and Firstfruits were celebrated at the time of the barley harvest. Together, they constituted an eight-day festival extending from the fourteenth to the twenty-first of *Nissan*. Passover therefore occurred midway through the month, coinciding with the appearance of the full moon.

Today the Jewish Passover festival centers on the commemoration of the Exodus (*Yetsi'ah Hamonit*); the deliverance of the ancient Israelites from Egypt under the leadership of Moses. In the past it was also an agricultural festival that marked the beginning of the grain harvest. For Messianic believers the festival has added significance. It contains strong overtones of the death, burial, and resurrection of Yeshua.

I. Passover or *Pesakh*

"The Lord's Passover begins at twilight on the fourteenth day of the first month [*Nissan*]. On the fifteenth day of that month the Lord's Feast of Unleavened Bread begins; for seven days you must eat bread made without yeast." (Lev. 23:5–6)

Passover and the Exodus

On the night of the last and most dreadful plague of Egypt, "the death of the firstborn," the Israelites were instructed to prepare a special meal. It is still commemorated in the Jewish Passover Seder today. Each family had to select a year old male lamb or kid (*seh*), without defect, and slaughter it at twilight—being careful not to break any of its bones. Moses then told them to take some of the lambs' blood and paint it on the doorframes of their houses. This was done to ensure that when the "angel of death" saw the blood, he would "pass over" their homes—so that no firstborn Israelite males would die that night. The Israelites were instructed to then roast the meat over their fires and to eat it with bitter herbs and unleavened bread.

"The animals you choose must be year-old males without defect, and you may take them from the sheep or the goats. Take care of them until the fourteenth day of the month, when all the people of the community of Israel must slaughter them at twilight. Then they are to take some of the blood and put it on the sides and tops of the doorframes of the houses where they eat the lambs. . . . The blood will be a sign for you on the houses where you are; and when I see the blood, I will pass over you. No destructive plague will touch you when I strike Egypt." (Exod. 12:5–13)

The Jewish Passover *Seder*

The first night of the Jewish Passover, *Pesakh*, is called "*Seder* night." The word Seder means "order" or "arrangement"; referring to the specific order of events found in the Passover booklet—the *Hagadah*. The Passover Seder begins with a question that is asked by the youngest child in the family: "Why is this night different from all other nights?" The father of the household, seated at the head of the table, answers four such questions during the meal.

Before him, a large platter, containing seven bowls of food, commemorates different aspects of the Exodus account. The *matzah* bread in the center is called "the bread of slavery and affliction." The *kharoset*—a mixture of apple, nuts, cinnamon, and wine—represents the bricks and mortar used by Hebrew slaves in the construction of Egyptian edifices. Horse-radish and lettuce—"bitter herbs"— symbolize the bitterness of this period. A lamb's shank bone serves as a reminder of the Passover lamb. An egg and a bowl of salt water also feature in this meal; the latter representing the salty tears shed by the suffering Israelites.

Four cups of Passover wine (*yayin*) are consumed during the meal. Each one is referred to as "a cup of salvation," because each relates to one of four promises of salvation found in the Book of Exodus:

> "Therefore, say to the Israelites: 'I am the Lord, and I will bring you from under the yoke of the Egyptians [1]. I will free you from being slaves to them [2], and I will redeem you with an outstretched arm and with mighty acts of judgment [3]. I will take you as my own people, and I will be your God [4].'" (Exod. 6:6–7)

For the Jews, this holiday does not merely commemorate the Exodus. Above all, it symbolizes the right of every individual to be free. Originally, the Israelites reclined on the floor as they shared this meal, but today a cushion is placed on each family member's chair. The cushions symbolize freedom and well being, as opposed to affliction and oppression.

Yeshua as the Passover Lamb
Yeshua died in Jerusalem at the time of the annual Jewish Passover (*Pesakh*) in approximately A.D. 30; about one thousand three hundred years after the time of Moses and the Exodus. Because it was the time of year when Jews celebrated freedom from bondage, an attitude of mute resistance was manifested toward the Romans who were occupying Palestine. Judas Iscariot apparently believed that a means of attaining freedom had been provided in Yeshua; that his "*rabbi*" was the conquering royal Messiah. But Yeshua was destined to come *first* as an atoning sacrifice—and only much later as a king.

Because Yeshua fulfilled all of God's requirements regarding the Passover Lamb, he is often referred to as "the Lamb of God" or "the Passover Lamb." He was sinless and therefore "a male without defect or blemish." He died on the "altar" of a Roman crucifixion stake on the eve of Passover. As with all Passover lambs not a single bone of his body was broken. The blood that poured from his side was not applied to the doorframes of Israelite homes to protect firstborn males from the "angel of death." Yeshua's followers believe that when the Father sees those who are "covered by Yeshua's blood," he sees only his Son, "the Lamb without blemish," and "passes over" their sins.

Therefore as the children of Israel were saved from *physical* death, so Yeshua's blood saves his followers from *spiritual* death. Similarly, the Israelites were freed from *physical* slavery, whereas in Yeshua mankind has been offered the opportunity to be released from *spiritual* slavery to the old nature. Yeshua is therefore viewed as being the perfect sin offering; the ultimate unblemished male Passover lamb.

Passover was commemorated as a national celebration from the time of the wilderness period. After the destruction of Herod's Temple, ritual blood sacrifices ceased altogether and Passover reverted to its earliest form—an intimate family celebration. This has continued to this day.

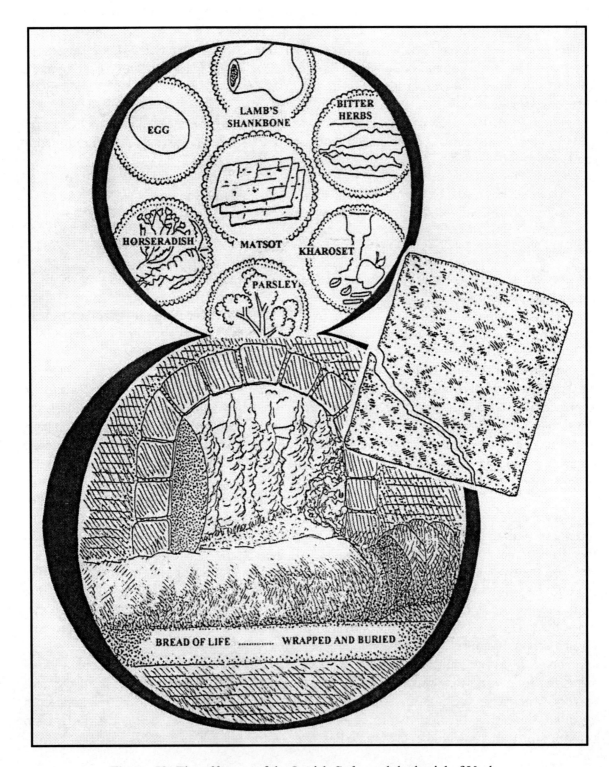

Figure 58: The *afikomen* of the Jewish *Seder* and the burial of Yeshua

Figure 59: The Feast of Firstfruits and the Resurrection

II. Feast of Unleavened Bread or *Khag HaMatzot*

"Celebrate the Feast of Unleavened Bread, because it was on this very day that I brought your divisions out of Egypt. Celebrate this day as a lasting ordinance for the generations to come. In the first month [*Nissan*] you are to eat bread made without yeast, from the evening of the *fourteenth* day until the evening of the *twenty-first* day. For seven days no yeast is to be found in your houses." (Exod. 12:17–19)

The terms "Passover" and "Feast of Unleavened Bread" are often used interchangeably, because during this eight day holiday the Israelites were permitted to eat only unleavened bread.

The Unleavened Bread of the Exodus
Before the Israelites left Egypt, they were instructed to bake unleavened bread. They left in haste. There was no time for their bread to rise. It was the season of the barley harvest, so barley flour, not wheat flour was, in all probability, used in the making of that Passover bread.

The Jewish Passover M*atzah*
Because leaven is *fermented* dough, it symbolizes that which is unclean, tainted or sinful. To this day, careful preparation for Passover—or Feast of Unleavened Bread—includes the cleansing of Jewish homes of all traces of *khametz*, the forbidden leaven. And only *matzot* (plural of *matzah*) are eaten during this eight-day holiday. They form the centerpiece of every Passover *Seder* plate, every Seder table. By rabbinic decree, matzah has to be pierced, striped, and have a bruised appearance. It replicates the ultimate *korban*; the crucified Messiah.

Matzah as a Picture of Yeshua Messiah (Isaiah 53)
   1. *Matzah* is *pierced*, reminding us of the wound in his side: "he was pierced for our transgressions."
   2. *Matzah* has a *bruised* appearance, reminding us of the blows to his head and body: "he was crushed [or bruised] for our iniquities. . ."
   3. *Matzah* is *striped*, reminding us of the marks of the thirty-nine lashes: "by his wounds [or stripes] we are healed."
   4. *Matzah* is *unleavened*, reminding us of his sinless nature: "he had done no violence, nor was any deceit in his mouth."

Yeshua as the Jewish afikomen. Within the context of the *Seder*, Yeshua is therefore symbolized in the sinless Passover Lamb—the shank bone—and in pure unleavened *matzah* bread. There is, however, one more picture of the Messiah in this meal. From the three pieces of matzah in the center of the plate, the middle piece—the *afikomen*—is removed, broken, and wrapped in a piece of linen. It is then hidden somewhere in the room. The children are later asked to search for it until they find it.

   Herein lies an image of Yeshua's body: removed from the stake in haste—it was the day of preparation for the Passover—wrapped for burial, and then hidden from sight in the tomb. On the third day, his "children" searched for him and found him (John 19 and 20).

194

Yeshua and the barley harvest. In ancient Israel, barley (*se'orah*) was the grain of the poor. It was a common crop, because it grew in infertile, rocky soil. Wheat (*khitah*), harvested about six weeks later, was used more by the wealthy and in priestly offerings. How appropriate it is that Yeshua, the unleavened "Bread of Life," fulfilled the New Covenant agreement during the time of the barley harvest—not the wheat harvest.

He was born in *Bet-lekhem*—the "House of Bread"—in a *humble* makeshift shelter (*sukkah*). He grew up among the *common* people of Nazareth. During his ministry he served the *poor*, sick, lame, blind, deaf, and mute. His harvest was primarily a "barley harvest," not a "wheat harvest." It was a harvest of the "poor in spirit" (Matt. 5:3) —and he himself became poor, "of no reputation," in order to immeasurably enrich the lives of others (2 Cor. 8:9).

> "Speak to the Israelites and say to them: 'When you enter the land I am going to give you and reap its harvest, bring to the priest a sheaf of the first grain you harvest. He is to wave the sheaf before the Lord so it will be accepted on your behalf; the priest is to wave it on the day after the Sabbath.' " (Lev. 23:10–11)

III. Firstfruits or *HaBikkurim*

The third spring feast, the Feast of Firstfruits or *HaBikkurim*, was celebrated on the first Sunday following the day of Passover—"on the day after the Sabbath." (Lev. 23:11) Because Passover was always celebrated on *14 Nissan*, the date of Firstfruits varied. It could fall on any of the days from 15 to 21 Nissan.

On *HaBikkurim*, during the time when Israelites worshipped at the Tabernacle or Temple, sheaves from the first harvested grain and the firstfruit of the flocks were presented to the priests. Acting as intermediaries between God and Israel, the priests then waved the sheaves before the Lord, thereby sanctifying them as offerings.

Yeshua and the Feast of Firstfruits
It was on the day of Firstfruits—the first Sunday after the Passover Sabbath—that Yeshua was resurrected. He became the "firstfruit" offering of a New Covenant harvest of believers—and the first to rise to eternal life. Notice the words of the Seder blessing over the Passover *matzah*: "Blessed art thou, O Lord our God, King of the universe, who bringest forth bread from the earth." On the third day after the crucifixion, the God of Israel did, indeed, "bring forth Bread from the earth." Early on that Sunday morning, Yeshua, "the Bread of Life," rose from the dead. A little later that day, his followers found their "*afikomen.*"

Throughout the centuries, believers have continued to "break the bread" ("the bread of affliction") and "drink the cup" ("the cup of salvation"), in remembrance of the priceless gift of salvation bequeathed to humanity during the Feast of Passover in approximately A.D. 30.

Jewish and Gentile Sabbaths
The first Messianic believers continued to attend synagogues and observe Jewish customs. However, because Yeshua died on a Friday (or Thursday, according to some scholars) — before sundown on the eve of Passover—and rose from death on Sunday, "the third day," Sunday came to be referred to as "The Lord's Day." Initially, both Saturday and Sunday

195

were therefore observed as holy days, but eventually Constantine permanently changed the day of the Christian Sabbath from Saturday, the seventh day of the Jewish week, to Sunday, the first day of the week.

8. Iyar: Grain Harvest and *Sfirat Ha'Omer*. *Iyar* was the time of the general grain harvest. This month falls between the barley firstfruit offering of *Nissan* and the wheat firstfruit offering of *Sivan*.

The Counting of the Sheaves (*Sfirat Ha'Omer*)

For observant Jews, the forty-nine days that make up the seven weeks between the second day of Passover and the day of *Shavu'ot* (Weeks or Pentecost), are carefully counted. This is a time of introspection and self-assessment—and a time spent anticipating a mighty act of God during the approaching Feast of Shavu'ot. The Hebrew name for this period is derived from an evening prayer recited by Jews during this interval in their sacred year. It is known as *Sfirat Ha'Omer*, meaning "The Counting of the Sheaves."

> "From the day after the Sabbath, the day you brought the sheaf of the wave offering, count off seven full weeks." (Lev. 23:15)

Yeshua and *Sfirat Ha'Omer*

It was during this period that Yeshua made his many supernatural appearances as the risen Messiah. His true identity finally became self-evident. A great body of witnesses was established who would testify concerning the Resurrection, resulting in the dissemination of a message of comfort and hope that would extend to "the four corners of the earth."

> "God raised up this Yeshua! And we are all witnesses of it!" (Acts 2:32; JNT page 156)

> After his suffering, he showed himself to these men and gave many convincing proofs that he was alive. He appeared to them over a period of forty days and spoke about the kingdom of God (Acts 1:3).

> [H]e appeared to Peter, and then to the twelve. After that, he appeared to more than five hundred of the brothers at the same time. . . . Then he appeared to James, then to all the apostles, and last of all he appeared to me [Paul or *Sha'ul*] also. . . . (1 Cor. 15:5–8)

9. Sivan: Tending of Vines, Wheat Harvest, and the Last Spring Feast. The month of *Sivan* marked the beginning of the wheat harvest. It was also the season of vine tending. The grapevines (*gefen*) were weeded, irrigated, and pruned; preparing them to bear much fruit (grapes: *anavim*).

IV. Feast of Weeks or *Shavu'ot*

> "Count off fifty days up to the day after the seventh Sabbath, and then present an offering of new grain to the Lord. From wherever you live, bring two loaves made of two-tenths of an ephah of fine flour, baked with yeast, as a wave offering of firstfruits to the Lord. . . . Then sacrifice one male goat for a sin offering and two lambs, each a year old, for a fellowship

offering. The priest is to wave the two lambs before the Lord as a wave offering, together with the bread of the firstfruits. They are a sacred offering to the Lord for the priest." (Lev. 23:16–20).

Seven weeks after Passover, on the sixth day of *Sivan*, the fourth spring feast was celebrated. It was the Feast of Weeks: known in Hebrew as *Shavu'ot*; and in Greek, as "Pentecost," meaning "Fiftieth Day." New wheat grain, two loaves of leavened bread, a male goat, and two lambs were presented to the Lord as firstfruit priestly offerings.

The Jewish *Shavu'ot*

Jews celebrate "The Giving of the *Torah*" at this time in their calendar, believing that Moses received the Law on fiery Mt. Sinai seven weeks after the Passover of the Exodus. During this two-day pilgrim festival, the focus is on two biblical figures: Moses, the Lawgiver; and Ruth, whose story of loyalty and gentleness is associated with the wheat harvest.

Shavu'ot and Pentecost

Unlike the unleavened *matzah* of Passover—associated with the sinless Messiah—the two leavened loaves of *Shavu'ot*, containing impure fermented dough, relate to the imperfect nature of mankind. The giving of the Law, or *Torah*, to sinful men and women during Shavu'ot forms a perfect equivalent to a profound life-changing event that took place on this day in Jerusalem—exactly seven weeks after the Passover death of Yeshua.

Before his ascension, Yeshua promised that he would not leave his followers as "orphans" and told them to wait in Jerusalem for the gift of the Holy Spirit (*Ruach HaKodesh*). On the day of *Shavu'ot* (Pentecost) the covenant of "heart circumcision" was fully realized. Many who had gathered for the festival were inwardly transformed as God wrote his *Torah* on their hearts and minds by means of his Spirit. Beginning with those Jews, the phenomenon of Spirit baptism has continued down the centuries among multi-cultural believers across the globe.

> "This is the covenant I will make with the house of Israel after that time," declares the Lord. "I will put my law in their minds and write it on their hearts. I will be their God, and they will be my people. . . . I will forgive their wickedness and will remember their sins no more." (Jer. 31:33–34; Heb. 10:16–17; JNT page 304)

The Spirit was first poured out on Yeshua's disciples *(talmidim)* in an "upper room" in Jerusalem and, later, on thousands of others in the streets of the city. Jews from all nations heard the spirit-filled disciples proclaiming the news concerning the Messiah in their own languages. The Spirit had enabled those unschooled Galileans to speak with great eloquence in "foreign tongues." As a result, three thousand Jews were added to the number of Yeshua's followers that day (Acts 2:5–11, 41). Pentecost is therefore often referred to as "the birthday of the Church."

The same number of Israelites—three thousand—had died at Mt. Sinai thirteen centuries earlier. During Moses' absence on the mountain, while God's *Torah* was being given to humanity for the *first* time, they'd degenerated into idol worship. At Pentecost three thousand were given new life thereby balancing the scales of divine justice and mercy.

Figure 60: The Feast of Weeks and the Day of Pentecost

A particular portion of the Book of Ezekiel is read during the Jewish *Shavu'ot* service every year. It paints a picture of a violent wind—a whirlwind (AV)—with a raging fire at its center. The head of each of the four living creatures mentioned bears an image of a man, lion, ox, and eagle—undoubtedly symbolic of the House of Israel:

> I looked, and I saw a windstorm coming out of the north—an immense cloud with flashing lightning and surrounded by brilliant light. The center of the fire looked like glowing metal, and in the fire was what looked like four living creatures. (Ezek. 1:4–5)

Therefore, how appropriate it was that the two irrepressible forces of fire and wind heralded the anointing of God's Spirit on Yeshua's Jewish followers on the day of Pentecost:

> The festival of *Shavu'ot* arrived, and the believers all gathered together in one place. Suddenly there came a sound from the sky like the roar of a violent wind, and it filled the whole house where they were sitting. Then they saw what looked like tongues of fire, which separated and came to rest on each one of them. They were all filled with the *Ruach HaKodesh* [Holy Spirit] and began to talk in different languages, as the Spirit enabled them to speak. (Acts 2:1–4; JNT page 154)

For believers in Yeshua, Pentecost—*Shavu'ot*—is therefore associated with the giving of God's Law by means of his Spirit. Christianity's first "fiftieth day" was a day of jubilee (*yovel*); a day of great celebration, rejoicing, and thanksgiving. It marked the beginning of a new epoch. Millions have since been inwardly transformed and regenerated by the Spirit. This restoration of mankind to the Creator has not been accomplished by overthrowing societies or entire civilizations. It has been accomplished by individuals being drawn to *Y-H-V-H* one-at-a-time, over a period of two thousand years.

> "I tell you the truth, unless a kernel of wheat falls to the ground and dies, it remains only a single seed. But if it dies, it produces many seeds." (John 12:24)

Yeshua Messiah, the firstfruit of the New Covenant, died, was buried, and rose during the time of the three spring feasts. On the day of the fourth feast, *Shavu'ot*, the Spirit was poured out on a Jewish firstfruit harvest of believers; equipping them to continue his work. The sap (Spirit) that flowed through the main vine (the Messiah) had entered its first new branches (followers); cleansing, transforming, and preparing them to bear much fruit. (Analogy based on John 15:1–6)

Between Spring and Autumn

10. Tammuz: First Ripe Grapes and the First Emissaries. The Mediterranean region is known as much for its ancient vineyards, as for its fig and olive trees. By the tenth month of the agricultural year, the first ripe grapes were ready for harvest. Today an image of an enormous bunch of grapes, supported on a pole between two Israelites, is used as an emblem for the Promised Land. This relates to the report brought back to Moses by his twelve scouts. They said that Canaan was a land of abundance, a land "flowing with milk and honey."

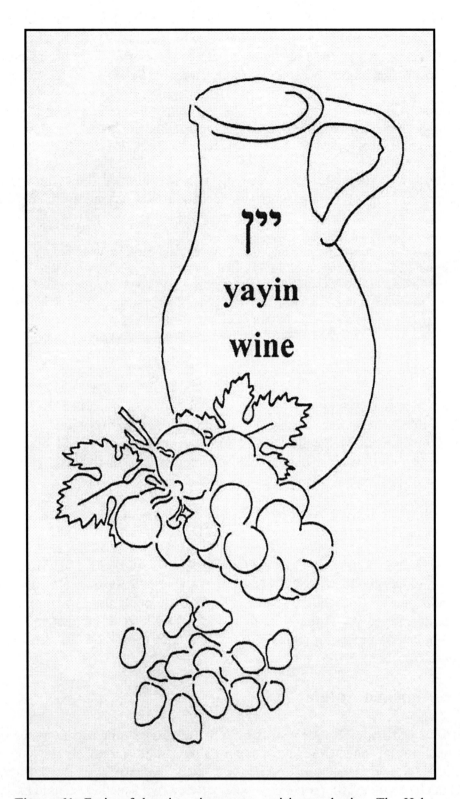

Figure 61: Fruits of the vine: ripe grapes, raisins, and wine. The Hebrew word is pronounced *yayin*, meaning "wine"

The first generation of spiritually anointed believers matured in their faith over a period of time. As they went out "into all the world" (Mark 16:15), people would have noticed the quality of their lives. Their inward transformation would have been evident in their demeanor—the presence of the Spirit has always been manifested in the lives of regenerated believers. "The fruits of the Spirit"—love, joy, peace, patience, kindness, goodness, faithfulness, gentleness, and self-control (Gal. 5:22)—as well as God-given courage and the message of forgiveness and eternal life, would have attracted others to belief in Yeshua.

This Messianic "vine" spread steadily throughout the Mediterranean region—but not without opposition. For nearly three hundred years, up until the time of the conversion of Constantine, believers were persecuted. The more intense the persecution, however, the more rapid the dissemination of the gospel: "The blood of the martyrs is the seed of the Church!"

> Furthermore, we know that God causes everything to work together for the good of those who love God and are called in accordance with his purpose: If God is for us, who can be against us? . . . Who will separate us from the love of the Messiah? Trouble? Hardship? Persecution? Hunger? Poverty? Danger? War? (Rom. 8:28–35; JNT page 209)

In the larger context, because this is a "fallen world," those who trust and obey the God of Israel have always been "foreigners" and "strangers." Very often, the greater an individual's love for God, the greater the ostracism by others. Conversely, the Scriptures indicate that times of suffering are frequently God's way of disciplining and refining those whom he loves. Therefore such experiences should not rob believers of their faith or equilibrium.

> "My son, don't despise the discipline of *Adonai* [*Y-H-V-H:* the Lord] or become despondent when he corrects you. For *Adonai* disciplines those he loves and whips everyone he accepts as a son." . . . he disciplines us in a way that provides genuine benefit to us and enables us to share in his holiness. (Heb. 12:5–6, 10; JNT page 308)

11. Av: Summer Fruit and a Harvest of Gentiles. Various fruits ripened during the long, hot, dry summers. Dates, pomegranates, melons, apples, and nuts, harvested in the month of *Av,* added color to tables and variety to diets. The harvest of summer fruit will be compared to the "time of the Gentiles"; alluded to in the Book of Romans (11:25).

Toward the end of the fourth century, once Christianity had become the state religion of the Roman Empire, it spread quickly among a *variety* of European civilizations. Gentiles—as opposed to Jews—soon dominated the Faith. Later, through trade, conquest, colonization and missionary work, the gospel gradually spread to the rest of the world.

The establishment of Christian nationalism in many gentile countries blurred the distinction between sincere and nominal belief, however. Over the centuries, certain disreputable deeds have therefore been performed "in the name of" the Messiah by "Christian" governments, church institutions, and nominal believers. People of other religions—not distinguishing between sincere and nominal Christianity—have often rejected the Faith on this basis.

Although Yeshua's first followers formed vibrant, closely-knit communities, the word *"ekklesia"* ("church") occurs in only two instances in the Gospels. He honored his religious heritage by regularly going to the Temple, attending synagogue, and celebrating the Hebrew

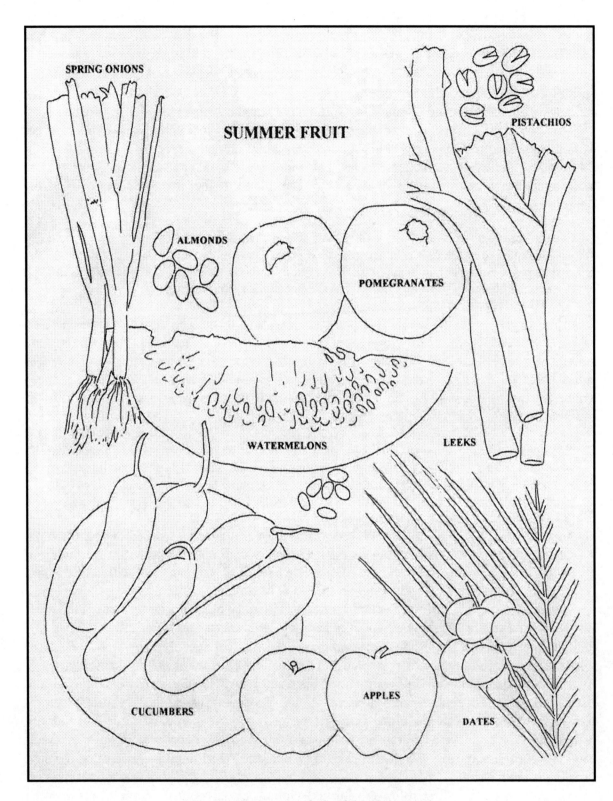

Figure 62: Summer fruit of the Holy Land

feasts, but the complex gentile systems of organized religion that would develop were in complete antitheses to the utter simplicity of Yeshua's original teachings. He spoke to his followers in informal situations: on a lakeshore or hillside, as he walked along a country road, during a meal. His primary concern was for those in need and for individuals who would allow *Y-H-V-H* to reign in their hearts and become effective members of his kingdom.

Yeshua was bitingly critical of religious leaders who undermined the integrity of Jewish worship with their arrogant self-righteousness. He consistently stressed the importance of an honest "living" faith, as opposed to dutifully going through the motions of institutionalized religion.

Despite the desensitizing and often destructive effects of nominal Christianity, true believers in Yeshua have continued to bear abundant fruit down the centuries—and have had an immensely civilizing effect on their societies. Nominal Christianity has *not* arrested the flow of the Spirit. The God of Israel has gathered to himself an abundant crop of gentile "summer fruit."

12. *Elul*: Olive Harvest and the House of Israel. The olive harvest is particularly important, because it directly precedes the High Holy Days of the Hebrew calendar. In ancient times, olives (*zeytim*) were one of the primary crops of the Mediterranean region. Every village had its own olive grove and press. When the ripe olives were harvested in early autumn, they were shaken from the trees or fell as branches were beaten with sticks. After being gathered, they were processed in one of two ways: either crushed for their oil (*shemen*), or pickled, to make them edible. Olives and their oil were valuable both in the home and as marketable products.

Olives were the most common fruit of ancient Israel—and the most prized. The humble olive symbolized sovereignty (Judges 9:9). Olive oil was blended with various spices and resins in order to produce the sacred "oil of anointing"—used in the ordination of kings, priests, and prophets. In worship, olive oil fueled the *menorah*. In fact the olive *tree* itself symbolized the nation of Israel.

"I have called you a thriving olive tree." (Jer. 11:16)

Elul in the Jewish Calendar

Elul is the month of preparation for the most sacred holy days of the Jewish year. It marks the beginning of a forty-day period known as *Teshuvah*, meaning "repentance" or "return." This extends from the first day of *Elul*, to the Day of Atonement on the tenth day of *Tishrei*. In synagogues a *shofar*, or ram's horn trumpet, is blown on each day of the month, calling Jews to repentance. Psalm 27, which speaks of God's people finding comfort and refuge in his presence in times of trouble, is read repeatedly.

The Jews believe that Moses went up onto Mt. Sinai on the sixth day of *Sivan* in order to receive the first set of commandments. On his return forty days later, he found the Israelites worshipping the golden calf. In his anger, he destroyed the stone tablets. They teach that he then spent *another* forty days outside the camp, before ascending the mountain for the second time—on the first day of *Elul*. After pleading with God for forty days to *forgive* his people, the Israelites were pardoned on the tenth day of *Tishrei*—the Day of Atonement. (Remember that in the Scriptures the number *forty* is frequently associated with a new phase in God's plan of salvation and with periods of probation, trial, and chastisement.)

Figure 63: Because the olive tree is an ancient symbol for the House of Israel, the olive harvest relates to the gathering and restoration of this nation

Elul and the Gathering of Israel

If we link the gathering of olives in the agricultural calendar to the days of *Teshuvah* in the sacred calendar, an interesting image is suggested—the House of Israel, "the thriving olive tree," returning to God in repentance, in preparation for the High Holy Days.

Since the establishment of the State of Israel in 1948, millions of Jews have returned to their homeland. On the international stage, thousands are also being drawn to Yeshua and proclaiming him to be the Messiah. Furthermore, the Spirit is subtly restoring the Hebrew heritage to numerous *gentile* Christians by means of the Messianic Movement. The receptive attitude of these Jews and Gentiles to new dimensions of the Hebrew heritage is an astonishing phenomenon. All of these things are manifestations of an urge to "return" to Hebrew origins.

Before being gathered, olives are *shaken* and *beaten* from olive trees; not gently picked. In the same way, the violence of the Holocaust preceded the gathering of Israel in the modern era. We're told that the restoration of the tribes and a period of extreme worldwide suffering, or "tribulation," will precede the second coming of Yeshua (Matt. 24:21–22; Mark 13; Rev. 7:14). Are we perhaps witnessing the beginnings of the "ultimate olive harvest"; the gathering of the whole House of Israel before "the great and dreadful day of the Lord" (Mal. 4:5–6)?

"His [Israel's] splendor will be like an *olive tree*. . . ." (Hos. 11:16)

Autumn Feasts

Caution in the Matter of Biblical Prophecy

Because Yeshua's death, burial, and resurrection—and the baptism of the Spirit— correlated precisely with the four spring feasts of Israel, it's reasonable to assume that unfulfilled messianic prophecies will find their parallels in the remaining three autumn feasts. However, it is presumptuous for any believer to make emphatic predictions regarding prophecy. Its realization can only be accurately gauged in retrospect. We can only wait, watch, and speculate with respect to the disclosure of the divine plan and should guard against prescribing to God—and misleading his people.

Interpretations vary as to the order in which these things will occur. Although it is probably true to say that many of the signs of which Yeshua spoke are increasingly evident in our modern world, essential spiritual realities remain in the present. An obsessive and fearful preoccupation with interpretations of prophecy and predictions concerning the future has never been conducive to a healthy state of mind. Believers are told only to "wait on the Lord," to "serve him" and to be ready for his coming. Only the Father knows "that day and hour."

"No-one knows about that day or hour, not even the angels in heaven, nor the Son, but only the Father." (Mark 13:32)

"[T]he Son of Man will come at an hour when you do not expect him." (Luke 12:40)

In the following analysis of the last three feasts, tentative connections will be made between unfulfilled prophecies and the Hebrew tradition—based on what the author considers logical or appropriate. This is not an attempt to propose yet another end-time doctrine.

1. Tishrei: Season of Ploughing and the Feasts of Autumn. In the agricultural calendar, *Tishrei* was a time of preparation for the coming growing season. In the sacred calendar, events reached their climax in the celebration of the three autumn feasts of Trumpets, Atonement, and Tabernacles. The olive harvest therefore heralded the approach of a new agricultural cycle *and* the climactic culmination of the sacred year.

V. Feast of Trumpets or *Yom Teru'ah*

> The Lord said to Moses, "Say to the Israelites: 'On the first day of the seventh month you are to have a day of rest, a sacred assembly commemorated with trumpets blasts.' " (Lev. 23:24)

In ancient times each feast, and the new moon of all Hebrew months, was signaled by blasts of the *shofar*. When the new moon appeared on the first day of the seventh month of *Tishrei*, the use of the shofar was more prominent. A special feast was held that was called the Feast of Trumpets, or *Yom Teru'ah* ("The Day of Blowing"). This fifth sacred feast was also called "The Last Trump."

Rosh HaShanah and the Feast of Trumpets

Today, the Jewish New Year, or *Rosh HaShanah*, is celebrated on this first day of *Tishrei*. As with all Jewish holidays, it begins and ends at sundown. A special family meal is shared. Food is laid out on a white tablecloth—symbolic of innocence and newness—two candles are lit, a prayer of thanksgiving is offered, a cup of sweet wine is poured out, and a blessing is given. On this occasion sweet *khallah* bread is served and slices of apple are dipped in honey; the sentiment being that the coming year will be as sweet as the bread, apples, and honey. On the following day, worship is conducted in synagogues.

Rosh HaShanah marks not only the beginning of the New Year, but the commencement of the ten High Holy Days of the Jewish year. These ten days, known as the "Days of Awe" or *Yamim Nora'im*, culminate on the Day of Atonement or *Yom Kippur* and are viewed as a time of preparation for Yom Kippur.

Jews believe that on the first day of *Tishrei*, God writes down names in the Book of Life. This book consists of three sections: one for the righteous, one for the wicked, and one for those who fall between the two extremes. The ten day grace period allows time for believers, by means of heart-felt repentance, to reverse any negative judgments that may have been made against them. While confessing past sins and reciting *slikhot*—prayers and poems of forgiveness —they address God as both King and Judge of the Universe and openly assess the quality of their lives.

The singing of the *Halel*, or hymns of praise, is forbidden during *Yamim Nora'im*. This would be most inappropriate during a season of such solemn repentance. Because *Rosh HaShanah* opens a period of divine judgment, it is also known as *Yom HaDin*, meaning "Day of Judgment."

The first day of *Tishrei* therefore relates to four concepts: New Year, the Feast of Trumpets, the commencement of the ten Days of Awe, and judgment.

When a trumpet [*shofar*] sounds in a city, do not the people tremble? (Amos 3:6)

Days of Awe and the Jewish '*Akedah*

The Hebrew word '*Akedah* means "binding." It relates specifically to the binding of Isaac—'*Akedat Yitzkhak*—and to the concept of sacrificing one's dearest. Although the story of the (near) sacrifice of Isaac is read on a regular basis in many synagogues throughout the year, particular emphasis is placed on this account during the Days of Awe. The Jewish *Talmud* teaches that because Abraham had been willing to sacrifice his son, God viewed this as an act that had actually been performed.

Days of Awe and Messianic Belief

In terms of Messianic belief, the focus on the sacrifice of a dearly beloved only son by a loving father occurs at precisely the right time in the Jewish calendar. During the Days of Awe, although also trembling under the judgment of God, sincere believers are able to give him thanks. For them it is a matter of claiming what has already been accomplished through the sacrifice of Yeshua; of being confident that they have been forgiven, not as a result of their own efforts, but by "grace"—the undeserved favor of God.

Yeshua and the 'Akedah. Several interesting parallels can be drawn between Isaac and Yeshua:

Isaac and Yeshua

1. Both Isaac and Yeshua were physical descendants of Abraham. (Gen. 21:3 and Matt. 1:1)

2. Both were "sons of promise." (Gen. 22:2, 17:19 and John 3:16; Luke 2:29–32)

3. Both were cherished by their fathers. (Gen. 22:2; Matt. 3:17)

4. Their miraculous births were foretold by angelic beings.
 (Gen. 8:10–13 and Luke 1:26–35)

5. Both carried their "wood of sacrifice" to a hill of sacrifice (Mt. Moriah and Golgotha).
(Gen. 22:2–6 and John 19:17)

6. Both went willingly to their deaths, like lambs led to the slaughter.
(Gen. 22:9 and Acts 8:32)

7. Neither was deserving of death.

8. Both survived to see their progeny: Yeshua's "children" being his followers; Isaac's being Esau and Jacob. (Gen. 25:21 and Heb. 2:10)

9. Through both, "all nations of the earth have been blessed." (Gen. 22:18 and Heb. 2:10)

The shofar and the return of the Messiah. Certain New Testament writings suggest that Yeshua, the Jewish Bridegroom, will come for his blood-bought bride in the manner of the ancient Hebrew marriage tradition. They indicate that he returned to his Father's house on the day of his ascension; that he is presently *preparing a place* for his bride; and that on his return, shouting and blasts of a *shofar* will herald his arrival. We are also told that he will come for his bride unexpectedly, "like a thief in the night."

> In my Father's house are many places to live. If there weren't, I would have told you; because I am going there to prepare a place for you. Since I am going and preparing a place for you, I will return to take you with me; so that where I am, you may be also. (John 14:2–3; JNT page 141)

> "This Yeshua, who has been taken away from you into heaven, will come back to you in just the same way [in the clouds] as you saw him go into heaven." (Acts. 1:11; JNT page 153)

In the following excerpts, notice how frequently the *shofar* is linked to the return of the Messiah.

> "Then the sign of the Son of Man will appear in the sky, all the tribes of the Land will mourn, and they will see the Son of Man coming on the clouds of heaven with tremendous power and glory. He will send out his angels with a great *shofar*; and they will gather together his chosen people from the four winds, from one end of heaven to the other." (Matt. 24:30–31; JNT page 35)

> For the Lord himself will come down from heaven with a rousing cry, with a call from one of the ruling angels, and with God's *shofar*; those who died united with the Messiah will be the first to rise; then we who are left still alive will be caught up with them in the clouds to meet the Lord in the air; and therefore we will always be with the Lord. (1 Thess. 4:16–17; JNT page 276)

> Look, I will tell you a secret—not all of us will die! But we will all be changed! It will take but a moment, the blink of an eye, at the final *shofar.* For the shofar will sound, and the dead will be raised to live forever, and we too will be changed. (1 Cor. 15:51–52; JNT page 236)

Remember that the Feast of Trumpets and Days of Awe fall within *Teshuvah,* a forty-day period of repentance that starts in *Elul.* If the Messiah returns on *1 Tishrei,* on the "Day of Blowing" (of the *shofar*), it will assuredly be "a sacred assembly," full of awe and repentance that welcomes him. After a betrothal period that has spanned the centuries, he will gather up his bride and escort her to his Father's house for the ultimate "High Holy Days."

> The Spirit and the bride say, "Come!" (Rev. 22:17)

Days of Awe for Yeshua's bride. Although the sins of Yeshua's bride have been paid for, we are told that remaining "dead works" will have to be burned away. Removing the last vestiges of impurity and worldliness will render her holy and spotless—spiritually "virginal." It would be most fitting if this purging process took place during the final Days of Awe; the time of probation, trial, and chastisement.

Figure 64: The Feast of Trumpets and the "final *shofar*"

[E]ach will be rewarded according to his work. For we are God's co-workers; you are God's field, God's building. . . . But let each one be careful how he builds. For no one can lay any foundation other than the one already laid, which is Yeshua the Messiah. Some will use gold, silver and precious stones in building on this foundation; while others will use wood, grass or straw. But each one's work will be shown for what it is; the Day will disclose it, because it will be revealed by fire—the fire will test the quality of each one's work. If the work someone has built on the foundation survives, he will receive a reward; if it is burned up, he will have to bear the loss: he will still escape with his life, but it will be like escaping through a fire. (1 Cor. 3:8–15; JNT page 222)

Two witnesses. We are told that prior to appearing before God's throne, a group of prophesying witnesses will continue his earthly work. They are referred to as the "firstfruits" of the final harvest of nations. In the Book of Revelation, these men are referred to as the "two witnesses," "two olive trees," or "two lamp stands"; possibly indicating that they will be descendants of the two ancient kingdoms of Ephraim and Judah—the original "olive tree." This, in turn, links them to the 144,000 virtuous celibate male Israelites—twelve thousand from each of the twelve tribes of Israel—mentioned in the following scriptures:

Then I heard the numbers of those who were sealed: 144,000 from all the tribes of Israel. (7:4)

And I will give power to my two witnesses, and they will prophesy for 1,260 days. . . . These are the two olive trees and two lamp stands that stand before the Lord of the earth. (11:3–4)

Then they heard a loud voice from heaven saying to them, "Come up here." And they went up to heaven in a cloud, while their enemies looked on. (11:12)

Then I looked, and there before me was the Lamb, standing on Mount Zion, and with him 144,000 who had his name and his Father's name written on their foreheads. (14:1)

These are those who did not defile themselves with women. . . . They were purchased from among men and offered as firstfruits to God and the Lamb. (14:4)

VI. Day of Atonement or *Yom Kippur*

"The tenth day of this seventh month is the Day of Atonement. Hold a sacred assembly and deny yourselves, and present an offering made to the Lord by fire." (Lev. 23:27)

In Old Testament times, the Day Atonement, or *Yom Kippur* ("Day of Covering"), was the only day of the year on which the high priest of Israel was permitted to enter the Most Holy Place in the Tabernacle or Temple. He did not wear his usual distinctive attire—crown, ephod, and breastplate—just a simple white linen robe, symbolic of purity. It was extremely important that he remained in a state of ritual purity on that most somber and sacred of holy days; avoiding anything that might render him "unclean."

His first duty was to sacrifice a bullock and to offer it as atonement for the sins of the priesthood. He carried hot coals from the brazen altar to the smaller altar in the Holy Place and then sprinkled fresh incense onto them; thereby creating a smoke screen that partially hid the ark from view. The blood of the sacrifice was then sprinkled on the mercy seat and on the ground before the ark. During this procedure his white robe became splattered with blood.

When lots had been cast to determine which of two male kid goats would be sacrificed for the atonement of the sins of the nation, the same procedure was followed. The high priest then took the second goat—the "scapegoat," or *azazel*, and, with his hands on its head, openly confessed the sins of the Israelites before God. The scapegoat—escape goat—was then driven from the camp, signifying that the community was being separated from its sins; that their sins were being carried away into the desert by the goat. Finally, the carcasses of the bullock and first goat were taken outside the camp and burnt.

It was also on this day alone, as the high priest offered the blood of the bullock and the kid in the Most Holy Place, that he was permitted to utter—"*Y-H-V-H*"—the sacred personal name of the God of Israel.

The Significance of the *Azazel*

Between 515 B.C. and A.D. 70, the *azazel* or "scapegoat," was driven over a cliff; ensuring that it didn't return. The *Talmud* records that a piece of red yarn was tied to one of the goat's horns, and that up until approximately A.D. 30, on inspection, the wool always turned white—signifying that the Israelites had been purified from sin. This no longer happened after the death of the Messiah. It remained red. From a Messianic perspective, this phenomenon is explained by the fact that the ultimate atoning sacrifice had been accomplished for all time, in the death of Yeshua. The goat of the sin offering and the azazel were no longer necessary.

> "Come now, let us reason together," says the Lord. "Though your sins are like scarlet, they shall be as white as snow; though they are red as crimson, they shall be like wool." (Isa. 1:18)

The Jewish *Yom Kippur*

Since the destruction of Herod's Temple in A.D. 70, Jews have not offered blood sacrifices—nor have they had the assurance of forgiveness enjoyed by their forefathers. Nevertheless, the *shofar* still sounds as a call to worship on the eve of *Yom Kippur*.

The color white predominates in synagogues and in the attire of worshipers. It is said to symbolize purity, death, and the equality of all people before God. The *Kol Nidre* or "All Vows" prayer—a beautiful opening prayer, which is sung—marks the beginning of twenty-four hours of fasting and praying. Worshipers plead and tremble as they expose themselves to the judgment of the Almighty. They acknowledge transgressions in thought, word, and deed against others and against God. The themes of repentance, prayer, and charity are repeatedly emphasized. In this way, they attempt to be united with God on the deepest level possible. *Yom Kippur* the only holy day that is not a feast, but a solemn fast, and it demands *everything* from the sincere Jewish worshiper. Jewish martyrs are also remembered on this day of intense introspection. The events of the forty days of *Teshuvah* reach their climactic conclusion at sunset on Yom Kippur with the opening of the ark, the exclamation from the exhausted worshipers, "*Shema Yisra'el*" ("Hear, O Israel"), and with a final blast of the *shofar*.

Yom Kippur as a Day of Judgment

According to the writings of the Hebrew prophets, a final day of reckoning—the "great and dreadful day of the Lord" (Mal. 4:5–6)—will reveal the judgment of God on all who have shown little or no remorse for sins committed against God and humanity. This concept relates strongly to *Yom Kippur*; it is the *final* day of *Teshuvah* and the *last* of ten days of judgment. The urgency and intensity of Jewish repentance on the Day of Atonement serves as an annual reminder of this decisive future event.

> But by your stubbornness, by your unrepentant heart, you are storing up anger for yourself on the Day of Anger, when God's righteous judgment will be revealed; for he will pay back each one according to his deeds. (Rom. 2:5–6; JNT page 200)

> But who can endure the day of his coming? Who can stand when he appears? For he will be like a refiner's fire or a launderer's soap. (Mal. 3:2)

> "Surely the day is coming; it will burn like a furnace. All the arrogant and every evildoer will be stubble, and that day that is coming will set them on fire," says the Lord Almighty. (Mal. 4:1)

A Final *Yom Kippur*

The Scriptures suggest that a time will come when, instead of Levitical high priests offering the blood of sacrifices for the sins of Israel in the Most Holy Place, or the Messiah, as the eternal High Priest, entering the presence of his Father in order to intercede on behalf of believers, Yeshua's holy bride will actually *accompany* him into the divine throne room.

The Messiah will present "an offering made to the Lord by fire"—his pure, radiant "blood-bought" bride. Her sins will have been completely erased. When believers stand in the presence of their awesome "thrice holy God," enveloped in his *Sh'khinah* glory, they will be united with him on the deepest and highest level possible. If this occurs, solemn *Yom Kippur* will be transformed into a day of jubilation, a day of sublime "at-one-ment" with the God of Israel. In the Book of Revelation we find an image of such a triumphant congregation:

> [T]here before me was a great multitude that no-one could count, from every nation, tribe, people and language, standing before the throne and in front of the Lamb. They were wearing white robes and were holding palm branches in their hands. And they cried out in a loud voice: "Salvation belongs to our God, who sits on the throne, and to the Lamb." (Rev. 7:9–10)

> "These are they who have come out of the great tribulation; they have washed their robes and made them white in the blood of the Lamb." (Rev. 7:14)

Figure 65: (opposite) A high priest of Israel in the Most Holy Place on the Day of Atonement, and Yeshua and his bride in the throne room of God. The Hebrew word on the throne is pronounced "*khay*," meaning "living." It alludes to the Living God

VII. Tabernacles or *Sukkot*

"So beginning with the fifteenth day of the seventh month [*Tishrei*], after you have gathered the crops of the land, celebrate the festival to the Lord for seven days; the first day is a day of rest, and the eighth day also is a day of rest. On the first day you are to take choice fruit from the trees, and palm fronds, leafy branches and poplars, and rejoice before the Lord your God for seven days. . . . All native-born Israelites are to live in booths [*sukkot*] so your descendants will know that I had the Israelites live in booths when I brought them out of Egypt. I am the Lord your God." (Lev. 23:39–43)

The Feast of Tabernacles was the last of three annual pilgrim festivals that every male Israelite was required to attend. It marked the end of the sacred year and the beginning of a new agricultural year. Above all, it commemorated God's providence to the nation during their forty-year sojourn in the wilderness of Sinai. The Feast of Tabernacles was celebrated five days after *Yom Kippur*, from 15–22 *Tishrei.*

The Hebrew term for this eight-day feast is *Khag HaSukkot,* meaning "Feast of Booths." Here the term "Tabernacles" does not relate to the wilderness *Mishkan*, or "Dwelling Place"—the Tabernacle—but to the flimsy makeshift structures or booths (*sukkot*) that sheltered the Israelites after their hurried exodus from Egypt. During Old Testament times, each native-born Israelite was required to live in a *sukkah* (booth), constructed of tree boughs and palm fronds, for the first seven days of the feast.

Special sacrifices were made during this eight-day period; including the offering of seventy bulls. For centuries rabbis have taught that the bulls had particular significance. Because they were associated with offerings made on behalf of a nation or nations, they maintain that these animals represented the seventy gentile nations that descended from Noah—that the bulls were sacrificed in order to ensure the welfare of the Gentiles.

Sukkot and the Jews

The Feast of Tabernacles, a time of celebration, is referred to by Jews as "The Season of Our Rejoicing." Makeshift shelters are still erected in gardens and synagogues, but are now decorated with vines, colored lights, "treats," and fruit. (The inclusion of fruit possibly relates to the fact that in ancient times, Tabernacles, also known as the Festival of Ingathering, marked the end of the fruit harvest. Leafy shelters provided shade for workers in open fields.) Although various modern materials may be used in their construction, the booths are still sometimes made simply from tree boughs and palm fronds. Meals are eaten in the *sukkot* and some go so far as to sleep in them overnight.

Tabernacles and the "Wedding of the Lamb"

Assuming that Yeshua returns on the Feast of Trumpets, his bride is purged from dead works during the Days of Awe and presented to the Father on the Day of Atonement, the "wedding of the Lamb" will surely coincide with the Feast of Tabernacles.

This seventh feast and the ancient Hebrew marriage tradition provide subtle images of the ultimate union between the Bridegroom and his bride. They correlate in several respects: Tabernacles marked the end of a *period of waiting* for the completion of the fruit harvest and the sacred year. The wedding feast marked the end of a prolonged period of betrothal. In both, the concept of living in unusual *"dwelling places"* for *seven days* is significant: in *sukkot* during the week of Tabernacles; in the bridal chamber, during the "bridal week."

Figure 66: The *sukkah* (booths) of Tabernacles appear above the holy city of Jerusalem, the future dwelling place of the Messiah

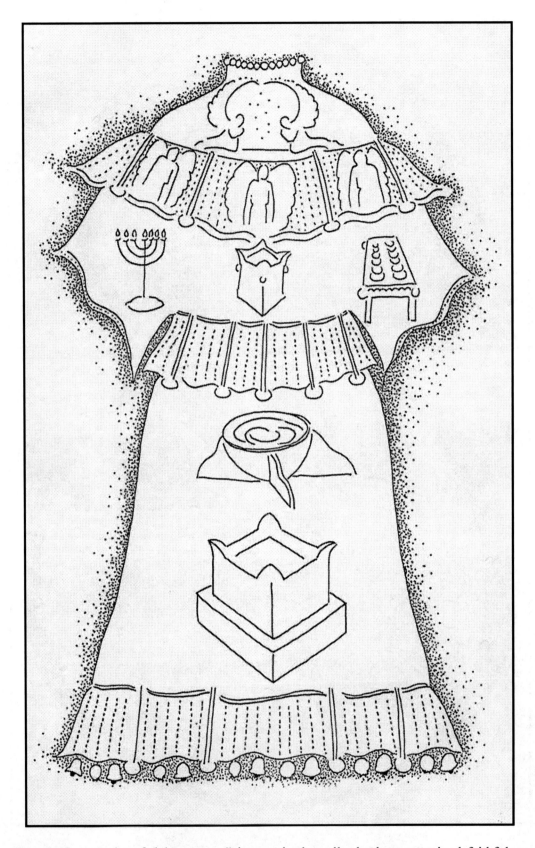

Figure 67: A "robe of righteousness" is promised to all who have remained faithful; to those who have persevered during the "Journey through the Tabernacle"

Images of the Messiah and his Bride in the Poetic "Song of Songs"

- Let the king bring me into his chambers (1:4).
- All beautiful you are, my darling; there is no flaw in you (4:7).
- How delightful is your love, my sister, my bride! (4:10).
- I liken you, my darling, to a mare harnessed to one of the chariots of Pharaoh (1:9).
- The fragrance of your garments is like that of Lebanon (4:11).
- You are a garden locked up, my sister, my bride; you are a spring enclosed, a sealed fountain (4:12).
- Your plants are an orchard of pomegranates with choice fruits. . . . (4:13).
- I am a rose of Sharon, a lily of the valleys. . . Like a lily among thorns, is my darling among the maidens (2:1–2).
- I am my lover's [beloved's], and my lover [beloved] is mine. . . . (6:3).

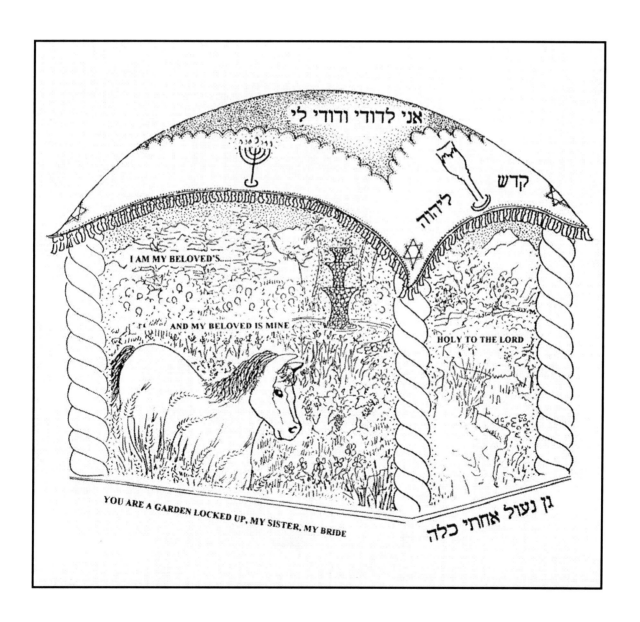

Tabernacles celebrated the union of Israelites with their *provider* as he *dwelt among* them in the wilderness. A Hebrew marriage was consummated as the couple *dwelt together* in the place *provided* by the groom. Both were occasions of great *celebration*.

The Ultimate Bridal Week

Yeshua's "bride," having been made ready by means of the final "refining fire," will undoubtedly be suitably attired for the "bridal week." She will be adorned with the "beauty of holiness"—clothed in clean, fine linen wedding garments: "robes of righteous-ness."

> "I am the Lord, who makes you holy." (Lev. 20:7)

> "Let us rejoice and be glad and give him glory! For the wedding of the Lamb has come, and his bride has made herself ready. Fine linen, bright and clean, was given her to wear." (Rev. 19:7–8)

Perhaps during the week of Tabernacles, the bride will rejoice in the loving presence of her Bridegroom—"in the place prepared for her." And perhaps as their marriage is consummated in a holy spiritual union, she will stand unveiled before him with absolutely no remorse. She will have been made sinless, inwardly "virginal."

The Great Day of the Feast or *Hoshana Rabbah*

In ancient times, Tabernacles ended with a solemn assembly and a day of rest. The priests made the final sacrifices. The year came to an end. This eighth and final day of *Sukkot* later became known among the Jews as "The Great Day of the Feast"— in Hebrew, *Hoshana Rabbah* (John 7:37).

> "[O]n the eighth day, hold a sacred assembly and present an offering made to the Lord by fire. It is the closing assembly; do no regular work." (Lev. 23:36)

Hoshana Rabbah and the Jews. During the period of the second Temple (Herod's Temple), Hoshana Rabbah became a holiday during which Jews prayed for rain for the next growing season. They congregated at the Temple, holding citron fruit (*etrog,* similar to lemons) and waving willow (*'aravot*), myrtle (*hadasim*), and palm branches (*lulavim*). These twigs and branches were tied together and then waved up, down, and in the different directions of the compass; indicating the omnipresence of God.

On that day, the high priest took new wine and ceremonially clean or "living" water from the Pool of Siloam and, accompanied by blasts of the temple *shofars*, poured them onto the holy altar. Then, while passages of Scripture relating to rain were read aloud, the Jews prayed for the "latter rain" (Zech. 10:1; Isa. 44:3). It was on the Great Day of the Feast that Yeshua made the following proclamation regarding the indwelling Spirit:

Figure 68: (overleaf) Beneath a Jewish wedding canopy, or *khuppah*, are images that reflect some of the terms of endearment recorded in the Song of Songs. English translations of the drawing's Hebrew Scriptures appear within the illustration

Now on the last day of the festival, *Hoshana Rabbah*, Yeshua stood and cried out, "If anyone is thirsty, let him keep coming to me and drinking! Whoever puts his trust in me, as the Scripture says, rivers of living waters will flow from his inmost being!" (John 7:37–38; JNT page 130)

The Rejoicing of the *Torah*

Also on the eighth day (eighth day in Israel, ninth day outside of Israel), the Jews celebrate "The Rejoicing of the *Torah*" or *Simkhat Torah*. This ritual marks the completion of the sacred Jewish year. It is a day of thanksgiving during which Torah scrolls are held up high and there are processions of singers and dancers. The last and first passages of the Torah—the last in Deuteronomy, the first in Genesis—are read aloud in synagogues. As Torah scrolls are rolled back to the beginning of Genesis, the old sacred year closes and a new year commences. Deuteronomy ends with the following powerful words:

Since then, no prophet has risen in Israel like Moses, whom the Lord knew face to face, who did all those miraculous signs and wonders the Lord sent him to do in Egypt. . . . For no one has ever shown the mighty power or performed the awesome deeds that Moses did in the sight of all Israel. (Deut. 34:10–12)

And Genesis begins with these words:

In the beginning God created the heavens and the earth. (Gen. 1:1)

Yeshua and the Rejoicing of the *Torah*

As in *Hoshana Rabbah*, there are strong messianic overtones in this traditional Jewish holiday. Among first century believers, Yeshua was frequently referred to as "The Living *Torah*." In the Book of Revelation (22:13), he claimed the title, "The First and the Last, the Beginning and the End." The final words of Deuteronomy, read on *Simkhat Torah*, appear to have their fulfillment in Yeshua; he was "a prophet like Moses." And the first verse in Genesis has its counterpart in the Gospel of John in the following excerpt, alluding to Yeshua—The Living Torah:

In the beginning was the Word, and the Word was with God, And the Word was God. He was with God in the beginning. All things came to be through him, and without him nothing made had being. In him was life, and the life was the light of mankind. (John 1:1–4; JNT page 118)

The Wedding Supper of the Lamb

How appropriate it will be if the final day of Tabernacles, "The Great Day of the Feast," coincides with the glorious "wedding feast of the Lamb"—if the harvest of souls from every nation on Earth, and the union of the Messiah and his bride, is celebrated on that day. Perhaps a magnificent royal procession, accompanied by singing and dancing, will be led by Yeshua. Perhaps a future *Simkhat Torah* will bring the old order to an end and usher in the new millennium of rest and peace. That would be the ultimate "season of rejoicing" and thanksgiving.

Blessed are those who are invited to the wedding supper of the Lamb! (Rev. 19:9)

219

Figures 69, 70, 71: A joyful procession to the Feasts of Tabernacles during the millennial reign. "Your procession has come into view, O God, the procession of my God and King into the sanctuary. In front are the singers, after them the musicians; with them are the maidens playing tambourines. Praise God in the great congregation; praise the Lord in the assembly of Israel." (Ps. 68:24–26)

Tabernacles and the City of Jerusalem

The Scriptures make the promise that Yeshua will not appear as a sacrificial lamb the second time, but as "Lord of Lords and King of Kings"—the mighty Lion of Judah. (Rev. 19:11–21) He will rule mankind from Jerusalem as King of the Earth (*Melekh Ha'Olam*) and there will be a thousand years of peace. Then, because Jerusalem will be the *dwelling place* of the Ruler of the Earth (*Ribbon Ha'Olam*), it will finally be the "City of Peace."

> The kingdom of the world has become the Kingdom of our Lord and his Messiah, and he will rule forever and ever! (Rev. 11:15; JNT page 344)

> "Yet in the towns of Judah and the streets of Jerusalem that are deserted, inhabited by neither men nor animals, there will be heard once more the sounds of joy and gladness, the voices of bride and bridegroom, and the voices of those who bring thank offerings to the house of the Lord. . . ." (Jer. 33:10–11)

The Scriptures indicate that the Feast of Tabernacles is the only feast that will continue to be celebrated during the millennial reign. It will be an international holiday until the heavenly holy city, the New Jerusalem, descends to Earth, and *Y-H-V-H* comes to dwell eternally among his people.

> Then the survivors from all the nations that have attacked Jerusalem will go up year after year to worship the King, the Lord Almighty, and to celebrate the Feast of Tabernacles. (Zech. 14:16)

In the Book of Revelation the symbol of a richly adorned bride also refers to the New Jerusalem. It is described as an exquisite city. There will be no temple, because the Lord Almighty and the Lamb will be its temple. There will be no need for the sun or moon to shine on it, because the *Sh'khinah* glory of God will be its light and the Lamb its lamp. Death and mourning will cease, and no impure person or object will be permitted to enter; only those whose names are written in the Lamb's Book of Life.

> Then I saw a new heaven and a new earth, for the first heaven and the first earth had passed away. . . . I saw the Holy City, the new Jerusalem coming down out of heaven from God, prepared as a bride beautifully dressed for her husband. And I heard a voice from the throne saying, "Now the dwelling of God is with men, and he will live with them. . . . He will wipe every tear from their eyes. There will be no more death or mourning or crying, for the old order of things has passed away." He who was seated on the throne said, "I am making everything new! (Rev. 21:1–4)

> Then the angel showed me the river of the water of life . . . flowing from the throne of God and of the Lamb down the middle of the great street of the city. On each side of the river stood the tree of life, bearing twelve crops of fruit, yielding its fruit every month. And the leaves of the tree are for the healing of the nations. . . ." (Rev. 22:1–2)

In this final reference to the Tree of Life, we are reminded of humanity's rebellion against God; the initial cause of the separation between the Creator and his creation. Once Adam and Eve had eaten from the Tree of the Knowledge of Good and Evil, they were banished from Eden. In this way they were prevented from eating from the Tree of Life and bearing the burden of their sins forever. (Gen. 3:22) This concept suggests that humanity will only be permitted to eat from the Tree of Life again, once a state of purity, or *holiness*, has been restored.

During the Feast of Tabernacles the ancient Israelites were told to take palm fronds, leafy branches, poplars, and choice fruit from the trees and rejoice before the Lord (Lev. 23:40). This indicates that this feast was, at least in part, a celebration of the harvest. *Etrog* (choice fruit), *lulavim* (palm fronds), *'aravot* (leafy branches), and *hadasim* (myrtle branches), feature in Jewish worship to this day.

Does this practice foreshadow the eventual restoration of humanity's privilege to eat from the Tree of Life—while enjoying eternal tender communion with the Ruler of the Universe (*Ribbon Ha'Olam*)?

"I, the Lord—with the first of them and with the last—I am he." (Isa. 41:4)

HOLY . . . HOLY . . . HOLY. . . *KADOSH . . . KADOSH . . . KADOSH*

Peace
Shalom
שלום

The Lord bless you and keep you; the Lord make his face shine upon you and be gracious to you, the Lord turn his face toward you and give you peace.
(The Aaronic Blessing; Numbers 6:24–26)

My peace I give to you.
(Words of Yeshua; John 14:27)

Amen
אמן

Figure 72: *Leshon HaKodesh*: Hebrew, the "Holy Language" of the Sinai Covenant

Appendix I

The Hebrew Language

'Ivrit: A Holy Language

Hebrew, or *'Ivrit*, is referred to as the language of Canaan or Judah in the Scriptures; and by the Jews, as the Sacred or Holy Language—*Leshon HaKodesh*. The latter reflects that it constitutes a direct and powerful link to the ancient Hebrew roots of the Faith; to the covenant made between God and the community of Israel at Sinai. The preservation of this language of the *Torah* is one of the most valuable components of the Jewish heritage.

The origins of this western Semitic language extend back beyond 2000 B.C. Hebrew was the vernacular of the ancient Israelites up until the Babylonian exile in the sixth century B.C. and then Aramaic, the common street language of the Mesopotamians (closely related to Hebrew), was adopted for everyday use.

Hebrew script developed in stages over time, attaining its modern day form in about the tenth century A.D. It has always been used in sacred and literary contexts. The *Tanakh* (OT), written between 1500 and 300 B.C., is principally a Hebrew document, but certain chapters were originally written in Aramaic (found in Ezra, Jeremiah, and Daniel).

Then the [Babylonian] astrologers answered the king [Nebuchadnezzar II] in *Aramaic*, "O king, live forever! Tell your servants the dream, and we will interpret it." (Dan. 2:4)

Alexander the Great (335–323 B.C.) used the *Greek* culture and language as a means of unifying his territories and Greek was still the universally accepted means of communication for the purposes of trade in first century Roman Palestine. Although Aramaic continued to be the vernacular during that period, New Testament manuscripts were therefore originally written in Greek. Babylonian Aramaic is sometimes referred to as the "Hebrew tongue" in the New Testament; because a Jew who was Aramaic speaking, as opposed to Greek speaking, was referred to as a "Hebrew."

She [Mary Magdalene] turned toward him and cried out in Aramaic, "*Rabboni!*" (John 20:16)

Yeshua and his followers probably spoke Aramaic on a daily basis, but they would also have had a working knowledge of Hebrew and Greek. It has therefore been suggested by certain scholars that the Gospels might originally have been written in Aramaic and later translated into Greek. What *is* certain is that Yeshua was literate:

The scroll of the prophet Isaiah was handed to him. Unrolling it he found the place where it is written. . . . (Luke 4:17)

And Yeshua proceeded to read, in Hebrew, from the Book of Isaiah (61:1–2).

It was only after the State of Israel was established in 1948, that Hebrew was revived to become its official language. Immigrant Jews returning from "the four quarters of the earth" have been encouraged to attend intensive language classes at the *Ulpan*. This has not only facilitated social interaction, it has restored Hebrew as a *living* language in modern-day Israel.

Yiddish ("Jewish German"), the Germanic language of central and eastern European *Ashkenazi* Jews—or Jews of such descent—is approximately one thousand years old. It developed out of the dialects of medieval Italian and French Jews, but also came to include German, Slavic, and Hebrew-Aramaic elements. Although Yiddish is not pure Hebrew, it is written from right to left in Hebrew characters.

Learning the Language

General principles:

- Hebrew is written from right to left. When reading a Hebrew book, one starts by opening the "back" cover and then progresses toward the "front" cover.
- The Hebrew alphabet consists of only twenty-two consonant letters; as opposed to the twenty-six vowel and consonant letters of the Latin alphabet.
- Hebrew has five consonants that sometimes act as vowels (*alef, heh, vav, yod, 'ayin*), but there are no pure vowels as such.
- Although upper and lower case letters are used in most Hebrew transliterations, no differentiation is made between cases in written Hebrew.
- As in French, Hebrew normally distinguishes between the masculine and feminine genders.
- Entire words are not spelt out as in the English language; instead, sets of Hebrew consonants form "word frames" into which vowel sounds are inserted.
- There are five *sofit* letters (*khaf, mem, nun, feh, tzadi*). They are slightly modified when used as the last letters in a word.
- Pointed Hebrew, also known as dotted or deficient Hebrew, features a system of points that indicate the correct articulation of the vowel sounds. These points were first added to Hebrew script in about the sixth century A.D., to ensure the preservation of the traditional pronunciation. Today this form is reserved for the Holy Scriptures, prayer books, and poetry.
- Unpointed or "*plene*" Hebrew is used casually, in everyday life. This is closer to the original form of the language, because the deciphering of the vowel sounds is determined not by points, but by conjecture; based on the context of the word. It is this form that is the vernacular in modern day Israel. It is this casual unpointed form that appears in this book, thereby simplifying the learning process.
- There are four Hebrew characters that represent more than one sound (*bet, kaf, shin, peh*). In pointed Hebrew, the differences are indicated by means of a dot within or on top of the letter.
- The twenty-two Hebrew letters also serve as a numeral system, similar to the Roman numeral system. When used as such, the letters are apostrophized. Hebrew numerals designate the days of the week, months, and years on Jewish calendars. Elsewhere ordinary digits are used.

When learning any new language, it is necessary to first become familiar with its building blocks; its alphabet. Because this can be a demanding exercise, a child-like Hebrew "picture alphabet" has been designed by the author to make the process more enjoyable. Once the Hebrew alphabet, or *alef bet*, has been mastered, the thrill of deciphering ancient Hebrew words will become a reality as characters are strung together and sounded out. Because this section is intended to serve only as an introduction to the language, apart from the page of blessings and proclamations, only individual words and short phrases are featured.

The term "transliteration" refers to the spelling of the words of one language (in this case Hebrew) in the letters of another language (in this case English). Hebrew transliteration spelling therefore varies, but this is not critical. The sole objective of any transliteration is simply to clarify the *enunciation* of the words of a foreign language.

The Hebrew Alphabet or *Alef Bet*

"*Sofit*" letters appear above the standard Hebrew characters (11, 13, 14, 17, and 18).
(Bold type indicates emphasis in pronunciation.)

ח	ז	ו	ה	ד	ג	ב	א
KHET	ZAYIN	VAV	HEH	DALET	GIMEL	BET	ALEF
8	7	6	5	4	3	2	1
		ן			ך		
ע	ס	נ	מ	ל	כ	י	ט
'AYIN	SAMEKH	NUN	MEM	LAMED	KAF	YOD	TET
16	15	14	13	12	11	10	9
					ץ	ף	
ת	ש	ר	ק	צ	פ		
TAV	SHIN	RESH	KUF	TZADI	PEH		
22	21	20	19	18	17		

Transliteration Guidelines

Throughout this book, the transliteration of Hebrew words has been based on the traditionally accepted model—which is not always self-explanatory. Readers will be able to approximate the *actual* sounds of spoken Hebrew by following these guidelines:

- Use the long *oo* sound (as in f*oo*d) whenever a *u* vowel appears, and the long *ee* sound (as in f*ee*d) whenever an *i* vowel appears. For example: the word Dav*i*d is pronounced Dav*ee*d; *Yerushalayim, Yerooshalayeem*; and *Yeshua, Yeshooa*.
- All single *e* vowels at the ends of words and all *ei* combinations should be pronounced as in the *ey* of the English word "th*ey*." For example: *Eloheinu*, as *Eloheynoo*; *Kol Nidre*, as *Kol Needrey*; and *Moshe* as *Moshey*.

229

PROPERTIES OF THE TWENTY-TWO HEBREW LETTERS
(Bold type indicates the sounds of the Hebrew characters.)

Hebrew		Sound	(as in)	Sofit Letters
1. ALEF	א	a or e	bar or yes	
2. BET	ב	b or v	boy or vet	
3. GIMEL	ג	g	get	
4. DALET	ד	d	dog	
5. HEH	ה	h	hug	
6. VAV	ו	va/ve/vee	very	
7. ZAYIN	ז	z	zero	
8. KHET	ח	kh/ch	Bach or Loch	
9. TET	ט	t	tart	
10. YOD	י	y	yarn	
11. KAF	כ	k or kh/ch	key or Bach	ך: Khaf Sofit (undotted Kaf)
12. LAMED	ל	l	love	
13. MEM	מ	m	main	ם: Mem Sofit
14. NUN	נ	n	nine	ן: Nun Sofit
15. SAMEKH	ס	s	soap	
16. 'AYIN	ע	a or e	bar or yes	
17. PEH	פ	p or f	pot or for	ף: Feh Sofit (undotted Peh)
18. TZADI	צ	tz	Ritz	ץ: Tzadi Sofit
19. KUF	ק	k	key	
20. RESH	ר	r	guttural r (as in French)	
21. SHIN	ש	sh or s	shell or sad	
22. TAV	ת	t	tart	

230

- Each *kh* consonant digraph should be pronounced as a *guttural g*; as in the *ch* of the name Ba*ch* (the German composer) or the word Lo*ch* (a Scottish lake). Words such as *khitah* and *Samekh*, for example, contain this guttural sound. Hebrew transliterations often feature both the *ch* and *kh* combinations, but in the interests of clarity, the *ch* combination—and the letter *c*—have been minimized in this book. *Ch* and *c* have only been used in such words as *Ruach HaKodesh*, *Mashiach*, and *Cohen* in order to correspond with the transliteration spelling used in selected Jewish New Testament (JNT) quotations.
- Bear in mind that the Hebrew "ha" is equivalent to the English "the" and that it frequently appears as a prefix. For example: *Ruach HaKodesh* means *the* Holy Spirit and *HaShem* means *The* Name (of God). The "ha" prefix is linked by means of an apostrophe when a word begins with a vowel, as in *ha'olam* (*the* world or universe), and a short dash in common nouns such as *lekhem ha-panim* (showbread: literally, "bread of *the* faces").
- The letters *alef* and *'ayin*, as breaks or pauses, are indicated by means of apostrophes, as are other breaks in vowel and consonant enunciation. For example *Yisra'el* and *Sh'khinah*.

How the "Vowels" Function

There are no pure vowels as such in the Hebrew language, but five of the Hebrew consonants frequently function as vowels or semi-vowels. Here is a summary of the rules that govern the use of the letters *alef, heh, vav, yod,* and *'ayin*, as consonants and as vowels.

1. *ALEF:* א

Alef is a semi-vowel. It is often represented by means of an apostrophe in its transliteration and affects the sounds of adjacent letters in the following ways:

- At the beginning or in the middle of a word: *a* as in *far* or *e* as in *less*
- When followed by a *vav* (אוֹ): *o* or *u* (oo)
- When followed by a *yod* (אִ): *i* (ee) or *ei* (ey)
- Before a double *yod* (אִי): *ay* as in *my*
- An *alef* at the end of a word: *a* and, very rarely, *o*

2. *'AYIN:* ע

The function and properties of the semi-vowel *'Ayin*, are similar to those of *Aleph*. It too is often represented by an apostrophe in its transliteration and affects the sounds of adjacent letters.

- At the beginning of a word: *a* as in *far* or *e* as in *less*
- When followed by a *vav* anywhere in the word (עוֹ): *o* or *u* (oo)
- When followed by a *yod* (עִ): *i* (ee) or *ei* (ey)
- Before a double *yod* (עִי): *ay* as in *my*

Figure 73: The "vowels" of the Hebrew alphabet (highlighted)

- When ending a word, it reads as *e'a* (as in *yode'a*) or as *a* (as in f*a*r)
- When preceded by a *vav* at the end of a word (ﬠﬡ): *u'a* (oo'a) or *o'a*

3. *HEH:* ה

- At the beginning of a word, when not followed by a "vowel": *ha, he,* or *hi* (hee)
- A *heh* in the middle of a word: *ha* or *he*
- A *heh* at the end of a word: *ah*
- A *heh* followed by a *yod* (הי): *hi* (hee)
- A *heh* followed by a *vav* (הו): *hu* (hoo)

4. *VAV:* ו

- As a consonant: *va, ve,* and *vi* (vee)
- As a vowel: *o* as in m*o*re or (oo) as in f*oo*d
- When opening or closing a word the *vav* is single, but when inside a word (with unpointed spelling), it is doubled (וו).
- The double *vav* (וו) also sometimes reads *vo* or *vu* (voo)

5. *YOD:* י

- As a consonant at the beginning of a word, when not followed by a "vowel": *yi* (yee), *ya,* or *ye*
- A *yod* followed by a *vav* (יו): *yo* or *yu* (yoo)
- A double *yod* in the middle of a word (יי): *ya* or *yayi* (yayee)
- A double *yod* (יי) at the end of a word: *ay*
- A *yod* at the end or in the middle of a word: *i* (ee) or *ei* (ey), as in th*ey*.

Using the Picture Alphabet and Glossary

In the following Hebrew picture alphabet and glossary, a simplified transliteration appears directly beneath the Hebrew characters. It is written "in reverse," from right to left, thereby mirroring the above characters. This is intended to facilitate the deciphering process for the uninitiated.

Although upper and lower case letters are normally used in transliteration spelling, in Hebrew itself, no differentiation is made between the two. Therefore, in the reverse transliteration in this section only upper case letters are used. The selection of Hebrew words is intended to reflect not only the dominant themes in the book, but also something of the rich tapestry of the Hebrew heritage as a whole.

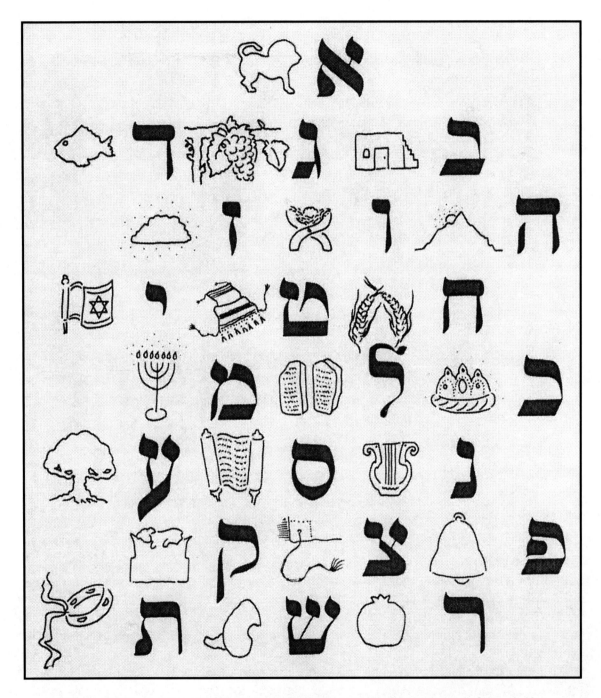

Figure 74: Twenty-two Hebrew images that correspond with the letters of the *alef bet*

A HEBREW PICTURE ALPHABET

Link the following words to the Hebrew images and characters in the accompanying illustration. (Upper case, bold type indicates the sounds of the letters in the "alef bet.")

		Hebrew Letter	Hebrew Transliteration	Hebrew with Reverse Transliteration	English Translation
1.	א	Alef	**A**ri	א ר י I / R / **A**	Lion
2.	ב	Bet	**B**ayit	ב י ת T / Y / **B**	House
3.	ג	Gimel	**G**efen	ג פ ן N / F / **G**	Grapevine
4.	ד	Dalet	**D**ag	ד ג G / **D**	Fish
5.	ה	Heh	**H**ar	ה ר R / **H**	Mountain
6.	ו	Vav	**V**elad	ו ל ד D / L / **V**	Infant
7.	ז	Zayin	**Z**ahav	ז ה ב V / H / **Z**	Gold
8.	ח	KHet	**KH**itah	ח י ט ה AH / T / I / **KH**	Wheat
9.	ט	Tet	**T**alit	ט ל י ת T / I / L / **T**	Prayer shawl
10.	י	Yod	**Y**isra'el	י ש ר א ל EL / ' / R / S / **Y**	Israel
11.	כ	Kaf	**K**eter	כ ת ר R / T / **K**	Crown
12.	ל	Lamed	**L**ukhot HaBrit	ל ו ח ו ת T / O / KH / U / **L** ה ב ר י ת T / I / R / B / HA	Tablets of the Law
13.	מ	Mem	**M**enorah	מ נ ו ר ה AH / R / O / N / **M**	Lampstand
14.	נ	Nun	**N**evel	נ ב ל L / V / **N**	Harp or lyre

15.	ס	Samekh	Sefer Torah	ס פ ר R / F / S ת ו ר ה AH / R / O / T	Torah scroll
16.	ע	'Ayin	'Etz	ע ץ ETZ / '	Tree, wood, or stick
17.	פ	Peh	Pa'amon	פ ע מ ו ן N / O / AM / ' / P	Bell
18.	צ	TZadi	TZitzit	צ י צ י ת T / I / TZ / I / TZ	Ritual fringe
19.	ק	Kuf	Korban	ק ו ר ב ן N / B / R / O / K	Sacrifice
20.	ר	Resh	Rimon	ר י מ ו ן N / O / M / I / R	Pomegranate
21.	ש	SHin	SHofar	ש ו פ ר R / F / O / SH	Ram's horn trumpet
22.	ת	Tav	Tof	ת ו ף F / O / T	Tambourine or drum

TRANSLITERATION CHART

A	א ה ע
B	ב
D	ד
E	א ה ע
F	פ ף
G	ג
H	ה ח
I (ee)	י
K	כ ק
KH (ch)	כ ח
L	ל
M	מ ם
N	נ ן
O	ו
P	פ
R	ר
S	ס ש
SH	ש
T	ט ת
TZ	צ
U (oo)	ו
V	ו וו ב
Y	י
Z	ז

236

English-Hebrew Glossary
From Aaron to Zion

Vowels accentuated by bold type indicate emphasis in pronunciation

English	Transliteration	Hebrew with Reverse Transliteration
		אהרן
Aaron	Aharon	N / R / H / A
		אברהם
Abraham	Avraham	M / H / R / V / A
		כל נדרי
All Vows Prayer	Kol Nidre	E / R / D / N L / K
		אלוהים
Almighty God	Elohim	M / I / H / O / L / E
		שקד
almond	shaked	D / K / SH
		מזבח העלה
altar of burnt offerings	mizbe'akh ha'olah	AH / L / ' / HA KH / B / Z / M
		מזבח הקטורת
altar of incense	mizbe'akh ha-ketoret	T / R / O / T / K / HA KH / B / Z / M
		אמן
Amen	Amen (So be it. It is true)	N / M / A
		תפוח
apple	tapu'akh	KH / U / P / T
		אייר
April/May	Iyar	R / A / Y / I
		אשר
Asher	Asher	R / SH / A
		כפרה
atonement	kapparah	AH / R / P / K
		חוצפה
audacity, insolence, nerve	khutzpah	AH / P / TZ / U / KH
		אלול
August/September	Elul	L / U / L / E
		סתיו
autumn	stav	V / A / T / S
		בבל
Babylon	Bavel	L / V / B
		שעורה
barley	se'orah	AH / R / O / ' / S
		כיור
basin or laver	kiyor	R / Y / I / K
		פעמון
bell(s)	pa'amon (pa'amonim)	N / O / AM / ' / P

		בנימין
Benjamin	Binyamin	N / I / M / Y / N / B
		בית–לחם
Bethlehem	Bet-Lekhem	M / KH / L - T / E / B
		אירוסים
betrothal	eirusim	M / I / S / U / R / EI
		ברכה
blessing/benediction	brakhah	AH / KH / R / B
		דם
blood	dam	M / D
		כחול
blue	kakhol	L / O / KH / K
		עבדות
bondage/slavery	'avdut	T / U / D / AV / '
		סוכה
booth(s)	sukkah (sukkot)	AH / K / U / S
		ילד
boy	yeled	D / L / Y
		פליז
brass	pliz	Z / I / L / P
		לחם
bread	lekhem	M / KH / L
		חשן
breastplate	khoshen	N / SH / KH
		כלה
bride	kallah	AH / L / K
		חתן
bridegroom	khatan	N / T / KH
		קבורה
burial	k'vurah	AH / R / U / V / K
		לוח שנה
calendar	lu'akh shanah	AH / N / SH KH / U / L
		מחנה
camp	makhaneh	H / N / KH / M
		כנען
Canaan	Kena'an	AN / ' / N / K
		ארז
cedar	erez	Z / R / E
		הבדלה
ceremony ending the Sabbath	Havdalah (Separation)	AH / L / D / V / HA
		להתראות!
Cheerio!	Lehitra'ot!	! / T / O / ' / R / T / H / L
		כרובים
cherubim	k'ruvim	M / I / V / U / R / K

238

children	yeledim	ילדים M / I / D / L / Y
Children of Israel	B'nei Yisra'el	בני ושראל EL / ' / R / S / Y EI / N / B
Christians	Notzri—followers of the Nazarene	נוצרי I / R / TZ / O / N
Circumcision (Covenant of)	Brit Milah	ברית מילה AH / L / I / M T / I / R / B
city	kiryah	קריה AH / Y / R / K
citron/lemon	etrog	אתרוג G / O / R / T / E
clay	khomer	חומר R / M / O / KH
cloud	ha'anan	הענן N / AN / ' / HA
copper	nekhoshet	נחושת T / SH / O / KH / N
cornerstone	even pinah	אבן פינה AH / N / I / P N / V / E
Counting of the Sheaves	Sfirat Ha'Omer	ספירת העומר R / M / O / ' / HA T / R / I / F / S
covenant or contract	brit	ברית T / I / R / B
crown	keter	כתר R / T / K
curtain or veil	parokhet	פרוכת T / KH / O / R / P
Dan	Dan	דן N / D
date	tamar	תמר R / M / T
date palm	dekel	דקל L / K / D
daughter	bat	בת T / B
David	David	דוד D / V / D
day(s)	yom (yamim)	יום M / O / Y
Day of Atonement	Yom Kippur	יום כיפור R / U / P / I / K M / O / Y
Day of Judgment	Yom HaDin	יום הדין N / I / D / HA M / O / Y

		ימים נוראים
Days of Awe	Yamim Nora'im	M/I'A/R/O/N M/I/M/Y
		מות
death	mavet	T/V/M
		טבת
December/January	Tevet	T/V/T
		גלות
Diaspora (Dispersion of the Jews)	Galut	T/U/L/G
		תלמיד
Disciple(s)/student(s)	talmid (talmidim)	D/I/M/L/T
		ביצה
egg	beitzah	AH/TZ/EI/B
		מצרים
Egypt	Mitzrayim	M/I/R/TZ/M
		שמונה
eight	shmoneh (or Khet)	EH/N/O/M/SH
		אליהו
Elijah	Eliyahu	U/H/Y/L/E
		מזוזה
encased scroll on Jewish doorposts	mezuzah	AH/Z/U/Z/M
		אפרים
Ephraim	Efrayim	M/I/R/F/E
		יציאה
Exodus	Yetzi'ah Hamonit	AH/'/I/TZ/Y
		המונית
		T/I/N/O/M/HA
		משפחה
family	mishpakhah	AH/KH/P/SH/M
		אבא
father/daddy	abba/ab (avinu: our father)	A/B/A
		חג
feast or celebration	khag	G/KH
		פסח
Feast of Passover	Pesakh	KH/S/P
		סוכות
Feast of Tabernacles	Sukkot	T/O/K/U/S
		חג המצות
Feast of Unleavened Bread	Khag HaMatzot	T/O/TZ/M/HA G/KH
		שביעות
Feast of Weeks/Pentecost	Shavu'ot	T/O/'/U/V/SH
		אדר
February/March:	Adar	R/D/A

		חמישים
fifty	khamishim (or Nun)	M / I / SH / I / M / KH
		תאנה
fig	te'enah	AH / EN / ' / T
		אש
fire	esh	SH / E
		ביכורים
Firstfruits	Bikkurim	M / I / R / U / K / I / B
		דג
fish	dag	G / D
		חמש
five	khamesh (or Heh)	SH / M / KH
		פישתן
flax/linen	pishtan	N / T / SH / I / P
		קמח
flour	kemakh	KH / M / K
		חליל
flute	khalil	L / I / L / KH
		מזון
food	mazon	N / O / Z / M
		סליחה
forgiveness, pardon ("Excuse me!")	slikhah (Slikhah!)	AH / KH / I / L / S
		ארבעים
forty	arba'im (or Mem)	M / I / ' / B / R / A
		ארבה
four	arbah (or Dalet)	AH / B / R / A
		יום ו'
Friday (sixth day)	Yom Vav or Yom Shishi	VAV M / O / Y
		יום שישי
		I / SH / I / SH M / O / Y
		גד
Gad	Gad	D / G
		גליל
Galilee	Galil	L / I / L / G
		גן עדן
Garden of Eden, Paradise	Gan 'Eden	N / ED / ' N / G
		אבן טובה
gemstones	even tovah	AH / V / O / T N / V / E
		ילדה
girl	yaldah	AH / D / L / Y
		שמחה
gladness/joy	simkhah	AH / KH / M / S
		אל
God	El	L / E

English	Transliteration	Hebrew
God Most High	HaElyon	העליון N / O / Y / L / E / HA
gold	zahav	זהב V / H / Z
Good evening!	'Erev tov!	ערב טוב! ! / V / O / T V / R / E
Good morning!	Boker tov!	בוקר טוב! ! / V / O / T R / K / O / B
gown	simlah	שמלה AH / L / M / S
grapes	'anavim	ענבים M / I / V / AN / '
grapevine	gefen	גפן N / F / G
Hallelujah!	Halleluyah! (Praise "Yah": Y-H-V-H)	הללויה ! / AH / Y / U / L / L / HA
hand, Torah pointer or memorial	yad	יד D / Y
harvest (noun)	katzir	קציר R / I / TZ / K
Hebrew	'Ivrit	עברית T / I / R / IV / '
Hebrew Bible (OT)	Tanakh	תנ"ך KH / / N / T
Hebrew Feast(s)	mo'ed (mo'adim) ("my feasts")	מועד ED / ' / O / M
Herod's Temple (Second Temple)	Bayit Sheni	בית שני I / N / SH T / Y / B
high priest	cohen gadol	כוהן גדול L / O / D / G N / H / O / C
holiness or sanctity	kodesh	קודש SH / D / O / K
Holocaust	HaSho'ah (Annihilation)	השואה AH / ' / O / SH / HA
Holy Ark	Aron HaKodesh	ארון הקודש SH / D / O / K / HA N / O / R / A
Holy City	'Ir HaKodesh	עיר הקודש SH / D / O / K / HA R / I / '
Holy Language (Hebrew)	Leshon HaKodesh	לשון הקודש SH / D / O / K / HA N / O / SH / L
Holy One	HaKadosh	הקדוש SH / O / D / K / HA

Holy Place	HaKodesh	הקודש SH / D / O / K / HA
Holy Scriptures	Kitvey HaKodesh	כתבי הקודש SH / D / O / K / HA Y / V / T / K
Holy Spirit	Ruach HaKodesh	רוח הקודש SH / D / O / K / HA KH / U / R
honey	dvash	דבש SH / V / D
horn	keren	קרן N / R / K
house	bayit	בית T / Y / B
hundred	me'ah	מאה AH / ' / M
husband, master, lord	ba'al	בעל AL / ' / B
"I Am"	Hayah	היה H / Y / H
I am sorry	Ani-*metz*ta'**er**	אני מצטער ER / ' / T / TZ / M I / N / A
Isaac	Yitzkhak	יצחק K / KH / TZ / Y
Israel	Yisra'**el**	ישראל EL / ' / R / S / Y
Issachar	Yissa'khar	יששכר R / KH / S / S / Y
Jacob	Ya'akov	יעקב V / AK / ' / Y
January/February	Shvat	שבט T / V / SH
Jericho	Yerikho	יריחו O / KH / I / R / Y
Jerusalem	Yerushalayim	ירושלים M / Y / L / SH / U / R / Y
Jesus	Yeshua (Salvation)	ישוע A / U / SH / Y
Jewish laws, legends, and morals	Talmud	תלמוד D / U / M / L / T
Jews	Yehudim ("Those who praise")	יהודים M / I / D / U / H / Y
Jordan	Yarden	ירדן N / D / R / Y
Joseph	Yosef	יוסף F / S / O / Y

Joshua	Y'hoshu'a	יהושע
		U / A / SH / O / H / Y
Jubilee	Yovel	יובל
		L / V / O / Y
Judah	Yehudah	יהודה
		AH / D / U / H / Y
Judea	Yihudah	יהודה
		AH / D / U / H / Y
July/August	Av	אב
		V / A
June/July	Tammuz	תמוז
		Z / U / M / T
kibbutz (communal farm)	kibbutz (pl. kibbutzim)	קיבוץ
		TZ / U / B / I / K
king	melekh	מלך
		KH / L / M
kosher food	kasher	כשר
		R / SH / K
lamb	keves	כבש
		S / V / K
lamb or kid	seh	שה
		H / S
lampstand (Jewish)	menorah	מנורה
		AH / R / O / N / M
Land of Israel	Eretz Yisra'el	ארץ ישראל
		EL / ' / R / S / Y TZ / R / E
Leah	Le'ah	לאה
		AH / ' / LE
Levi	L'vi	לוי
		I / V / L
life	khayim	חיים
		M / I / AY / KH
light	or	אור
		R / O
lily	khavatzelet	חבצלת
		T / L / TZ / V / KH
Lion of God	Ari'el	אריל
		L / I / R / A
Listen!/Hear!	Shema!	שמע
		A / M / SH
living/alive	khay	חי
		AY / KH
Lord, the	Adonai (Y-H-V-H)	אדוני
		AI / N / O / D / A
Lord's Glory, the	Sh'khinah	שכינה
		AH / N / I / KH / SH

244

(Heavenly Spirit)

Lord of Lords	Adonai Ha'Adonim	אדוני AI / N / O / D / A האדונים M / I / N / O / D / A / HA
Lord our God	Adonai (Y-H-V-H) Eloheinu	יהוה אלהינו U / N / EI / H / L / E H / V / H / Y
love	ahavah	אהבה H / V / H / A
lyre/harp	nevel	נבל L / V / N
Manasseh	M'nasheh	מנשה H / SH / N / M
March/April	Nissan	ניסן N / S / I / N
marriage contract	ketubah	כתובה AH / B / U / T / K
Mary/Miriam	Miryam	מרים M / Y / R / M
May/June	Sivan	סיון N / V / I / S
Melchizedek	Malki-Tzedek	מלכי-צדק K / D / TZ - I / K / L / M
mercy seat or atonement cover	kapporet	כפרת T / R / P / K
Messiah/Christ	Mashiach ("Anointed One")	משיח CH / I / SH / M
milk	khalav	חלב V / L / KH
miracle	nes (or pele)	נס S / N
Monday (second day)	Yom Bet or Yom Sheni	יום ב' BET M/O/Y יום שני I / N / SH M / O / Y
month(s)	khodesh (khodashim)	חודש SH / D / O / KH
moon	levanah	לבנה AH / N / V / L
Mosaic Law/Pentateuch	Torah	תורה AH / R / O / T
Moses	Moshe	משה E / SH / M

		קודש קודשים
Most Holy Place	Kodesh Kodashim	M / I / SH / D / O / K SH / D / O / K
		אמא
mother	ima	A / M / I
		תל
mound/hill	tel (site of ancient cities)	L / T
		הר
mountain	har	R / H
		שבעה
mourning for close Jewish relative (7 days)	shiv'ah ("sitting shiv'ah")	AH / ' / V / SH
		הדס
myrtle branch(s)	hadas (hadasim)	S / D / H
		נפתלי
Naphtali	Naftali	I / L / T / F / N
		גוי״ם
nations (esp. gentile)	goyim	M / Y / O / G
		נצרת
Nazareth	Natzrat (or Natzeret)	T / R / TZ / N
		ברית חדשה
New Covenant/Testament	Brit Khadashah	AH / SH / D / KH T / I / R / B
		ראש השנה
New Year (Day of Trumpets)	Rosh HaShanah (Yom Teru'ah)	AH / N / SH / HA SH / O / R
		תשע
nine	tesha (or Tet)	A / SH / T
		לא
no	lo	O / L
		כסלו
November/December	Kislev	V / L / S / K
		חשון
October/November	Kheshvan (or Markheshvan)	N / V / SH / KH
		שמן
oil	shemen	N / M / SH
		זית
olive or olive tree	zayit	T / Y / Z
		אחד
one	ekhad (or Alef)	D / KH / E
		עץ אחד
"one stick"	'etz ekhad	D / KH / E ETZ / '
		פסח
Passover	Pesakh	KH / S / P
		חרוסת
Passover food paste (apples, nuts, cinnamon)	kharoset	T / S / O / R / KH

		סדר
Passover meal	seder (order, arrangement)	R / D / S
		הגדה
Passover narrative	Hagadah (tale or story)	AH / D / G / HA
		שלים
peace (often a greeting)	shalom	M / O / L / SH
		תפילין
phylacteries	t'fillin	N / I / L / I / F / T
		נעים
plagues	nega'im	M / I / ' / G / N
		רימון
pomegranate(s)	rimon (rimonim)	N / O / M / I / R
		הגבורה
"Power", The	HaG'vurah (Y-H-V-H)	AH / R / U / V / G / HA
		זמר
praise with music	zamar	R / M / Z
		הלל
praise/exult	hallel	L / L / HA
		ידה
praise/thanksgiving	yadah	AH / D / YA
		תפילה
prayer	t'fillah	AH / L / I / F / T
		שלית
prayer shawl	talit	T / I / L / T
		כוהן
priest(s)	cohen (cohanim)	N / H / O / C
		נביא
prophet	navi	- / I / V / N
		ארגמן
purple	argaman	N / M / G / R / A
		רב
rabbi	rav (teacher, sage, master)	V / R
		רחל
Rachel	Rakhel	L / KH / R
		שופר
ram's horn trumpet	shofar	R / F / O / SH
		רבקה
Rebekah	Rivkah	AH / K / V / R
		לשמוח
rejoice	lismo'akh	KH / O / M / S / L
		שמחת תורה
"Rejoicing of the Torah"	Simkhat Torah	AH / R / O / T T / KH / M / S
		תשובה
repentance	t'shuvah	AH / V / U / SH / T
		תחייה
resurrection	tekhiyah	AH / Y / I / KH / T

		שיבה
return	shivah	AH / V / I / SH
		עלייה
return to Israel	'aliyah	AH / Y / I / AL / '
		ראובן
Reuben	Re'uven	N / V / U / ' / R
		צדיק
righteous person	tzadik	K / I / D / TZ
		צדק
righteousness, justice	tzedek	K / D / TZ
		ציציות
ritual fringe (s)	tzitzit (tzitziyot)	T / I / TZ / I / TZ
		נהר
river	nahar	R / H / N
		חלוק
robe	khalluk	K / U / L / KH
		שושנה
rose	shoshanah	AH / N / SH / O / SH
		ריבון העולם
Ruler of the World (or Universe)	Ribbon Ha'Olam	M / L / O / ' / HA N / O / B / I / R
		חלה
Sabbath bread loaf (sweet, leavened)	khallah	AH / L / KH
		קורבן
sacrifice or gift to God	korban	N / B / R / O / K
		עקידה
Sacrificing One's Dearest	'Akedah	H / D / E / AK / '
		סנהדרין
Sanhedrin	Sanhedrin	N / I / R / D / H / N / S
		שרה
Sarah	Sarah	AH / R / S
		שטן
Satan	Satan (accuser, adversary, obstacle)	N / T / S
		שבת
Saturday (the Sabbath)	Shabbat (or Yom Shabbat)	T / B / SH
		שאול
Saul	Sha'ul	L / U / ' / SH
		מושיע
savior/deliverer	moshi'a	A ' I / SH / O / M
		שני
scarlet	shani	I / N / SH
		ימי
sea	yami	I / M / Y

248

		עונה
season(s)	ʻonah (ʻonot)	AH / N / O / ʻ
		תשרי
September/October	Tishrei	E / R / SH / T
		שבעה
seven	shivʻah (or Zayin)	AH / ʻ / V / SH
		לחם הפנים
showbread	lekhem ha-panim ("bread of the faces")	M / I / N / P / HA M / KH / L
		כסף
silver	kesef	F / S / K
		שמעון
Simeon	Shim'on	N / O / ʻ / M / SH
		עוון
sin	ʻavon (or khet)	N / O / AV / ʻ
		לשיר
sing	lashir	R / I / SH / L
		שש
six	shesh (or Vav)	SH / SH
		כיפה
skullcap	kippah (Yiddish: yarmulka)	AH / P / I / K
		שלמה
Solomon	Shlomoh	H / M / L / SH
		בית ראשון
Solomon's Temple (First Temple)	Bayit Rishon	N / O / SH / I / R T / Y / B
		בן
son	ben (or bar)	N / B
		בן דוד
Son of David	Ben David	D / V / D N / B
		בר מצווה
son of the commandment (daughter)	bar mitzvah (bat mitzvah)	H / V / TZ / M R / B
		אביב
spring	aviv	V / I / V / A
		מגן-דוד
Star of David	Magen-David	D / V / D - N / G / M
		כוכב
star(s)	kokhav (kokhim)	V / KH / O / K
		אבן
stone(s)	even (avanim)	N / V / E
		רחוב
street	rekhov	V / O / KH / R
		אבן נגף
stumbling stone	even negef	F / G / N N / V / E

Sukkot palm branch(s)	lulav (pl. lulavim)	לולב V / L / U / L
summer	kayitz	קיץ TZ / Y / K
sun	shemesh	שמש SH / M / SH
Sunday (first day)	Yom Alef or Yom Rishon	יום א׳ ALEF M/O/Y יום ראשון N / O / SH / I / R M / O / Y
synagogue	bet-knesset	בית-כנסת T / S / N / K - T / E / B
Tabernacle	Mishkan (Dwelling Place)	משכן N / K / SH / M
Tabernacles, Feast of	Sukkot	סוכות T / O / K / U / S
table of showbread	shulkhan lekhem	שלחן לחם M / KH / L N / KH / L / SH
Tablets of the Covenant	Lukhot HaBrit	לוחות הברית T / I / R / B / HA T / O / KH / U / L
tambourine or drum	tof	תוף F / O / T
ten	'eser (or Yod)	עשר R / ES / '
Ten Commandments	'Aseret HaDibrot	עשרת T / R / AS / ' הדיברות T / O / R / B / I / D / HA
tent(s)	ohel (pl. oholim)	אוהל L / H / O
Tent of Meeting	Ohel Mo'ed	אוהל מועד ED / ' / O / M L / H / O
Thank you	Todah	תודה AH / D / O / T
The [Lord's] Name	HaShem	השם M / SH / HA
"The Great Day of the Feast"	Hoshana Rabbah (lit.: "Great Hosanna")	הושענא רבה H / B / R A / N / A / SH / O / H
thirty	shloshim (or Lamed)	שלושים M / I / SH / O / L / SH
thousand(s)	elef (pl. alafim)	אלף F / L / E
three	shalosh (or Gimel)	שלוש SH / O / L / SH

		כס מלכות
throne	kes malkhut	T/U/KH/L/M S/K
		יום ה ׳
Thursday (fifth day)	Yom Heh or	HEH M/O/Y
	Yom Khamishi	יום חמישי I/SH/I/M/KH M/O/Y
		עיר
town	‘ir	R/I/‘
		הורה
traditional Hebrew dance	horah	AH/R/O/H
		שבטם ושראל
Tribes of Israel	Sh‘vatim Yisra‘el	EL/‘/R/S/Y M/T/V/SH
		יום ג ׳
Tuesday (third day)	Yom Gimel or	GIMEL M/O/Y
	Yom Shlishi	יום שלישי I/SH/I/L/SH M/O/Y
		עשרים
twenty	‘esrim (or Kaf)	M/I/R/ES/‘
		שתים
two	sh‘tayim (or Bet)	M/I/T/SH
		עולם
universe or world	‘olam	M/L/O/‘
		מצה
unleavened bread	matzah (pl. matzot)	AH/TZ/M
		כינור
violin	kinnor	R/O/N/I/K
		עלמה
virgin or young woman	‘almah	H/M/AL/‘
		מים
water	mayim	M/Y/M
		חתונה
wedding	khatunah	AH/N/U/T/KH
		חופה
wedding canopy or ceremony	khuppah	AH/P/U/KH
		יום נשואים
wedding day	yom nisu‘im	M/I/‘/U/S/N M/O/Y
		יום ד ׳
Wednesday (fourth day)	Yom Dalet or	DALET M/O/Y
	Yom Revi‘i	יום רביעי I/‘/I/V/R M/O/Y
		שבוע
week(s)	shavu‘a (pl. shavu‘ot)	A/‘/U/V/SH
		חיטה
wheat	khitah	AH/T/I/KH

		לבן
white	lavan	N / V / L
		א י ש ה
wife	ishah	AH / SH / I / -
		ש מ מ ה
wilderness	shmamah	AH / M / M / SH
		ע ר ב ה
willow branch(s)	'aravah (pl. 'aravot)	H / V / AR / '
		י י ן
wine	yayin	N / Y / Y
		ח ו ר ף
winter	khoref	F / R / O / KH
		ע ץ
wood, tree or stick	'etz	ETZ / '
		ע ו ל ם ה ב א
world to come, heaven, paradise	'olam ha-ba	A / B / H M / L / O / '
		ע ב ד
worship/serve	abad	D / B / A
		י ה ו ה
Y-H-V-H: "He that is"	Y-H-V-H (Not spoken by Jews)	H / V / H / Y
		ש נ ה
year(s)	shanah (pl. shanim)	AH / N / SH
		ח מ ץ
yeast or leaven	khametz	TZ / M / KH
		כ ן
yes	ken	N / K
		ב ב ק ש ה !
You're welcome!	B'vakashah!	! / AH / SH / K / V / B
		ז ב ו ל ו ן
Zebulun	Z'vulun	N / U / L / U / V / Z
		צ י ו ן
Zion	Tziyon	N / Y / I / TZ

Seven Hebrew Proclamations and Blessings

1. Hear O Israel, the Lord our God, the Lord is one!
Shema Yisra'el, Adonai [Y-H-V-H] Eloheinu, Adonai [Y-H-V-H] ekhad!
שמע ישראל יהוה אלהינו יהוה אחד!
!D/KH/E H/V/H/Y U/N/EI/H/L/E H/V/H/Y EL/'/R/S/Y A/M/SH

2. God be praised! / Blessed be The Name!
Barukh HaShem!
ברוך השם!
!M/SH/HA KH/U/R/B

3. Peace be upon you
Shalom aleikhem
שלום עליכם
M/KH/EI/L/A M/O/L/SH

4. Blessed are you, O Lord our God, King of the Universe!
Barukh atah, Adonai [Y-H-V-H] Eloheinu, Melekh Ha'Olam!
ברוך אתה יהוה אלהינו מלך העולם!
!M/L/O/A/H KH/L/M U/N/EI/H/L/E H/V/H/Y AH/T/A KH/U/R/B

5. Here is Yeshua, the salvation of Israel!
Hineh Yeshua, yeshuat Yisra'el!
הנה ישוע ישועת ישראל!
!EL/'/R/S/Y T/A/U/SH/YE A/U/SH/YE EH/N/H

6. A great miracle happened here! ("Here!" [*poh*] in Israel; "there!"[*sham*] elsewhere in the world.)
Nes gadol hayah poh! (The first Hebrew letters of these words [נ ג ה פ] are printed on the sides of Jewish dreidels.)
נס גדול היה פה!
!H/P H/Y/H L/O/D/G S/N

7. Come back! Return!
Shuv!
שוב!
!V/U/SH

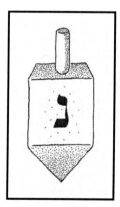

Figure 75: A Jewish dreidel. The letter *nun* represents the Hebrew word *nes*; meaning "miracle"

253

THE HEBREW NUMERAL SYSTEM

The Hebrew calendar governs all holy days: days of remembrance, *bar mitzvah*s, circumcisions, marriage rituals, and so on. These dates are never quoted as ordinary numbers, only as numerals. And of the two methods for writing the days of the week, one makes use of the numeral system. Hebrew numerals relate specifically, therefore, to the concept of time.

The Hebrew numeral system is relatively simple. Because it is based on the alphabet, Hebrew letters become numerals. The first nine letters of the alphabet, *alef* to *tet*, denote the "ones"; numerals from *one to nine*. The next group of nine letters, *yod* to *tzadi*, denote the "tens"; numerals from *ten to ninety*. The remaining four letters, *kuf* to *tav*, denote the first four "hundreds." All of these are apostrophized in order to indicate that they are numbers and not letters.

To form a number with two digits, two numerals are used. In the numeral 34, for example, 30 is written first and then 4 is added: 30 + 4 (*lamed - dalet*). In this instance, the last numeral (reading from right to left) is preceded by quotation marks. The numeral 34 therefore looks like this: לֿ ד. The same procedure is followed for the numerals from 100 to 499. The numeral 324, for example, is formed by adding three numbers: 300 + 20 + 4 (*shin - kaf - dalet*) and looks like this: שׂ כ ד. For the numerals 499 to 999, Hebrew letters are linked together to denote the additional hundreds. Hence, the numeral for 999 is formed as follows:

400 + 400 + 100 + 90 + 9—(*tav - tav - kuf - tzadi - tet*):

תתקצ"ט.

With thousands, the word *alafim* is written in the place of the thousands' comma. For example the year A.D. 2000 was the Hebrew date 5760. It is formed in this way:

5 + thousand + 400 + 300 + 60—(*heh - alafim - tav - shin - samekh*):

ה׳ אלפים תש"ס

In practice, however, only the last three digits are quoted when referring to a year, so this is quoted simply as "760"—תש"ס.

The date *Av 24*, would be written *kaf-dalet Av*: כ"ד אב.

There are two exceptions with regard to the above procedure. The form of the numerals for numbers 15 and 16 have been changed, because each of these combinations would result in two letters, which, in part, would spell the name *Y-H-V-H*, the sacred name of God (י׳ ה ו ה). The *Torah* forbids this name to be used casually. Therefore, instead of forming these numerals by the addition of 10 + 5 (י"ה) and 10 + 6 (י"ו), they are formed by the addition of 9 + 6 (ט"ו) and 9 + 7 (ט"ז).

254

Hebrew Numerals
Bold type indicates emphasis in pronunciation

Basic	Numerals			Other Examples	
# 1	ALEF	א	# 12	YOD-BET	י״ב
# 2	BET	ב	# 34	LAMED-DALET	ל״ד
# 3	GIMEL	ג	# 86	PEH-VAV	פ״ו
# 4	DALET	ד	# 157	KUF-NUN-ZAYIN	קנ״ז
# 5	HEH	ה	# 286	RESH-PEH-VAV	רפ״ו
# 6	VAV	ו	# 324	SHIN-KAF-DALET	שכ״ד
# 7	ZAYIN	ז	# 499	TAV-TZADI-TET	תצ״ט
# 8	KHET	ח	# 500	TAV-KUF	ת״ק
# 9	TET	ט	# 573	TAV-KUF-'AYIN-GIMEL	תקע״ג
# 10	YOD	י	# 600	TAV-RESH	ת״ר
# 20	KAF	כ	# 632	TAV-RESH-LAMED-BET	תרל״ב
# 30	LAMED	ל	# 700	TAV-SHIN	ת״ש
# 40	MEM	מ	# 747	TAV-SHIN-MEM-ZAYIN	תשמ״ז
# 50	NUN	נ	# 800	TAV-TAV	ת״ת
# 60	SAMEKH	ס	# 900	TAV-TAV-KUF	תת״ק
# 70	'AYIN	ע	# 999	TAV-TAV-KUF-TZADI-TET	תתקצ״ט
# 80	PEH	פ	# 1000	ALEF-ALAFIM	א׳ אלפים
# 90	TZADI	צ	# 50,000	NUN-ALAFIM	נ׳ אלפים
# 100	KUF	ק	# 76,450	'AYIN-VAV-ALAFIM-TAV-NUN	ע״ו אלפים ת״ן
# 200	RESH	ר	# 5760	HEH-ALAFIM-TAV-SHIN-SAMEKH	ה׳ אלפים תש״ס
# 300	SHIN	ש	Exceptions:		
# 400	TAV	ת	# 15: TET-VAV (9 + 6)		ט״ו
			# 16: TET-ZAYIN (9 + 7)		ט״ז

255

Appendix II

Messianic Prophecies of the *Tanakh*
(Old Testament)

The Torah scroll images demonstrate that all of these things were written down "in advance." Hebrew prophets anticipated the Messiah hundreds of years before his birth. Observe how well the messianic prophecies relate to Yeshua of Nazareth.

It "was written" that he would be the following:

1. A Jew: a descendant of the tribe of Judah, the royal line of David:
Gen. 49:10   2 Sam. 7:12– 13   Isa. 9:6, 11:1–5   Jer. 23:5   Matt. 1:2–3, 6   Luke 3:33
Acts 11:23   Rom. 1:4   Heb. 7:14

2. Called *Y-H-V-H*, the sacred name of the God of Israel:
Isa. 9:5–6   Jer. 23:5–6   Rom. 10:9   Phil. 2:9–11

3. Born in Bethlehem of a pure young maiden (Mary or *Miryam*):
Mic. 5:1   Isa. 7:14   Matt. 2:1   Luke 2:4–7   Matt. 1:18–2:1   Luke 1:26–35

4. Preceded by a messenger (John the Baptist or *Yokhanan*):
Isa. 40:3–5   Mal. 3:1   Matt. 3:1–3   Luke 1:17; 3:2–6

5. Anointed by the Spirit of God:
Isa. 11:2, 61:1   Ps. 45:8   Matt. 3:16   John 3:34   Acts 10:38

6. A prophet like Moses (*Moshe*):
Deut. 18:15, 18   Acts 3:20–22

7. One bringing healing and spiritual liberation to his people:
Isa. 61:1–2   Isa. 35:5–6, 42:18   Luke 4:18–19   Numerous examples; such as Matt. 11:5

8. One with a priestly ministry comparable to that of Melchizedek (*Malki-Tzedek*):
Ps. 110:4   Heb. 5:5–6, 6:20, 7:15–17

9. One who would enter Jerusalem in triumph, riding on a donkey:
Zech. 9:9   Matt. 21:1–11   Mark 11:1–11

10. Betrayed by a friend and sold for thirty pieces of silver:
Ps. 41:9, 55:13–15   Zech. 11:12   Matt. 26:15, 21–25, 47–50   John 13:18–21
Acts 1:16–18

11. Pierced through his hands and feet, but die without bones being broken:
Ps. 22:1   Zech. 12:10   Exod. 12:46   Ps. 24:31   Matt. 27:35   Luke 24:39
John 19:18, 34–37, 20:35   Rev. 1:7

12. Buried among the rich and then raised from the dead:
Isa. 53:9–10   Ps. 2:7, 16:10   Matt. 27:57–60, 28:1–20   Acts 2:23–36, 13:33–37
1 Cor. 11:4–6

13. One who would ascend to heaven:
Ps. 16:11, 68:19, 110:1   Luke 24:51   Acts 1:9–11, 7:55   Heb. 1:3

14. One who would become the foundational cornerstone of a new covenant:
Isa. 28:16   Ps. 118:22–23   Matt. 21:42   Eph. 2:20   1 Pet. 2:5–7

15. Accepted by the gentile nations of the earth:
Isa. 11:10, 42:1–4, 49:1–12   Matt. 12:21   Rom. 15:10

16. A king:
Ps. 2:6   Ezek. 37:22   John 18:33, 37, 19:19   Luke 23:38   Rev. 19:16

Bibliography

Alexander, David and Pat, eds., producers. *The Lion Handbook to the Bible*. Herts, England: Lion Publishing, 1973.

Alexander, Pat, ed. *The Lion Encyclopedia of the Bible* (*Life and Times, Meaning and Message, A Comprehensive Guide*). Herts, England: Lion Publishing, 1986.

Askarabbi.com (Website drawing on the knowledge of a team of Jewish rabbis.)

Baltsan, Hayim. *Webster's New World Hebrew Dictionary*. New York: Prentice Hall, Simon & Schuster, Inc., 1992.

Belt, Don, "World of Islam." *National Geographic Magazine*. (Official Journal of the National Geographic Society.) January 2002.

Boyd, James P. *Bible Dictionary*. Ottenheimer Pub. Inc. Distributed by Crown Publishers, Inc., New York, 1957.

Bryant, T. Alton, ed. *The New Compact Bible Dictionary*. Grand Rapids, Michigan: Zondervan Pub., 1967.

Bullinger, E.W. *Numbers in Scripture*. Grand Rapids, Michigan: Kregel Publications, 1967.

Compton's Interactive Encyclopedia (*Home Library CD-ROM*): *Version 1.0*. Chicago, Illinois: Developed by Compton's NewMedia, Inc., Softkey Multimedia Inc., 1997.

Fruchtenbaum, Dr. Arnold. *Hebrew Christianity: Its Theology, History & Philosophy*. Tustin, California: Ariel Ministries Press, 1983.

Gardner, Helen. *Art Through the Ages* (Sixth Edition). Revised by Horst De La Croix and Richard G. Tansey. New York, Chicago, San Francisco, Atlanta: Harcourt Brace Jovanovich, Inc., 1975.

Goodrick, Edward W., and John R. Kohlenburger III. *The NIV Exhaustive Concordance*. Associate editors, Donald L. Potts and James A. Swanson. Grand Rapids, Michigan: Zondervan Publishing House, 1997.

Dowley, Dr. Tim, John H.Y. Briggs, Dr. Robert D. Linder, David F. Wright, eds. *The History of Christianity: A Lion Handbook*. Herts, England: Lion Publishing, 1977.

Hastings, James, ed. *Dictionary of the Bible*. (Revised Edition by Frederick C. Grant & H.H. Rowley). New York: Charles Scribner's Sons, 1963.

The Holy Bible containing the Old and New Testaments in the King James Version. Nashville: Thomas Nelson Publishers, 1977.

The Holy Bible. New International Version containing The Old Testament and The New Testament. Grand Rapids, Michigan: Zondervan Bible Publishers, 1984.

The Illustrated Bible Dictionary. (3 Volumes) Lane Cove, NSW, Australia: Hodder & Stroughton; Leicester, England: Inter Varsity Press; and Wheaton, Illinois: Tyndale House Publishers, 1980.

Illustrated Dictionary & Concordance of the Bible. New York: Macmillan Publishing Company, London: Collier Macmillan Publishers, 1986. (Copyright: The Jerusalem Publishing House, Ltd.)

Isaacs, Ronald H. *Sacred Seasons: A Sourcebook for the Jewish Holidays*. Jason Aronson, Inc., 1997.

Kohlenberger, John R. III, ed. *The NIV Interlinear Hebrew-English Old Testament*. Grand Rapids, Michigan: Zondervan Publishing House, 1987.

Levitt, Zola and Jeffrey L. Seif. *The House That God Built. The Tabernacle in the Wilderness*. Zola Levitt Ministries, Inc., 1989.

Levitt, Zola. *The Miracle of Passover*. Dallas, Texas: Zola Levitt Ministries, Inc., 1977.

——*The Seven Feasts of Israel*. Dallas, Texas: Zola Levitt Ministries, Inc., 1979.

"The Lost Tribes of Israel / Where are the Ten Lost Tribes?" Nova On-line article, pbs.org, 2000.

Martell, Hazel Mary. *The Kingfisher Book of the Ancient World: From the Ice Age to the Fall of Rome*. Larousse Kingfisher Chambers, Inc./Scholastic Inc., 1998.

May, Herbert G., ed. *Oxford Bible Atlas*. Second Edition. London, New York: Oxford University Press, 1974.

Metzger, Bruce M. and Michael D. Coogan, eds. *Oxford Companion to the Bible*. New York, Oxford: Oxford University Press, 1993.

New American Standard Bible. La Habra, California: Collins World, the Lockman Foundation, 1973.

259

The New World Dictionary-Concordance to the New American Bible. Stamply, C.D. Enterprises. World Bible Pub., 1970.

Pink, A.W. *An Exposition of Hebrews*. Grand Rapids, Michigan: Baker Book House, 1954.

——*The Gospel of John*. Grand Rapids, Michigan: Zondervan Publishing House, 1945.

Scharfstein, Sol. *Understanding Jewish History Part 1 (From the Patriarchs to the Expulsion from Spain)*. Hoboken, New Jersey: KTAV Publishing House, Inc., 1996.

Sephardic Jews, The. *The Jerusalem Connection Magazine*; Conclusion, Page 33; Special Edition; September-October, 2006.

Silberling, Kay, Ph.D., Daniel Juster, Th.D., David Sedaca, M.A. "The Ephraimite Error." Article submitted to International Messianic Jewish Alliance, Dec. 1999.

Stern, David. *Complete Jewish Bible*. Clarksville, Maryland and Jerusalem, Israel: Jewish New Testament Publications, Inc., 1998.

——*Jewish New Testament*. Jerusalem, Israel and Clarksville, Maryland: Jewish New Testament Pub., 1989.

Szulc, Tad, "Journey of Faith." Photographs by Reza. *National Geographic Magazine*. (Official Journal of the National Geographic Society.) December 2001.

Time Almanac 2002 with Information Please. Borgna Brunner, Editor in Chief: Published by Information Please (Part of Learning Network), 2001.

Ratnesar, Romesh. "Why Bush had to Act." *Time Magazine*. (Volume 159 No. 12)

Trepp, Leo. *The Complete Book of Jewish Observance*. New York: Behrman House, Inc., Simon and Schuster, 1980.

Turner, Reuben. *Jewish Festivals*. Vero Beach, Florida: Rourke Enterprises, Inc., 1987.

United States Catholic Conference, Inc., *Catechism of the Catholic Church* (1994).

Williams, Kevin. *The Holidays of God: The Spring Feasts*. Grand Rapids, Michigan: RBC Ministries, 2000.

——*The Holidays of God: The Fall Feasts*. Grand Rapids, Michigan: RBC Ministries, 2000.

Whiston, William A.M., trans. *Josephus (Complete Works)*. Foreword by William Sanford LaSor, Ph.D., Th.D. Grand Rapids, Michigan: Kregel Publications, 1981.

Wood, Angela. *Judaism*. New York: Thompson Learning; UK: Wayland Publishing Ltd., 1995.

The World Almanac and Book of Facts 2001 and 2002 Versions. World Almanac Education Group, Inc., Distributed by St. Martin's Press, 2001, 2002.

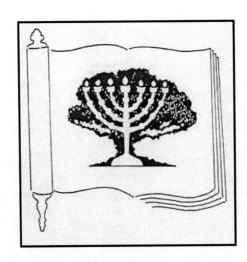

About the Author

Shelley Wood Gauld, a graduate of the University of KwaZulu-Natal in South Africa, is a former high school teacher of Religious Education, Art History, Drawing and Painting. Her illustrated memoir, *Much Bigger than Grownups: Chronicles of a Native South African*, traces her life path from an Apartheid era Zulu trading post, to the USA. It also describes the extraordinary circumstances that led to the creation of *Return to the Fountainhead of the Faith*. Shelley is presently living in Wheat Ridge, Colorado USA, with her husband and two daughters.

To preview, order, rate or review
e-book, paperback or hardcover versions of

Much Bigger than Grownups (© 2006)
&
Return to the Fountainhead of the Faith (Revised Edition: © 2006)

visit http://www.lulu.com/grownupsbook

These titles are also available from bookstores such as
Amazon.com and Barnes and Noble

For signed and discounted copies
e-mail author at grownupsbook@aol.com.

Changes in e-mail address will be posted with book descriptions on lulu.com at
http://www.lulu.com/grownupsbook

CPSIA information can be obtained at www.ICGtesting.com
Printed in the USA
BVOW021955220812

298514BV00001B/107/A

9 781430 308652